THE MASS AND MODERNITY

Jonathan Robinson
of the Oratory

The Mass and Modernity
Walking to Heaven Backward

*We advance to the truth by experience of error; we suc-
ceed through failures. We know not how to do right except
by having done wrong. . . . We know what is right, not
positively, but negatively—we do not see the truth at once
and make towards it, but we fall upon and try error, and
find it is not the truth. We grope about by touch, not by
sight, and so by a miserable experience exhaust the possible modes of acting till nought is left, but truth, remaining. Such is the process by which we succeed; we walk to
heaven backward.*

—John Henry Newman, *Parochial and Plain Sermons*

IGNATIUS PRESS   SAN FRANCISCO

Cover art:
Pietro Lorenzetti (c. 1306–1345)
The Last Supper, Fresco
Lower Church, S. Francesco, Assisi, Italy
Scala / Art Resource, N.Y.

Cover design by Riz Boncan Morsella

© 2005 Ignatius Press, San Francisco
ISBN 978-1-58617-069-1
ISBN 1-58617-069-4
Library of Congress Control Number 2005924112
Printed in the United States of America ∞

FOR DAVID AND DEREK
SINE QUIBUS NON

CONTENTS

PREFACE

There is no shortage of books today that discuss the life of
the Catholic Church in the modern world with a particular emphasis on the post-Vatican II liturgy. Often these writings shed more heat than light, sometimes because of their
shrill tone and intemperate language or their indiscriminate
dislike of anything "modern". All too often they suffer from
a markedly superficial analysis of the ideas behind the reforms.
Sometimes we do find a more rigorously intellectual
approach, but even that can be marred by an author's lack
of practical or pastoral experience. The present volume by
Fr. Robinson is notable for being the work of someone
who is a pastoral priest, an experienced spiritual director,
and a professional philosopher who has been a full-time
member of the Department of Logic and Metaphysics at
the University of Edinburgh and of the Department of Philosophy at McGill in Montreal. This is a rare combination
and explains why this volume is so refreshing and illuminating. The author knows well what he is talking about,
both in the theory and in the practice.

We find here a book that is friendly to the cause of
post-Vatican II liturgical reform but also willing to question the usefulness of much that has been promoted in
the name of that reform. We find here a circumspect critique of modernity based on the careful analysis of ideas
and their cultural ramifications. There is, for example, an
unusually attentive reading of Kant's *Religion within the Bounds
of Reason Alone* and Hegel's philosophy of religion. We

also find here an unwavering defense of the divine transcendence. This defense invokes the mystical writings of
Dionysius the Areopagite and is preceded by a survey of
recent sociological studies on secularization. Here the South-
ern writer and self-proclaimed "hillbilly Thomist" Flannery O'Connor rubs shoulders with Iris Murdoch, the
philosopher-novelist. Fr. Robinson speaks throughout with
the voice of a working parish priest who is undaunted by
the more impractical prescriptions of liturgical experts. He
is a bold analytical thinker with an uncommon ability to
cut through entrenched cant.

What will you not find in this book? The author endorses
no familiar party line, nor does he seek to initiate a new
party of his own. The modest liturgical reforms he does
propose at the end of the book may appear radical to some,
but that is a sure sign that they need to read the rest of the
book. What we have here is a well-constructed working-
kit for those who understand that any serious discussion of
the modern liturgy must be based on sound philosophical
and theological premises. I pray that this book might bring
to the current "liturgical wars" an infusion of the author's
own reasonableness, moderation, and reverent humility—
the humility with which he tackles the important liturgical
question: "What next?"

I do not mean to suggest that this is a book without
passion. No one who works his way through the following
pages can doubt Fr. Robinson's passionate devotion to the
sacred liturgy as the God-given means for the sanctification
of mankind. He has the strong conviction that without the
lure of the "beauty of holiness" as found in the liturgy, the
Church has nothing substantial to offer the world. This conviction is what informs Fr. Robinson's dissection of the obstacles and opportunities of modernity in relation to the

shibboleths and false turns of late twentieth-century liturgical reform.

A major influence on Fr. Robinson's insights has been
his experience as founder of the Toronto Oratory and, subsequently, his many years as its superior and parish priest.
Part of the Oratorian tradition, which, inspired largely by
the English Oratory, he established in Canada, is a love of
the Catholic Church's public worship. The sixteenth-
century founder of the Oratory in Rome, St. Philip Neri,
knew that divine worship was an essential way of raising
hearts and minds to God and, thus, changing lives for the
better. Since its beginnings, the Oratory of St. Philip Neri
has been known for the splendor of its liturgy. This love of
the liturgy, always going hand in hand with a deep love of,
and fidelity to, the Church, is something that the English
Oratory has taken pains to maintain. This was a patrimony
loyally transmitted by Newman and Faber from Rome to
nineteenth-century England, and this patrimony was later
fruitfully transplanted and has taken root in Canada's Toronto
Oratory.

At times our critics have not hesitated to accuse us of
being overly conservative or even obscurantist. I hope I can
be forgiven for citing here just one true anecdote. One Sunday morning in the early 1980s, a bright young priest (and
member of a distinguished religious order) stood outside
the church of the London Oratory in South Kensington at
about 12:15 P.M., watching several hundred of the faithful
leaving the Oratory church after the solemn Latin Mass had
ended. Later that week he said to me, "I just can't understand why so many young people go to that eleven A.M.
thing of yours." He asked himself, in a state of some per-
plexity, how it was that the hundreds of Mass attenders he
had seen included a high proportion of people under thirty

years of age. How was it that young families and young people could get anything out of a solemn Latin Mass (*Novus Ordo*), celebrated *ad orientem,* with polyphony and Gregorian chant? He could not understand why such a church and such a Mass were full. Indeed, he seemed to resent the fact. It seemed to him an aberration, a blot on the politically correct landscape of the liturgical establishment. I do not suggest that his question is easy to answer, beyond stating the obvious, that the crowds regularly attending such Masses clearly found something there to inspire and invigorate them. But if I had had Fr. Robinson's book to hand on that occasion, I would have been better able to steer this baffled and modern young cleric through the issues raised by his question and his prejudice.

I very much hope that this book becomes available to all those who do wonder what authentic worship is about and that it will help both clergy and laity to evaluate what they are doing when they approach the altar of sacrifice and how best to do it, for God's greater glory and for the good of all his people.

Ignatius Harrison, Cong. Orat.
Feast of Our Holy Father St. Philip

May 26, 2004

Acknowledgments

My first debt is to the members of the Toronto Oratory for their patience and support. In addition to Fr. David Roche and Fr. Derek Cross, to whom this book is dedicated, I am grateful to Fr. Daniel Utrecht for putting his proofreading skills to work on different versions of my manuscript.

Then I have to thank the members of the English Oratories, whose example of a serious concern with the liturgy of the Church has always been an inspiration to me. I think especially of the late Fr. Michael Napier, who did so much for me and the Toronto Oratory. It would be ungrateful for me not to single out Fr. Michael's successor, Fr. Ignatius Harrison, who has written the preface to this book. In addition, I have to thank two Oratorians from Newman's own House in Birmingham: Fr. Guy Nicholls, for his encouragement and interest, and Fr. Philip Cleevely, for his awkward and penetrating questions about many of the themes of this book.

I also wish to mention my legal and journalistic friends who have helped me to see things from standpoints that are neither academic nor ecclesiastical: to Charles Mark, Q.C., and David Brown, members of the Toronto Bar; to David Warren and Gerald Owen, both former editors of *The Idler*, and also to Philip Marchand and John Bentley Mays, for their advice at a crucial moment.

Finally, there is Anne Englund Nash, whose unsentimental and generous help has meant much more to me, and I think to this book, than she seems to believe.

INTRODUCTION

Knowledge, right principles, true thoughts, are not at their post; and the place lies open to the assault of false and presumptuous notions.

—Plato, *The Republic*

This book is about the reform of the worship of the Catholic Church undertaken after the Second Vatican Council. The fruits of that reform have often been apathy, bitterness, and triviality. It may be true that apathy, bitterness, and triviality are not the whole story, but they are indisputably prominent and help to create a situation whose gravity, it seems to me, is not sufficiently understood. The present liturgical situation matters. It matters not only for the internal or domestic health of the Church, but also for the effectiveness of her mission in the modern world.

The first part of this book takes a look at the destructive program, usually called modernity, which has been instrumental in creating the modern world. The modern world is a reality in which we all live, and it has in part been created by the ideas of modernity. Modernity itself, however, is a mind-set and not an all-encompassing environment. There is nothing, or should be nothing, in the Christian's concern for the modern world that requires accepting this mind-set. Yet many in the Church have accepted modernity in their effort to speak to the modern world, and I argue here that not nearly enough attention has been given to trying to disentangle the complex of ideas and half-formulated convictions that constitute this mindset, which is in fact inimical to Christianity. The result of trying to adapt the liturgy to meet the perceived needs of the world from the perspective of modernity weakens, not strengthens, the Church.

The second part deals with the world we live in today. One aspect of this world involves a fashionable scepticism about the benefits of the modern project. Nevertheless, the intellectual currents of this confused and confusing postmodern world impede the Church in her efforts to break free of the dubious inheritance of modernism and to draw society to the truth of the gospel.

In the third part, I maintain that the Paschal Mystery, made present in the Mass, is the key to understanding existence and provides the strength to break with the modern world and return to God.

The Sacrifice of the Mass is the heart of Catholicism because at every Mass the Paschal Mystery is made present on our altars.[1] The meaning of the Paschal Mystery is clearly stated in *Sacrosanctum Concilium*, the document of Vatican II on the liturgy:

> The wonders wrought by God among the people of the Old Testament were but a prelude to the work of Christ the Lord in redeeming mankind and giving perfect glory to God. He achieved His task principally by the paschal mystery of His blessed passion, resurrection from the dead, and

---

[1] "The Eucharist is . . . a sacrifice because it *re-presents* (makes present) the sacrifice of the cross, because it is its *memorial* and because it *applies* its fruit" (*Catechism of the Catholic Church*, 2nd ed. [Vatican City: Libreria Editrice Vaticana, 1997], 1366 [hereafter abbreviated CCC]).

glorious ascension, whereby "dying he destroyed our death and rising, he restored our life." [2]

The liturgy of the Eucharist is:

the summit toward which the activity of the Church is directed; at the same time, it is the fountain from which all her power flows. For the goal of apostolic works is that all who are made sons of God by faith and baptism should come together to praise God in the midst of His Church, to take part in her sacrifice, and to eat the Lord's supper.[3]

These passages are a wonderful and confident affirmation of Christ's continuing victory over sin and death, of his presence in the Eucharist, and of the true goal of the Church's apostolic activity. It was out of the conviction that the state of the Church's worship did not adequately convey these sublime truths that Vatican II mandated a modest revision of existing rites, but not the creation of wholly new ones. After 1965, however, when the Council ended, the reforms actually prescribed by the Council were speedily implemented and then left behind in the wake of new instructions and experiments. We have now reached the point that many concerned with the health of the Church have begun both to speak and to write about the need of at very least a reform of the reform.[4]

[2] *Sacrosanctum Concilium* 5, *The Documents of Vatican II*, ed. Walter M. Abbott, S.J. (New York: Herder and Herder, 1966) (hereafter abbreviated A), p. 139.

[3] *Sacrosanctum Concilium* 10 (A 142).

[4] For example, in an article entitled "Reform of the Reform?" Fr. John Parsons wrote: "Reform of the Liturgical Reform introduced into the Western Church during the 1950's and 1960's was the subject of a paper delivered by my friend Rev. Brian Harrison at Colorado Springs in 1995. It was that paper which moved Father Joseph Fessio, S.J., and others to launch the *Adoremus* movement to work toward such a reform" (*Sacred Music*, vol. 129, no. 2 [Summer 2002]: 4). There is a useful bibliography of books and articles on this subject in: Thomas M. Kocik, *The Reform of the Reform? A Liturgical Debate: Reform or Return?* (San Francisco: Ignatius Press, 2003).

They contend that the changes in Catholic worship since the Council are not a real development and perfection of existing rites but represent a brutal rupture with the strong and steady tradition of the worship offered to God by his Church.

One of the reasons for the reform of the liturgy was the conviction that the Church was faced with a new world and that this necessitated at least a new perspective on worship if it were to be viable in this changed environment. If ours is a new age, then a new effort has to be made to understand it, and so the Council called for the "entire People of God", particularly its "pastors and theologians", "to hear, distinguish, and interpret the many voices of our age, and to judge them in the light of the divine Word. In this way, revealed truth can always be more deeply penetrated, better understood, and set forth to greater advantage.[5]

The consequences, however, of this attempt at deeper penetration, better understanding, and more suitable presentation have not been reassuring. The net result of the changes has been the incorporation of principles and attitudes that should have no place in Catholic worship. This points us to what English philosophers would call the septic area in today's situation. The present condition of Catholic worship has come about because it has been shaped by principles and attitudes of secular modernity. The result is that the liturgy, instead of providing an alternative vision of life to that provided by secular modernity, now cooperates with and disseminates principles that are destructive of Catholicism.

The principles and attitudes that have created the modern world, and have entered so deeply into the life of the

---

[5] Vatican II, Pastoral Constitution on the Church in the Modern World, *Gaudium et Spes* 44 (A 246).

Church, can be studied from two different points of view. First of all, we can take such currents of thought as *enlightenment* or *romanticism* and see how they have influenced in a direct way the Catholic Church in the modern world. Then, secondly, there is the critical evaluation of the broad complex of philosophical ideas and attitudes that go to make up the background within which the Liturgical Movement, the Council itself, as well as the implementation of its liturgical decrees were developed.

One of the most obvious examples of the influence of modernity on Catholicism is the Liturgical Movement, and it was through the Liturgical Movement that many of the ideas that in fact distorted Catholic perceptions entered into the life of the Church. The Liturgical Movement brought the question of Catholic worship to the fore, and it is often said to have begun with the work of Dom Prosper Guéranger (1805–1875), the restorer of the French Benedictine Congregation at Solesmes in the first half of the nineteenth century.[6] The triumph and vindication of the movement were seen, at least by its supporters, to be the encyclical *Mediator Dei* of Pope Pius XII, issued in 1947.[7] The study of this movement and of the ideas that

---

[6] "Guéranger worked to make the liturgy of the Church known and loved because he saw it as the voice of the Bride speaking to the Bridegroom" (article "Liturgical Movement", in *New Catholic Encyclopaedia* [New York and St. Louis: McGraw-Hill, 1967]).

[7] Dom Lambert Beauduin, O.S.B., whom Fr. Aidan Nichols calls "father of the twentieth century Liturgical Movement", said of the document that it was: "A solemn, unique document by which the supreme authority rehabilitates the Liturgy—yesterday's Cinderella—in its rights and claims to primacy ... our Holy Father Pius XII is the first to explain in a magisterial document ... the basic prerogatives which entitle the Liturgy to a post of the first order in the spiritual life" (cited in Aidan Nichols, O.P., *A Pope and a Council on the Sacred Liturgy* [Farnborough: Saint Michael's Abbey Press, 2002], p. 7).

influenced the men who formed it is mainly an inquiry of a historical nature.

This historical inquiry has been developed with elegance and learning by scholars such as Fr. Aidan Nichols. For example, Fr. Nichols writes:

> Not enough attention was paid to certain ambiguities in the history of the liturgical movement either by those who brought about the Second Vatican Council's commitment to the "liturgical renewal", in the Constitution *Sacrosanctum Concilium*, or by those who subsequently worked to give that commitment concrete form in the revised liturgical books whose publication began with the issue of the reformed Roman Calendar in 1969.[8]

In his analysis of these ambiguities, Fr. Nichols discusses the Enlightenment and the Romantic Movement and the influence these movements had on important figures in the Liturgical Movement itself. This discussion is extremely well done, and my book may be looked on as trying to complete his historical work.

It is true that there are really very serious questions about how to reach the modern world with Christ's saving truth. We live in a world for which the language of traditional Christianity is a dead letter. The intellectual framework, the images, and the moral teaching of the faith no longer color the ordinary consciousness as they once did. We live, as Iris Murdoch put it, "in a scientific and anti-metaphysical age in which the dogmas, images, and precepts of religion have lost much of their power".[9] This weakening of the religious

---

[8] Aidan Nichols, O.P., *Looking at the Liturgy* (San Francisco: Ignatius Press, 1996), p. 11.

[9] Iris Murdoch, "Against Dryness", in *Existentialists and Mystics* (London: Chatto & Windus, 1997), p. 287.

aspect of the modern consciousness is usually called *secularization*; modern society has been secularized. Sometimes the word is used to ascribe the cause of this condition: people seem to be convinced that secularization is kind of force or irresistible current that is sweeping away faith. At other times the word describes what this force or current has brought about, that is, a secularized society.[10]

The fact that we live in a secularized society is just that—a fact. There are, of course, all sorts of questions that we can and should ask about the fact. We may wonder if secularization is a good or a bad aspect of our existence; we may debate about the various causes we believe have brought about this condition of our society; and we may differ as to whether we can or should try to alter this situation. None of this, however, changes the fact that we live in a world in which Christian belief is misunderstood, when it has been heard of, and is largely irrelevant to the day-to-day life of society.[11] Catholics have to take account of this state of affairs unless they are to be content with talking to so few people they will finish by talking only to themselves.

If we are to come to terms with a situation or condition, we have to know something about how it came to be. The situation in which the Church finds herself is no exception to this general rule. The *symptoms* of secularization may be easy enough to recognize, but if we are going to understand

---

[10] But, as Charles Taylor says, the term "is more a locus of questions than a source of explanations" (Charles Taylor, *Sources of the Self* [Cambridge, Mass.: Harvard University Press, 1989]). "It describes a process which is undeniable: the regression of belief in God, and even more, the decline in the practice of religion, to the point where from being central to the whole life of Western societies, public and private, this has become sub-cultural, one of many private forms of involvement which some people indulge in" (p. 309).

[11] See below, pt. 1, "Wingless Chickens".

secularization, and so see how a Christian should react to it, then we have to understand the convictions and beliefs that went into creating it. Ideas matter, and it is impossible to understand the present liturgical malaise without knowing something about the ideas that have shaped the way we all look at the world we live in. The Enlightenment as well as other philosophical and cultural movements have created a climate of opinion that is at best indifferent, if not deeply hostile, to the claims of Christianity. This feeds and will continue to feed a strong and effective ideology working against any "reform of the reform".

The notion of ideology has been thoroughly worked over and seems to mean any number of different things. I am using it here to mean a complex of principles, images, ideas, and emotional attitudes that direct conduct. By using the word *ideology*, I want to emphasize first of all that I do not think it has any necessary connection with true principles or right thinking; and, secondly, I want to make sure we understand we are not dealing with a mere theory that is liable to remain on paper. Ideology is powerful, and it is difficult to argue against because it is more than theory. What we who are interested in a more traditional liturgy are up against is an ideology that is powerful and well connected, and it is one that mixes Christian principles with convictions and attitudes that are inimical to Catholicism.[12]

---

[12] For example: Melissa Kay was, and perhaps still is, a member of the editorial staff of the Liturgical Committee of the National Conference of Catholic Bishops. In *It's Your Own Mystery: Guide for the Communion Rite*, cited in *Adoremus Bulletin*, vol. 8, no. 3 (May 2002), she has written that "the liturgical movement ... is engaged in a radical relocation of the experience of transcendence, and with that, a reinterpretation of its meaning." Ms. Kay acknowledges that there is a "long religious tradition in which transcendence relates to the otherness of God", but she goes on to tell us: "Transcendence can also be understood as a dynamism, an energy, a quality of being, open-

The Christian elements of this ideology are a concern for the community, for the poor and the marginalized; the non-Christian elements are an uncritical acceptance of large tracts of the Enlightenment, of nineteenth- and twentieth-century philosophy, which, step by step, are well on their way to destroying what remains of traditional Catholicism. The Enlightenment began by denying revelation in Jesus Christ, by neutering the doctrine of the Mystical Body, by denying the existence of God, and by discrediting the Resurrection of Jesus and the possibility of everlasting life. The nineteenth century went on to provide a theory in which the community became god. Put in this blunt way, I do not suppose many people would recognize these elements in the current ideology that drives an apparently insatiable desire for more liturgical change; but, recognized or not, they are the fuel driving the changes today.

The ideology that has created the modern world has ended with an approach to things that is often called postmodernism. Postmodernism may be summed up in the attitude that one set of opinions is as good as any other set, and this is so because there is no objectivity to be found in human experience. The very possibility of looking for a description of "the way things really are" is looked on as foolish. "That's your choice, and so long as you don't try to impose it on anyone else, you are entitled to it" sums up this attitude. There are no *grands-discours*, or general descriptions of reality, because, to put it bluntly, there is no reality to be described.[13]

---

ing from within and drawing toward the expansion and enrichment of life." If we examine *what* is said, then this passage has very little merit; on the other hand, what she writes is of great importance and influence because of her position.

[13] See below, pt. 2, chap. 1, "Postmodernism—Blowing It All Up".

I do not think anyone really believes this when it is his
own interests and convictions that are at stake. On the other
hand, the profession of postmodernism, with its view that
there is no truth but only stories of our own choice, poi-
sons the atmosphere we all breathe. This book is written
with the conviction that our relation to the truth is not
one of choice, and I have written in an attempt to describe
a situation, not to create a story. While it is true that we
are drawn to what is good and true in a way it is possible
to resist (and this introduces an element of choice), the pull
is there independently of our wishes, and that to which we
are drawn is not of our own making. Plato said this desire
for the good and the true was love, or, to use his word,
Eros, and while Eros can lead us badly astray, it is a gift that
enables us to go out beyond ourselves to the good that is
beautiful and true and is the only reality that will satisfy us
in any long-term way.[14]

We find this same combination of subjective and objective approaches in St. Thomas Aquinas. Human beings are
created with what St. Thomas calls an *inclinatio* for truth.[15]
Inclinatio here does not mean "inclination", which in English
has an element of choice or decision about it; we say, for
example, I incline to this point of view, but my mind could
be changed. The whole point about an *inclinatio* for St.
Thomas is that it designates a given fact about human nature.
One modern translation of the *Summa Theologiae* sometimes renders *inclinatio* as "natural appetite" or as "natural
tendency", or again as "bent".[16] Whichever word is used,

---

[14] See below, pt. 2, chap. 3, "Swimming against the Tide", pt. 3, chap. 2,
"With Desire I Have Desired".

[15] See, for example, *Summa Theologiae* 1a, 2ae, 94, 2.

[16] *Summa Theologiae* (Cambridge, Eng.: Blackfriars; New York: McGraw-
Hill, 1964–1969) (hereafter abbreviated STB), vol. 28 (1a, 2ae, 90–97).

however, the point to be grasped is that these appetites, tendencies, or bents are not the result of our choices. We may ignore *inclinationes*, try to suppress them, or deny that they exist, nonetheless, in Thomas' view, they are built-in aspects of what it means to be a human being. In discussing the *inclinatio* for the good, he says, "There is in man an appetite for the good (*inclinatio ad bonum*) of his nature as rational, and this is proper to him, for instance, that he should know truths about God and about living in society." [17]

This position of St. Thomas is called today *ethical realism*; on this view our judgments about right and wrong are ultimately based on the way things really are. I believe that unless some form of ethical realism can be established, then we are left with the dismal, dark, and dangerous prospect of a world in which there is no truth, no goodness, and no beauty other than what those in control happen to say is true, good, or beautiful. This is a somber prospect. In the words of John Rist:

> Such darkness is not to be understood rhetorically but in concrete terms of vanishing respect for human life; daily more "unjust" killing, torture, and every form of "callousness" and neglect both in public and in private. With morality, aesthetics will also disintegrate, as it did under the rule of the Nazi "artist" Hitler, for where there is no God, "beauty" is a matter of choice and merely (ultimately official) taste. [18]

[17] STB 1a, 2ae, 94, 2.

[18] John Rist, *Real Ethics* (Cambridge, Eng., and New York: Cambridge University Press, 2002), p. 283. Rist uses quotation marks for such "value terms" as *unjust* and the like because they have become, as he puts it, "transvalued" in a nonrealist universe. "It is this very perception which makes way for 'diabolical' transvaluations such as the Nazi; Heidegger is a ghastly warning figure" (p. 283, n. 26).

The malaise of the present liturgical situation in the Church presents us with an analogue to this retreat from ethical realism. If we think that liturgy is about the worship of a God who is, and who is no matter what we may feel or think about him, then our worship will be developed in terms of the vision of Isaiah, who saw the Lord "sitting upon a throne, high and lifted up";

> Above him stood the seraphim; each had six wings: with two he covered his face, and with two he covered his feet, and with two he flew. And one called to another and said: Holy, holy, holy is the LORD of hosts; the whole earth is full of his glory. (Is 6:1–3)

On the other hand, if we think, or act as though we thought, that liturgy is primarily about shifting human aims and aspirations, the result will be that worship, in losing its thrust toward God, will be replaced by a focus on the community and its purposes. But, "building community", however admirable and even necessary it may be, is no substitute for the worship of almighty God. This substitution of the interests of the community for the worship of God effectively destroys the significance of the liturgy for Christian living.

If the Eucharist is the "summit and source" of the Church's life, and if the worship of the Church has gone badly awry, then the mission of Christ's Mystical Body has been seriously compromised. This matters, and it matters not only for the Church; it matters for the world as well. It matters for the world because the Church, which St. Paul calls "the pillar and bulwark of the truth" (1 Tim 3:15), is speaking in muted tones about the Passion and death, the Resurrection and Ascension of Christ, and the world is poorer in consequence. The world is poorer because without the

Paschal Mystery, the world will never realize its destiny, which is that there should be "one Lord, one faith, one baptism, one God and Father of us all, who is above all and through all and in all" (Eph 4:4–6).

PART ONE

WINGLESS CHICKENS

This is a generation of wingless chickens, which I suppose is what Nietzsche meant when he said God was
dead.

—Flannery O'Connor, letter of July 20, 1955,
The Habit of Being

Something has gone drastically wrong with the worship of
the Church. It is important to see that this conviction, while
by no means universal, is shared by traditionalists and by
many who could in no way be called conservative or traditional. The Belgian primate Cardinal Danneels, who would
certainly be regarded as belonging to the "progressive" wing
of the Church, wrote in his diocesan newsletter:

> In the past Canon Law and the rubrics dominated every-
> thing: priests conformed to their prescriptions with an obe-
> dience which was sometimes puerile, for want of being
> enlightened. Today, the reverse is the case: it is the liturgy
> which must obey us and be adapted to our concerns, to
> the extent of becoming more like a political meeting or a
> "happening". "We are going to celebrate our own life
> experience!" [1]

I think the Cardinal is right, and I also believe he has
identified what has gone wrong: the liturgy is no longer
primarily the worship of God, but a celebration of our needs
and "our own life experience". It is quite true that many,

---

[1] Cited in: Mark Drew, "The Spirit or the Letter? Vatican II and Liturgical Reform", in *Beyond the Prosaic—Renewing the Liturgical Movement*, ed.
Stratford Caldecott (Edinburgh: T & T Clark, 1998), p. 50.

31

perhaps even most, people who still go to Mass are not
unduly upset by this. But this satisfaction, self-satisfaction if
Godfried Cardinal Danneels is right, has to be balanced with
two considerations.

In the first place, there is a recognition at the highest
levels in the Church that something like *a reform of the reform*
really is required; and this shows at very least that criticism
of the present liturgical arrangements is not based merely
on an unwillingness to change or on a contrariness that
refuses to accept the behest of legitimate authority. Secondly, there is the fact that, while those who still go to
Mass may be satisfied enough with the present arrangements, there has been a catastrophic falling off in attendance at Mass and in the influence of the Church. A far
greater number of non-practicing Catholics and the
unchurched find nothing in our rites, as currently celebrated, to draw them.

Joseph Cardinal Ratzinger in a series of important books
has argued that many of the ills in today's Church are directly
connected with both the way the liturgical reforms of the
post-Vatican II era were implemented and the way the liturgy is celebrated today.[2] Many liturgists and theologians
disagree with what the Cardinal has to say, but I do not see
how it is possible to deny that the Cardinal, as the Prefect
of the Congregation for the Doctrine of the Faith, was in
a unique position to see what is actually going on in the
worldwide Church. If he thinks there is a problem, then
most probably there is a problem. The officials of a liturgical commission in a particular diocese may tell us that

[2] For example, Joseph Ratzinger, *The Spirit of the Liturgy*, trans. John Saward
(San Francisco: Ignatius Press, 2000), and *God Is Near Us: The Eucharist, the
Heart of Life*, ed. Stephan Otto Horn and Vinzenz Pfnür, trans. Henry Taylor
(San Francisco: Ignatius Press, 2003).

everything is all right and that it is only extremists on both sides who are worried about the way things are, but it would seem the better part of rationality, if not ecclesial-political expediency, to give the Cardinal's point of view at least a hearing:

> I am convinced that the crisis in the Church that we are experiencing today is to a large extent due to the disintegration of the liturgy, which at times has even come to be conceived of *etsi Deus non daretur:* in that it is a matter of indifference whether or not God exists and whether or not he speaks to us and hears us.[3]

The Cardinal says here that there is in fact a crisis in the Church and that he thinks this crisis is intimately concerned with what he calls the *disintegration* of the liturgy. Many dissent from the Cardinal's position on various liturgical matters, but I have yet to see any argument to show that his description of the contemporary situation is wrong.

In addition to the well-known work of Ratzinger, I want to draw attention to another publication that may not be quite so well known: *The Reception and Actualization of Vatican II in the Light of the Jubilee of the Year 2000* is a large book written by a group of scholars and ecclesiastics who assembled in Rome for a private conference. It was edited by the rector of the Lateran University in Rome, Bishop Fisichella, and was published in 2000.[4]

One of the participants in the conference at the Vatican was Bishop Tena Garriga of the Congregation for Divine Worship. The Bishop did not hesitate to characterize much

---

[3] Joseph Ratzinger, *Milestones: Memoirs 1927–1977*, trans. Erasmo Leiva-Merikakis (San Francisco: Ignatius Press, 1998), pp. 148–49.

[4] R. Fisichella, ed., *Il Concilio Vaticano II: Recezione e attualità alla luce del Giubileo* (Cinisello Balsamo [Milan]: San Paolo, 2000).

modern worship in the Church as *auto-celebrations*,[5] that is, a celebration in which the community itself, with its aspirations and interests, becomes the focus of attention: "In the final analysis, the mystery of Christ takes second place, at very best, to the particular interests of the group ... as those who think of themselves as Church: not the *Body of Christ*, but only as *we*."[6] The Bishop goes on to write that today we are faced with a liturgy that is based on a vision of Christian living that is in practice exclusively horizontal, both in what concerns the fruits of the liturgy as well as with respect to the motivation for liturgical worship itself.[7]

Another series of talks that deserves to be noted was a world videoconference in September 2002 organized by the Vatican's Congregation for the Clergy. One of the speakers in the videoconference was Professor Gerhard Müller, who was subsequently appointed Bishop of Regensburg, a diocese in the southeast of Germany that has over a million Catholics. Bishop Müller said:

> A profound discrepancy can be found between the official liturgy and the lack of reception of its deeper meaning. In European countries participation in the Sunday eucharistic celebrations is drastically reduced. Many appear unaware that

[5] "Una liturgia che si chiamò 'desacralizzata' o 'secolarizzata', nei testi e nel rituale, e il cui centro di interesse andava passando, lentamente o rapidamente, dal mistero di Christo e dall'adorazione del Dio vivo alla riflessione ideologica o sociale e, in definitiva, *alla autocelebrazione*" (Tena Garriga, "La sacra liturgia fonte e culmine della vita ecclesiale", in ibid., p. 52 [my emphasis]).

[6] "In ultima analisi, il mistero di Cristo resta al massimo in secondo piano di fronte agli interessi propri dei gruppi, perché è, nello stesso modo, ciò che si pensa della Chiesa: non il 'corpo Christo', ma solamente il 'noi'" (ibid., p. 55).

[7] "Una visione quasi esclusivamente orizzontale della vita cristiana, della valutazione dei frutti delle celebrazoni, della motivazione stessa della liturgia" (ibid., p. 52). See below, pt. 1, chap. 5, "Hegel: God Becomes the Community".

this is an encounter with Jesus Christ, who has offered us
the gift of the Eucharist so that we may reach God in communion with the crucified and resurrected Lord, who is
the reason for our lives and makes sense of them.[8]

It is clear, then, that the criticism of the present state of
the liturgy is not always the work of disobedient malcontents
and that the process of desacralization and secularization
has not gone unnoticed by the highest authorities in the
Church.[9]

Further evidence that there is a problem can be seen from
the falling off of attendance at Mass and the increasing marginalization of the Church. It seems to be the practice of
those who defend the present liturgical arrangements to
emphasize that most people who go to Mass are happy with
what goes on in church. I do not think even this is true,
but the point here is to take seriously the fact that nowadays relatively few people in Europe and North America

[8] Professor (now Bishop) Gerhard Ludwig Müller of the University of
Munich, "Can Mankind Understand the Spirit of the Liturgy Anymore?"
Zenit.org., October 10, 2002, http://www.tcrnews2.com/liturgymuller.

[9] Cardinal Gustaaf Joos (in an interview with PUR magazine on March
26, 2004; http://johanneszentrum.kath.net/detail.php.id=7307) has been equally
frank about the refusal to see any divisions in the Church: "Ich will nur
soviel sagen: Nachdem wir 30–40 Jahre in Europa nach dem Mott 'keine
Polarisierung' gearbeitet haben und die Kirche heute noch 10 Prozent echte
Katholiken hat, glaube ich, dass es jetzt Zeit wird, wieder Farbe zu beken-
nen. Wir müssen den Leuten wieder klar sagen: 'Wenn Sie überzeugter Katholik sind, müssen sie das und das glauben; wenn Sie das nicht mehr glauben,
sind sie kein guter Katholik.'"

(I will only say this: Now that we in Europe have worked thirty to forty
years with the motto "no polarization", and the Church today has only 10
percent genuine Catholics, I believe it is now time to lay our cards on the
table once again. We must once again tell the people clearly, "If you are a
convinced Catholic, you must believe thus and so; if you don't believe that,
you are not a good Catholic.") An honest diagnosis of a disease does not
necessarily entail that we accept the prescription for its cure.

go to Mass in comparison to the recent past. To take Canada, for example, the following figures ought to be considered. In 1957 weekly attendance at Mass was 88 percent in Quebec and 75 percent outside the Province of Quebec; in 1975 those figures had dropped to 42 percent and 48 percent, and by 1990 they had plummeted to 28 percent and 37 percent. In the Canadian general social survey for 2000, those percentages were now 23 percent in Quebec and 29 percent outside.[10]

Few deny the figures, but they refuse to see that they have any connection at all with the damage done to the worship of ordinary Catholics by the liturgical changes; by "ordinary" I mean those without an interest in defending and promoting the changes, and "ordinary" here includes everyone else—well educated or not. Liturgists tend to be contemptuous of nonspecialists and all too often look on ordinary Catholics the way Marxists looked on the *Lumpenproletariat*.[11] For example, consider the following from the European liturgist Fr. Thierry Martens:

> It is in the Liturgy that dogma and moral teaching are experienced and tested for truth. Altering that really does amount to calling a great many things into question.... Seeing again the reactions of our faithful ... is enough to make us aware

[10] Reginald W. Bibby, *Restless Gods: The Renaissance of Religion in Canada* (Toronto: Stoddart, 2002), p. 20. This book was given a review article in *The Tablet*, August 31, 2002, p. 10, by Michael Higgins, who subjected the idea of a renaissance of religion in Canada to a sceptical analysis. However, the figures of "Good News Glibby", as the reviewer terms the author, are not in question.

[11] That is, as a necessary but unattractive element to bring about revolution; the *Lumpenproletariat* was a rabble, without any real stake in or understanding of society. Marx took the idea over from Hegel; see G. W. F. Hegel, *Hegel's Philosophy of Right*, trans. T. M. Knox (Oxford: Clarendon Press, 1949), p. 150.

how widespread is an attitude of setting one's face against changes and taking refuge in a series of taboos. . . . We may hope from the next Council for some important changes, and there is a danger that our faithful are not sufficiently open-minded for these.[12]

So, changing the liturgy alters the perception of the faithful about dogma and morals, and Fr. Martens is right about that; furthermore, the faithful are said not to be keen on more change, and he is right about that as well; finally, although I am not altogether sure what he means by taboo[13] here, it is clearly intended as derogatory; the faithful are not intelligent and open enough to accept the changes decided on by the liturgists.

At this point the supporters of the new arrangements usually introduce the idea of secularization[14] and say that the falling off of attendance at Mass has little if anything to do with the liturgical changes but everything to do with the fact that we live in a world in which religious language and religious symbols have become largely meaningless. It follows from this, although it is not often explicitly said, that the dramatic drop in the numbers of those practicing their faith would have happened anyway.

It is hard to refute arguments about contra-factual conditionals. That is, if someone wants to say that if the liturgical

[12] Quoted by Dom Charbel Pazat de Lys, O.S.B., "Towards a New Liturgical Movement", in *Looking Again at the Question of the Liturgy*, ed. Alcuin Reid, O.S.B. (Farnborough: Saint Michael's Abbey Press, 2003), pp. 100–101.

[13] In English, at least, *taboo* has to do with setting aside something as sacred; later on it was used to indicate that a person was ostracized from society. If the poor laity thought the Blessed Sacrament ought to be *taboo* so far as the liturgists were concerned, they are hardly to be blamed.

[14] See above, introduction, and below, pt. 2, chap. 2, "The Church in Society".

changes had *not* taken place, then the situation today would be the same, it is difficult to know what sort of argument could possibly lead him to change his mind. If liturgists with an investment in the project of liturgical reform continue to resist the thought that the new liturgical programs themselves might have a great deal to do with the falling away from the practice of the faith, others who have custody of the liturgy, and not just Cardinal Ratzinger, are beginning to articulate such a critique. Cardinal George of Chicago seems to be trying to put the record straight by pointing out that changes in a "symbol system" brought about a "limited concept" of the liturgy:

> In the post-conciliar period a limited understanding of the People of God has often led to a limited, horizontal concept of the subject of liturgy.... The liturgical reform was treated too much as a program and a movement for change, without enough thought being given to what happens to a community when its symbol system is disrupted.[15]

There is evidence, then, both from the authority of those in a position to know as well as from statistics, that a problem exists. In *The Mass and Modernity* I examine some of the most important of the ideas that lay behind the liturgists' "program for change". My aim is to show in some detail that ideas such as community, reason, science, modernism, and the like come trailing behind them a complex of ideas that have distorted the Catholic consciousness and so helped to deform the liturgical development of the modern Church.

First of all, there is the Enlightenment of the eighteenth century, whose principles and attitudes are still very much

---

[15] *Sacred Music*, vol. 130, no. 4 (Winter 2003): 26.

with us. Some of these principles and attitudes can be clearly
seen in the philosophies of Hume and Kant. But after the
eighteenth century came the nineteenth, with different ways
of understanding our existence, and these newer fashions
have become intertwined with the heritage of the Enlightenment. Among these influences there is Hegel's subtle and
far-reaching analysis of the state, civil society, and the community. Hegel, in his turn, was followed by Marx. I have
not devoted a special chapter to Marx because, so far as
Christianity is concerned, the damage to Catholic belief
had already been done by Hegel. When I say this, I am not
speaking about Marxism as a political movement that was
responsible for unparalleled damage to the Church and society, as well as being the cause of suffering on an untold
scale; but I am referring to the restructuring of the absolutely fundamental belief in God and about the nature of
the community. Viewed from the standpoint of the believer,
it does not matter a great deal whether these ideas are presented by a Hegelian or a Marxist. Marxism as the official
philosophy of communist states may, at the moment, be
largely quiescent, but the interest in Marxism is not dead,
and, indeed, there are those who say that with the end of
Stalinism we are now free to examine the whole question
without the intrusion of "irrelevant" political considerations.[16] We must also take account of the increasing

---

[16] For example, consider the following: "The Revolution in the revolu-
tions of 1989 has not 'destroyed' Marxism so much as it has dismantled post-
war state-Socialism. We have been given back the last two hundred years—in
life and in letters. All the debates, all the antinomies of modern state and
society addressed since Hobbes, Smith and Rousseau, have been re-opened
as well as the opportunity to resume examination of the connection between
liberalism and Fascism from which post-war Socialism has proved such a dangerous distraction" (Gillian Rose, *The Broken Middle* (Oxford: Blackwell, 1992),
p. xi).

importance of the social sciences, and especially of sociology, which is associated with the work of Comte.[17]

Part I, then, of this book is concerned with ideas. Once
ideas have become part of the intellectual furniture of an
age, they influence the way people look at life, what they
think is really important, and what they believe is worth
struggling for.[18] These very fundamental stances toward life
have been called absolute presuppositions,[19] and this phrase
expresses very well the unacknowledged but vital way that
intellectual positions condition and help to create the basic
attitudes of society, attitudes that shift and vary over the
centuries.

Ideas matter; but the ideas that matter most are taken for
granted. They have become so much a part of the intellectual landscape that they are only half recognized by most
people, even if their truth is accepted without question.
But we should recognize that these principles and ideas have
a history behind them, and the truth they now seem so

[17] See below, pt. I, chap. 6, "Comte: 'Policing the Sublime'".

[18] The intellectual dimension in the development of history covers a good
deal more than well-argued systems of thought. It also includes how these
systems are taken up into the consciousness of educated people who may
have very little firsthand knowledge of intellectual history. How ideas spread
as part and parcel of the nonspecialist consciousness is a complex subject,
and to discuss it in a satisfactory way would require an investigation that
would be partly sociological and would consist in as much hard data as could
be assembled about where and how people were actually educated, the avail-
ability of printed matter, who read what, and how ideas were exchanged
both within particular societies and between different societies. The investigation might also include a discussion of how fundamental convictions were
used to mold and strengthen particular ways of behaving in society. In addition there would have to be at least an elementary theory of how society in
its turn colors the interests and development of philosophy itself.

[19] R. G. Collingwood, *An Essay on Metaphysics* (Oxford: Clarendon Press,
1940), p. 31. I think Collingwood's theory is unacceptable as a metaphysics,
but it certainly expresses a reality at the level of experience.

obviously to possess is the result of hard-fought and often virulent clashes of opposing viewpoints. Eventually one set of ideas or another comes to be accepted as what "right-thinking" or "realistic" people accept. These fundamental presuppositions are the environment in which the Church has to function.

Ideas that influence people have been as productive of evil as they have of good. The most obvious case of this is the Enlightenment, whose basic principles most of us nowadays take for granted as being undeniably true and destined to endure. Such values as human rights, political liberty, due process in legal matters, the forbidding of torture, and religious toleration can be clearly traced, in their present formulation, back to eighteenth-century thinkers. The good effects of these principles are well summed up in a recent book: "When challenged to condemn torture in Argentina, war in Vietnam, or racism in the United States, where can we make our stand if not on principles enshrined in the Declaration of Independence and the Declaration of the Rights of Man and of the Citizen?" [20]

No one wants to dispute the truth of this so far as it goes, but it does not go far enough, because the influence of the Enlightenment has a good deal to answer for in addition to these emollient and uplifting sentiments. Indeed, there is a growth industry today in showing that a lot of what is considered objectionable about our modern world should be laid at the door of the Enlightenment. The Enlightenment is often looked on today as having a "dominating" view of reason that was really an instrument of control, and this has been an alienating force; furthermore,

[20] Robert Darnot, *George Washington's False Teeth*, cited in a review by Munro Price, *Times Literary Supplement*, August 8, 2003, p. 28.

it is also said to have tried to impose a Eurocentric view on
the rest of world and to have encouraged racism as well as
the oppression of women. It is also claimed that, in addition to these achievements, the origins of what has been
called totalitarian democracy must be laid at the door of
Enlightenment thinkers.

> A messianic political ideology, the mass mobilization of soci-
> ety to implement it, the treatment of political differences
> not as legitimate disagreements but as treason deserving death:
> these horrors first appeared not in Russia or Germany in
> the 1930s, but in France in 1793.[21]

This example shows that ideas have hooks, and they catch
onto other ideas. They tangle up other lines of thought in
a way that produces, not clear and distinct ideas, but an
amalgam that may have many attractive features but must
be handled with care. I do not think that nearly enough
care has been shown by churchmen in understanding and
evaluating these ideas that shaped the modern world, and,
as a result, it is the modern world that has begun to determine our understanding and preaching of the gospel, to
the detriment of our common Christian tradition. We can
see this, by way of an example central to this book, in the
way that Christ's redeeming sacrifice on the Cross for our
sins has receded from the center both of theological inquiry
and of the presentation of the Christian message.

Père de la Taille began his great work *The Mystery of
Faith* (first published in 1915) with the following words:
"In this treatise I deal first with the sacrifice and then with
the sacrament of the Body and Blood of the Lord, with the
sacrifice offered by our Lord Himself, before the sacrifice

[21] Price, ibid.

offered by us every day in our churches, with the Last Supper before the institution of the Mass." [22] The work caused a theological furor and was denounced by many in the Church. David Jones, the author of *Anathemata*, recounts meeting the eminent Dominican Fr. Vincent McNabb, "who looked at me and said that the whole proposition of the great French Jesuit was fraught with grave danger and was in fact heretical".[23] Yet, whatever the final judgment on Fr. de la Taille's work may be, we should see that both the Jesuit and the Dominican were operating within the same universe of discourse; they both thought the same things were important; they were both talking about the sacrifice of Christ and its relation to the Mass. It is this sense of a common heritage to be understood ever more deeply that seems to be disappearing in our day. This contrasts, I think sadly, with an earlier time when Fr. de la Taille could still boldly say, in the preface to his book, in words with which his Dominican critic would surely have agreed: "The real sources of theology are the documents of divine revelation; to one who denies the authority of these documents the theologian as such has nothing to say, *because theology is for believers.*"[24]

I have tried to explain why this sense of a common heritage seems to have disappeared and has all too often been replaced by the uncritical absorption of the principles of modernity. There are two aspects of my discussion that should be noticed. In the first place, the choice of the ideas for analysis has been dictated by the influence they have had

[22] Maurice de la Taille, *The Mystery of Faith* (New York and London: Sheed and Ward, 1940), p. vii.

[23] Words cited in René Hague, *A Commentary on the Anathemata of David Jones* (Wellingborough, Eng.: Christopher Skelton, 1977), p. 240.

[24] La Taille, *Mystery of Faith*, p. vii (my emphasis).

on the development of Christianity and, particularly, of the liturgy. As a result, the themes discussed may not be central to the thinker or movement from which they are taken, nor are the various thinkers treated in chronological sequence. For example, Kant thought that the phrase *sapere aude*— dare to know—showed what the Enlightenment was essentially about.[25] Whatever else he may have meant, he at least intended to assert that the problem of knowledge, and our attitude toward it, was the most important theme of the Enlightenment. Anyone writing a history of the Enlightenment would have to put this claim, and its ramifications, at the center of his account, even if he thought it were untrue. But my purpose is, not to provide such an account, but to show how various Enlightenment themes have played a role in the formation of the modern consciousness as it has impinged most directly on the Church. Furthermore, I discuss Kant before Hume (although chronologically Hume came before Kant) because Hume's clear repudiation of personal immortality represents a more extreme position than that of Kant, and it is Hume's denial, not Kant's complicated efforts to save the belief, that has won the day in non-Christian circles.

Secondly, while my selection of the ideas to be discussed is not the conventional list of topics to be found in a history of philosophy, the actual discussion of the ideas is deliberately a usual one. It is this usual understanding that has been influential, even when this understanding has been inadequate or defective. In dealing with the Enlightenment, for example, I have relied on standard modern works

---

[25] "*Sapere Aude*! Have the courage to use your own intelligence! is therefore the motto of the enlightenment" (*The Philosophy of Immanuel Kant*, ed. Carl J. Friedrich [New York: Modern Library, 1949], p. 132).

to set out what we could call the force or momentum of the movement. In doing this, however, I am certainly not agreeing with the unqualifiedly positive spin that is so often put on the principles of the Enlightenment in these standard interpretations.

This principle of selection has meant the exclusion of some familiar and important names. For example, in spite of the claim that Wittgenstein is one of the most important philosophers of the twentieth century, I have not discussed his work because it has had little direct influence on Catholicism. If his philosophy is understood as a revolutionary theory of meaning, it has not made the headway even in philosophical circles that its supporters believe it merits. This is certainly also true of the generality of theologians. Anthony Kenny, who is one of the world's leading interpreters of Wittgenstein's thought, has written: "Wittgensteinian scholarship has blossomed during the decade [1974–1984], ... but Wittgensteinian philosophy, as opposed to Wittgensteinian scholarship, has not made progress and some of the philosophical gains we owe to Wittgenstein seem in danger of being lost." [26]

Insofar as Wittgenstein's explicit remarks on religion are concerned, they translate into what I can only call a nondogmatic fideism based on an acute sense of moral failure.[27] "I believe that Wittgenstein was prepared by his own character and experience to comprehend the ideas of a judging God. But any cosmological conception of a Deity, derived from notions of cause or of infinity, would be repugnant to

[26] Anthony Kenny, *The Legacy of Wittgenstein* (Oxford: Blackwell, 1987), p. vii.

[27] Ray Monk in his *Ludwig Wittgenstein: The Duty of Genius* (London: Vintage, 1991), gives an account of this sense of moral failure and of its influence on Wittgenstein's thinking about religion.

him." [28] Wittgenstein's thought may be as intrinsically important as his supporters claim, but so far this has not shown
itself in terms of a Wittgensteinian revolution even in scholarly circles. Again, it is not criticism of the philosopher's
integrity to point out that the wrestling with sin and the
fear of judgment do not in themselves create a great theologian to whose influence attention must be paid.

Heidegger is another important figure in twentieth-
century philosophy whose work I have not discussed. [29] The
influence of Heidegger, unlike that of Wittgenstein, is apparently easy enough to detect in the thought of the Church.
Karl Rahner was a great (perhaps the great) influence on
postconciliar theology, and Rahner was deeply indebted to
Heidegger's teaching. In 1934 Rahner began studies for a
doctorate at Freiburg, and over the next four semesters he
attended virtually every lecture course and seminar that
Heidegger gave.

> [Rahner] was in the classroom when Heidegger echoed
> Nietzsche's condemnation of Christianity as "Platonism for
> the masses" and when he asserted that "a faith that does
> not constantly expose itself to the possibility of unfaith is
> not faith at all but a mere convenience." The effect of
> Heidegger's teaching was overwhelming. Thirty years later
> Rahner would remark that "although I had many good pro-

[28] Norman Malcolm, *Wittgenstein: A Religious Point of View?* (Ithaca, N.Y.:
Cornell University Press, 1994), p. 10. Malcolm knew Wittgenstein well and
published a memoir of him.

[29] "The ultimate worth of Heidegger's thought is still *sub judice*. Like his
great rival Hegel ... he is alternately worshipped, reviled, or sympathetically
assimilated to other, more accessible philosophers, especially Wittgenstein.... But his immense learning, his profound and innovative intelligence,
and, above all, his intense influence on modern thought, are not open to
doubt" (*The Oxford Companion to Philosophy*, ed. Ted Honderich [Oxford
and New York: Oxford University Press, 1995], p. 349).

fessors in the classroom, there is only one whom I can revere as my *teacher*, and he is Martin Heidegger." [30]

That, for better or for worse, seems clear enough, but it does not follow from this that Rahner should be called a Heideggerian. Rahner is often presented from the perspective of Heidegger's work, and this is not always warranted by what Rahner actually says. Furthermore it is doubtful whether Heidegger himself would have recognized himself in Rahner's work. [31] This is true, in part at least, because the two men had very different views about what could be said. Rahner himself wrote of Heidegger:

> Surely he has taught us *one thing*: that everywhere and in everything we can and must seek out that *unutterable mystery* which *disposes* over us, even though we can hardly name it with words. And this we must do even if, in his own work and in a way that would be strange for a theologian, Heidegger himself abstains from *speech* about this mystery, speech which the theologian must *utter*. [32]

Although Rahner uttered copiously on the sacraments, he had relatively little to say that touches directly on the liturgy. This "relatively little" has to be understood in relation to his enormous output, and in, for example, *The*

---

[30] Thomas Sheehan, "The Dream of Karl Rahner", *The New York Review of Books*, vol. 29, no. 1 (February 4, 1982).

[31] Thomas Sheehan, who espoused a well-regarded and very radical understanding of Rahner's thought, did not think Rahner was a Heideggerian, because, I take it, Rahner wanted to establish a (Kantian) basis for metaphysics while Heidegger wanted to overcome metaphysics altogether. See chap. 7, pp. 272–317, of *Karl Rahner: The Philosophical Foundations*, Continental Thought Series, vol. 9 (Athens, Ohio: Ohio University Press, 1987).

[32] Cited in ibid., p. xi.

Celebration of the Eucharist[33] he did deal directly with the Mass. But even here the focus is on theology and deals with the question "on which to determine how often Holy Mass should be celebrated". There is, however, one area where it could be argued that Heidegger's thinking has directly touched Catholic worship, and this is in the funeral Mass. The traditional Christian doctrine of immortality is said to have been recast by Rahner under Heidegger's influence, although once again, this seems to me to go far beyond anything Rahner says. However, it is true that there is a new understanding of death and resurrection, of Purgatory and heaven abroad, and this new understanding has radically altered a good deal of the Catholic's attitude toward death. I touch upon this in the chapter on Hume and atheism.[34]

Aside from this special case of immortality, much of Heidegger's work is the echo of themes to be heard in Hegel; that is, in spite of Heidegger's avowed purpose of leaving metaphysics behind, there are many aspects of his thought that do stand in the tradition of German Idealism.[35] I have dealt with these themes in my treatment of the influence of Hegel on the formation of the modern consciousness. Again,

[33] Karl Rahner, *The Church and the Sacraments* (Freiburg: Herder; Montreal: Palm Publishers, 1967). The title of the book in German is *Die vielen Messen und das eine Opfer* (the many Masses and the one Sacrifice). Three out of the five chapters of this book deal with what Rahner was still calling in 1963, when the book was first published, the Sacrifice of the Mass.

[34] Pt. I, chap. 4.

[35] "The drama [of the free and self-producing subject] give or take a few details, remains unchanged in Schelling and Hegel, and remnants of it survive through Schopenhauer, Feuerbach and Marx right down to Heidegger. What it lacks in cogency it amply supplies in charm, and even today its mesmerising imagery infects the language and agenda of Continental philosophy" (Roger Scruton, *A Short History of Modern Philosophy*, 2nd ed. (London: Routledge, 1995), p. 158.

insofar as Heidegger anticipates certain topics of post-modernism, I have covered this perspective on his work in the chapter on postmodernism.[36]

I contend that in trying to deal with modernity, the reformers of the Catholic liturgy have taken wrong turnings and made mistakes. The interesting question, though, is why these wrong turns of modernity seemed to be the right ones to make and the mistakes made seemed to be so attractive. I do not think that turning the wrong way and making mistakes are always the result of stupidity or ignorance or arrogance or even wickedness. The focus of my book is different from that of many current works because I provide an account of the philosophical and cultural background of the present liturgical malaise that is not entirely hostile to either the modern world or, much less, liturgical reform. On the other hand, wrong turnings and blind alleys are just that, and mistakes are mistakes. This is true even if the intentions in racing down dead-end streets are as authentic as anyone could wish and the motives for making mistakes seem to be pure as crystal. The wrong turnings taken and the mistakes made have their roots in disciplines that could have thrown light on how the gospel should be understood and lived in our own age but in fact have not. By this I mean, first of all, that sociology, metaphysics, moral philosophy, theology, and politics all color the way we understand the modern world; and, secondly, that this coloring has in fact pulled us away from faith and sent us off down blind alleys, when it has not encouraged us to follow "the easy way that leads to destruction" (cf. Mt 7:13).

It might be objected that theology, philosophy, and the social sciences seem a long way from Catholicism as it is

[36] Pt. 2, chap. 1, "Postmodernism—Blowing It All Up".

lived out in the Sunday worship of the parish and in the daily lives of believing Christians. This objection, while true about the perception of ordinary believers, is radically wrong if it is taken to mean that the creative work of thinkers and writers does not matter. In the long run, thinking and writing about religion, whether this thinking is positive or negative, well informed or badly informed, ends up affecting the way religion is practiced. But it also has to be said that the daily life of the Church is not affected *immediately* by new ideas or the reformulation of old ones. In one way or another she takes new ideas on board and absorbs them, sometimes it seems by a process of osmosis and at other times more directly, as happened at the Second Vatican Council and in the years that followed it. Yet, in neither case do these ideas have a direct influence on how people in the parish live their Catholicism, because the new ideas come mediated through the activity of various commissions and authorities in the Church. Nonetheless, these authorities and commissions have shown themselves to be open to all those forces in the world that have created modernity.

I do not suppose what I have said so far is particularly controversial. Serious intellectual work in any field requires a rigorous formation, intelligence, hard work, time, and freedom from practical concerns. In addition it usually requires a new vocabulary that is often difficult to recast in simpler language. High scholarly endeavors do not have a direct influence on the life of the Church because they are often very difficult to understand and usually require a specialized education to be assimilated. But they do end up having a vital role in how Catholics understand and practice their faith once they have been disseminated through widening circles of influence that recast and simplify them. These newer understandings of faith, and of the way it should be practiced, have created a sense that the worship of the Church is being radically restructured by hidden experts and impenetrable theologies. This sense, in turn, has caused suspicion, resentment, and unease. These reactions are understandable, and I sympathize with them. Yet I believe that the way to deal with this situation is, not by an unthinking and often brutal repudiation of modern thought and experience, but through an effort to see these developments for what they really are and then to judge them from the standpoint of faith.

I have understood "judging from the standpoint of faith" in a straightforward way, and in this book I have taken the traditional teachings of the Church as found in the *Catechism of the Catholic Church* for my reference point against which we can understand and evaluate the different forces at work on the Church. In the apostolic constitution *Fidei Depositum* (which serves as a preface or introduction to the *Catechism*), Pope John Paul II wrote that "the *Catechism* . . . is a statement of the Church's faith and of catholic doctrine, attested to or illumined by Sacred Scripture, the Apostolic Tradition, and the Church's Magisterium",[37] and then went on to state:

> I declare it to be a sure norm for teaching the faith and thus a valid and legitimate instrument for ecclesial communion. May it serve the renewal to which the Holy Spirit ceaselessly calls the Church of God, the Body of Christ, on her pilgrimage to the undiminished light of the Kingdom![38]

The *Catechism* does not say everything there is to be said about Catholicism, but it does "provide a norm for teaching

---

[37] *Fidei Depositum* 3.
[38] Ibid.

the faith". The *Catechism* enables us to say that intellectual positions that directly contradict it are disputing the Church's faith and Catholic doctrine.[39]

But what are, in fact, the salient characteristics of the current of modern experience that faith is negotiating in our time? They are well described by Czesław Miłosz, a Nobel Prize winner for literature:

> I lived at a time when a huge change in the contents of the human imagination was occurring. In my life Heaven and Hell disappeared, the belief in life after death was considerably weakened, ... the notion of absolute truth lost its supreme position, history directed by Providence started to look like a field of battle between blind forces.[40]

The inhabitants of this world are, to use Flannery O'Connor's phrase, *wingless chickens*:

> It is easy to see that the moral sense has been bred out of certain sections of the population, like the wings have been bred off certain chickens to produce more white meat on them. This is the generation of wingless chickens, which I suppose is what Nietzsche meant when he said God was dead.[41]

---

[39] "The most notable event in this pontificate [that is, of John Paul II], a pontificate providential in many respects, has been the publication of the *Catechism of the Catholic Church*, where the entirety of a most orthodox faith is found to be made explicit. This is an essential work because it stands as a visible point of reference, a norm declared and recognizable to everyone, and because, by this very fact, it judges and allows to be judged all expressions of faith" (John Borella, *The Sense of the Supernatural*, trans. G. John Champoux [Edinburgh: T & T Clark, 1998], p. 42).

[40] Czesław Miłosz, *To Begin Where I Am* (New York: Farrar, Straus and Giroux, 2001), p. 329.

[41] Flannery O'Connor, letter of July 20, 1955, *The Habit of Being*, ed. Sally Fitzgerald (Toronto: McGraw-Hill Ryerson, 1979), p. 90.

This is the modern world, or the postmodern world, a world whose inhabitants subsist on a badly digested mishmash of beliefs, a world that thinks it knows that science provides the answer to important questions and that religion is not true, even if it is sometimes thought to be useful in helping to create social cohesion by disguising the hard realities of life with suitable rites of passage or because it helps to underpin a desired morality. In general, though, the modern attitude views religion as at best superfluous when it is not actually harmful.

Wingless chickens are cripples who have had religion bred out of them. This means it is increasingly difficult to say anything about Catholicism that registers with our contemporaries, and not only with nonbelievers, but with Catholics as well. The message and mysteries of Christianity, whether loved or hated, are no longer part and parcel of most people's awareness, and, because of this, what Flannery O'Connor called "the accurate naming of the things of God" [42] has become almost intolerably difficult. It is all but impossible to name the things of God accurately because hardly anyone understands what is being talked about; or, if they do understand, they do not think it matters very much.

I have tried to write about what modernity has done to the worshipper in the pew. It is at Sunday Mass that the vast majority of practicing Catholics encounter the Church, and I am writing about the liturgy that they encounter. The encounter matters because in the liturgy we worship the God who is Father, Son, and Holy Spirit revealed to us through Christ. In the Eucharist we share in a unique and

---

[42] "I suppose when I say that the moral basis of Poetry is the accurate naming of the things of God, I mean about the same thing that Conrad meant when he said that his aim as an artist was to render the highest possible justice to the visible universe" (letter of January 13, 1956, ibid., p. 128).

mysterious way in his saving death, his Resurrection, and glorious Ascension, and we give a real assent to the truth that it is only in doing what God wants of us that we find the way to our own happiness, self-fulfillment, and finally the reward of everlasting life. If something has gone drastically wrong with the worship of the Church, our way back to God is effectively blocked.

When Newman wrote his great work *The Grammar of Assent*, he chose for its motto the words of St. Ambrose: "Non in dialectica complacuit Deo salvum facere populum suum". In the light of how Newman actually used this text, we could translate it as "it did not please God to save his people through a process of reasoning." Instead God *did* something. He sent his Son into the world to redeem the world. Newman believed that a Christian thinker had the obligation to remember he was not merely an academic theologian or philosopher but was responsible for understanding, guarding, and spreading the truth of the gospel. It should be obvious that this practical thrust means, not that Newman was anti-intellectual, but that he was concerned with how ordinary people could be believers and tried to help them. The analysis he provided may have been difficult enough to work with, but like St. Paul he was not ashamed of the gospel (see Rom 1:16) and wanted to show how belief was possible in the modern world without retreating into either obscurantism or liberalism. In this sense his work was *practical*.

My book follows Newman's example at least in this practical thrust.

CHAPTER ONE

THE ENLIGHTENMENT: DARING TO KNOW

[Enlightenment] knows that faith is opposed to pure insight, opposed to Reason and truth. Just as it sees faith in general to be a tissue of superstitions, prejudices, and errors, so it further sees the consciousness of this content organized into a realm of error in which false insight, common to the mass of people, is immediate, naïve, and unreflective.

—Hegel, *The Phenomenology*

The modern world is often looked on as a world that has shaken itself free from the bondage of religion, a bondage that over the centuries had imprisoned the human spirit and fettered the growth of freedom and rationality. The eighteenth century is usually said to mark the birth of a newer and truer account of the nature and destiny of mankind, and this improved view of things is called the Enlightenment.[1] It is the impact that the Enlightenment has had on

[1] The following citation is typical of this attitude: "During the later Middle Ages and the early modern age down to around 1650, western civilization was based on a largely shared core of faith, tradition and authority. By contrast, after 1650, everything, no matter how fundamental or deeply rooted, was questioned in the light of philosophical reason and frequently challenged or replaced by startlingly different concepts generated by the New Philosophy and what may still usefully be termed the scientific revolution" (Jonathan I. Israel, *Radical Enlightenment: Philosophy and the Making of Modernity, 1650–1750* [Oxford: Oxford University Press, 2001], p. 3).

Christianity that is of interest to us, not the enormously complex movement as a whole. Nonetheless, we should have at
least a very general idea of the standard interpretations of the
movement before trying to see how the movement has influenced the belief of Catholics and, therefore, the liturgy as well.

The Enlightenment is not merely a term devised by the
historian of ideas to describe a period in the history of the
modern European and American consciousness. It was also
deliberately used both by the people whose work created
the movement and by those who were inspired to follow
and develop its basic principles. In talking about the Enlightenment, then, we are referring to a movement that was in
part created by the use of the term itself. The movement
was created, developed, and cohered around explicit principles that constituted not only ideals but a practical program. A new world was being created, so they passionately
believed, and Eric Voegelin quite rightly characterizes this
belief as a "new consciousness of epoch".[2]

"The men of the Enlightenment", Peter Gay has written
in his two-volume interpretation of the Enlightenment,

> united on a vastly ambitious program, a program of secu-
> larism, humanity, cosmopolitanism, and freedom, above all
> freedom in its many forms—freedom from arbitrary power,
> freedom of speech, freedom of trade, freedom to realize
> one's talents, freedom of aesthetic response, freedom, in a
> word, of moral man to make his own way in the world.[3]

---

[2] Eric Voegelin, *From Enlightenment to Revolution* (Durham, N.C.: Duke
University Press, 1975): "Increasingly in the eighteenth century the sentiment grows that one age has come to its close and that a new age of Western
civilization is about to be born. We might well characterize this sentiment as
a new consciousness of epoch" (p. 3).

[3] Peter Gay, *The Enlightenment: An Interpretation* (London: Weidenfeld and
Nicolson, 1967), 1:3.

This movement has had a mixed press over the last three hundred years. For some it is almost axiomatic that the source of all that is best in modern civilization is to be found in the work of the men of the Enlightenment. Ernst Cassirer described it as "the period which discovered and passionately defended the autonomy of reason and which firmly established this concept in all fields of knowledge".[4] It is clear that Cassirer views this to have been a positive achievement of the first importance not only for the Enlightenment itself but for our own time. Even if we cannot restore in a simple-minded way the philosophy of the period, we should, he thinks, take to heart, and learn to apply to our own times, the lessons of the age that venerated reason and science as man's highest faculty. We must, he says: "find a way not only to see that age in its own shape but to release again those original forces which brought forth and moulded this shape".[5]

Peter Gay also sees the Enlightenment as a struggle for freedom. He views its operations as a family of *philosophes*[6] who worked within the cultural climate of an eighteenth-century world that was in part their own creation: "The philosophes' experience ... was a dialectical struggle to assimilate the two pasts they had inherited— the Christian and the pagan—to pit them against one another and thus to secure their independence. The

[4] Ernst Cassirer, *The Philosophy of the Enlightenment* (Princeton, N.J.: Princeton University Press, 1968), p. xi.

[5] Ibid.

[6] "*Philosophe* is a French word for an international type.... France fostered the type that has ever since been taken as *the* philosophe: the facile, articulate, doctrinaire, sociable, secular man of letters. The French philosophe, being the most belligerent, was the purest specimen" (Gay, *Enlightenment*, 1:10).

Enlightenment may be summed up in two words: criticism and power." [7]

Even for those who regard the Enlightenment with suspicion or open hostility, there is not much disagreement as to what it was about. Collingwood held it was an effort

> to secularize every department of human life and thought. It was a revolt not only against the power of institutional religion but against religion as such. Voltaire regarded himself as the leader of a crusade against Christianity, fighting under the motto *Écrasez l'infâme*, where *l'infâme* meant superstition, religion considered as a function of what was backward and barbarous in human life.[8]

Other interpreters, indeed, precisely *because* the Enlightenment marked the destruction of the religious view of man, hold that it must be viewed as having caused more harm than good to modern society. Voegelin, to take an example of this approach, writes that the eighteenth century has been "variously characterized as the century of Enlightenment and Revolution or alternatively as the Age of Reason" and then goes on to say:

> Whatever the merit of these designations they embody a denial of cognitive value to spiritual experiences, attest to the atrophy of Christian transcendental experiences and seek to enthrone the Newtonian method of science as the only valid method of arriving at truth. The apostatic revolt, for such it was, released a movement of ideas which would shape decisively the political structure of the West.[9]

---

[7] Ibid., 1:xiii.

[8] R. G. Collingwood, *The Idea of History* (Oxford: Clarendon Press, 1946), p. 76.

[9] Voegelin, *From Enlightenment to Revolution*, p. 3.

Whether we regard the Enlightenment as a betrayal of what was most valuable in the spiritual and political heritage of the West, or whether we see it as the source of what is best in our patrimony, in either case, no one doubts the importance of either the movement or the fact that the struggle against Christianity was central to it. If "moral man", to use Peter Gay's expression, were to make his way in the world, then he would have to escape from Christianity; and before man could become truly enlightened, much of Christianity would have to be destroyed. The men of the Enlightenment set about this work with a ready will. Bigotry, superstition, and the Christian story of man's redemption through the blood of Jesus Christ were all jettisoned as the great obstacles to the establishment of what the *philosophes* called "the religion of humanity".

The effects of the Enlightenment project are all around us in a variety of different ways. In addition to any number of particular doctrines, it is represented by an attitude of tolerance toward Christianity combined with an apparently benign interest in its precepts. Closer inspection often shows the tolerance to be no tolerance at all and the interest in its precepts to be anything but benign.

First of all, then, we have to have a more definite idea of what we are talking about when we use the term Enlightenment. Then we have to outline how Christians coped with what the more clear-headed of their number saw as a movement hostile to their faith. I have structured this outline on Bishop Berkeley's analysis of the intellectual currents of his own age written in 1732. He puts his analysis in the first person, and it is, I think, a more than slightly ironical comment on many of his fellow Christians.

Berkeley was the Anglican bishop of Cloyne and a distinguished philosopher. He was also, which does not perhaps follow necessarily from this fact, a perceptive and judicious observer of the intellectual movements of his time[10] and of their influence on Christianity. He is best known for his idealism, which, in an altered form, is still a powerful force in contemporary philosophy.[11] At first sight his thought usually occasions ridicule, because he taught in his beautiful English that "all the choir of heaven and furniture of the earth, in a word all those bodies which compose the mighty frame of the world, have not any subsistence without a mind", and the mind in which they subsist is the mind of God.[12] But the Bishop was no fool. He knew what he was about and would have had no difficulty with Dr. Johnson's kicking of a stone and saying, "Thus I refute Bishop Berkeley." It is true he analyzed the physical reactions of Johnson into what he called ideas; but call the ideas sense data, and we have the beginnings of a theory that is still influential. The sense-data theory has played an important role in twentieth-century English-speaking philosophy and owes much to him.

Apart from this technical aspect of his thought, Christians ought to remember that one of the driving forces behind his work was the effort to vindicate Christianity against the materialism of his age. This materialism went hand in hand with atheism; and both atheism and materialism he quite correctly saw were the inevitable outcome of the develop-

[10] "He was the most acute of critics, a writer of perfect grace and lucidity, and by temperament an enemy to all dullness, pedantry, and needless sophistication" (G. J. Warnock, *Berkeley* (Handsworth: Penguin Books, 1953), p. 12.

[11] "The contemporary theory which is most closely related to Berkeley's is the elaborate and much-discussed Phenomenalism. This might be described, in the simplest terms, as 'Berkeley without God'" (ibid., p. 236).

[12] George Berkeley, in *Selections from Berkeley Annotated*, ed. A. C. Fraser (Oxford: Clarendon Press, 1899), p. 36.

ment of the Enlightenment's repudiation of Christianity.
Berkeley knew what he was up against and was no sitter on
the fence. He said that the response of those interested in
Christianity, when faced with the dynamic of Enlightenment thought, went through three stages.[13] First they became
Latitudinarians. Latitudinarians was the name given to a large
group of Anglicans in the seventeenth century who, while
attached to Episcopal government and the forms of worship of the Anglican Church, regarded these attachments as
really unessential to Christianity. By the eighteenth century
it was taken to mean one who, "though not a sceptic, is
indifferent as to creeds and forms".[14] The Latitudinarian is
wearied of religious controversy and comes to think most
of the points that divide Christians have to do with things
that cannot be of importance for rational and cultured people: "Having observed several sects and subdivisions of sects
espousing very different opinions, and yet all professing Christianity, I rejected those points wherein they differed, retain-
ing only that which was agreed to by all, and so became a
Latitudinarian." [15]

But then our rational and cultured Christian begins to
reflect that it shows a very narrow mind to restrict the consideration of religion to what different Christians believe.
Surely, they begin to say to themselves, we should take into
account the beliefs of all those who accept the existence of

[13] "In a work of his mature years, *Alciphron* (1732), whose fly-leaf presents
it as 'An Apology for the Christian Religion against those who are called
Free-Thinkers', Berkeley traces the inevitable process of logic followed by
free thought in his day, beginning with its attack on the mysteries of Christianity and ending with the undermining of all faith in, or persuasion of, the
existence of a God" (Cornelio Fabro, *God in Exile*, ed. and trans. Arthur
Gibson [Westminster, Md.: Newman Press, 1968], p. 292).

[14] *Oxford English Dictionary*.

[15] Berkeley, cited in Fabro, *God in Exile*, p. 292.

God, and so they become deists. Deists were people who acknowledged the existence of a God but based this belief on reason and rejected the possibility of revelation. "Having afterward, upon an enlarged view of things, perceived that Christians, Jews and Mahometans had their different systems of faith, agreeing only in the belief of one God, I became a Deist." [16]

Finally, the deist sees everyone disagreeing about religion, so he gives up on the whole question of religion and becomes an atheist:

> Lastly, extending my view to all the other various nations which inhabit this globe, and finding they agreed on no one point of faith, but differed from one another, as well as from the aforementioned sects, even in the notion of God, in which there is a great diversity as in the methods of worship, I thereupon became an atheist.[17]

We could summarize the three stages of Berkeley's analysis by saying that, first, I gave up on revelation; then I gave up on the Church and sacraments; and then I gave up on God and the hope of an everlasting life with God in eternity.

[16] Ibid.
[17] Ibid.

CHAPTER TWO

LATITUDINARIANISM:
GIVING UP ON REVELATION

Cardinal de Bernis noted in his *Memoirs* that by 1720 it "was no longer considered well-bred to believe in the Gospels".

—Peter Gay, *The Enlightenment: An Interpretation*

There are few things more depressing than religious controversy, and over the centuries there has not only been controversy over religion but wars and rumors of wars fought in the name of various sorts of theological convictions. And, to make matters worse, some of those wars have been fought by Christians and against Christians over conflicting views as to what it was Jesus Christ came to earth to do and to teach. "Peace in our time" was one of the deepest urges of the eighteenth century, and this extended to religious questions.

There was a widespread sense that religious controversy had caused more suffering and bitterness than it was worth. Then, at the same time, there was the contempt of the *philosophes* themselves for religion in general and the ridicule they poured out on the doctrines of Christianity in particular. The result of the general longing for peace in society and the incessant and supercilious current of influential thought produced a crisis in religious confidence. The clergy

63

themselves had to live in a world in which "religious institutions and religious explanations were slowly being displaced from the centre of life to its periphery",[1] and the
response of the ecclesiastics in control of the various churches
was, in most places, a de facto, if not an explicit, acceptance of what they took to be the spirit of their age. Latitudinarianism is more of an attitude than a set of convictions,
but it was very real and very powerful.

> The real source of trouble, hard to diagnose and almost
> impossible to eradicate, was a bland piety, a self-satisfied
> and prosperous reasonableness, the honest conviction that
> churches must, after all, move with the times. This—the
> concessions to modernity, to criticism, science, and philos-
> ophy, and to good tone—this was the treason of the clerks.[2]

It is clear that Latitudinarianism is a response to secularization. Religion, it was felt, had been moved from the center; people wanted peace. Why stir up things for no good
purpose? This is not to say that religion suddenly disappeared; the trouble was that believers, like Berkeley himself, were somehow out of step with the temper of the times,
and they certainly did not provide a response that could
have stemmed the tide of cultivated agnosticism about Christian doctrine that dominated the age.[3]
The campaign to replace Christianity by this new and
rational religion of humanity had many facets. The most
important of these was the effort to destroy the Christian

[1] Peter Gay, *The Enlightenment: An Interpretation* (London: Weidenfeld and
Nicolson, 1967), 1:338.

[2] Ibid., p. 343.

[3] "Not only the poor, not only ignorant country clerics, but also profes-
sors and even bishops continued to believe in the Christian God" (ibid.,
p. 338).

view of revelation, a view that is clearly stated in the *Catechism of the Catholic Church*:

> Through an utterly free decision, God has revealed himself and given himself to man. This he does by revealing the mystery, his plan of loving goodness, formed from all eternity in Christ, for the benefit of all men. God has fully revealed this plan by sending us his beloved Son, our Lord Jesus Christ.[4]

The Enlightenment fought against this belief that God has shown himself in a unique and definitive way through Jesus Christ and ridiculed the conviction that this revelation imparts, as St. Paul says it, "a secret and hidden wisdom",[5] a "secret and hidden wisdom" that could be expressed in human language. It is this question of the verbalization of revelation that is the nub of the matter. It is one thing to think that God may have communicated, or shared, himself with us, but it is quite another to affirm that this communicating and sharing has some necessary connection with nouns, adjectives, verbs, and adverbs. It seems a bit crass, and for many unbelievable, to say that what revelation *means* is God's conveying a verbal message that then gets written down by different people in various ways. A great deal has been made of this difficulty, but before saying anything about it, we should see that we are really faced with two questions. The first of these is: What, in this activity of revealing, are we to understand by God's initiative and man's response? Secondly, what is the result of this activity?

---

[4] CCC 50.
[5] 1 Cor 2:7: "But we impart a secret and hidden wisdom of God, which God decreed before the ages for our glorification."

The first question is treated in a learned and fair way in a recent article by John Montag, S.J.,[6] in which he shows that the activity of God's revealing, and our part in this activity, is best understood by developing some of St. Thomas' ideas in the questions on prophecy in the *Summa Theologiae*. These questions concern in part the idea of the prophet's participating in God's own knowledge, rather than receiving a written or spoken message that he then hands on.

But this *how* of revealing is not really our concern here. What we do want to see is that the second question, that is, *what* is revealed, is very much of interest to us. St. Thomas never wrote a treatise on revelation, but we can find his position on the *what* of revelation in the questions on faith in the *Summa Theologiae*. The assent of faith is our response to God as the first truth; but the first truth is not a complex of statements (or a complex of anything else). Thomas insists that it is our adherence to God as the first truth that provides us with the means to believe in the particular assertions of Christianity, such as that God is a Trinity or that Christ is true God and true man and was born of the Virgin Mary. So, it is true and important to say that the part God plays in revelation cannot really be adequately understood as the dictation of a series of propositions; and, from our point of view, our faith is faith in the living God who cannot be grasped or understood through conceptual thinking. "[I]f we consider, in faith, the formal aspect of the object, it is nothing else than the First Truth. For the faith of which we are speaking, does not assent to anything, except

---

[6] "Revelation, the False Legacy of Suarez", in *Radical Orthodoxy*, ed. John Milbank, Catherine Pickstock, and Graham Ward (London and New York: Routledge, 1999), p. 38.

because it is revealed by God. Hence the mean on which faith is based is the Divine Truth." [7]

On the other hand, God as the first truth is simple, and we have no way of knowing anything about this nature except that it is. If God is to reveal something about himself that we can grasp, then it will have to be in a way that is suited to our capacities. We understand things by using *enuntiabilia*, that is, what can be enunciated, or propositions, or words.

> [T]he human mind knows in a composite way things that are themselves simple; this is quite the opposite of the divine mind, which in a non-composite manner knows things that are themselves composite. To apply this: consider the object of faith from its two perspectives. First, from the perspective of the reality believed in, and then the object of faith is something non-composite, i.e. the very reality about which one has faith. Second, from the perspective of the one believing, and then the object of faith is something composite in the form of a proposition. This explains why earlier theologians were correct in maintaining either alternative; there is a sense in which each is true. [8]

The purpose of this revelation by God is not merely to convey information, but to teach us how to live if we are to appropriate for ourselves the fruits of Christ's redemption. In the *Summa Theologiae*, St. Thomas teaches that revelation was necessary for man's salvation. Man was created for a purpose that surpasses anything he could have known if left to his own speculations about the meaning of existence.

---

[7] St. Thomas Aquinas, *Summa Theologica* 2, 2, 1, 1, trans. Fathers of the English Dominican Province (New York: Benziger Brothers, 1946–1948), 2:1169. (This translation is hereafter abbreviated STD.)

[8] STB 2, 2, 1, 2 (New Blackfriars translation).

He quotes the words of Isaiah to the effect that ear has not heard nor eye seen what things God has prepared for those that wait on him (see Is 64:4, Vulgate) and understands this to mean that, unless the nature of this destiny is revealed to us, then we could never do our part in seeking to obtain it for ourselves: "[T]he end must first be known by men who are to direct their thoughts and actions to the end. Hence it was necessary for the salvation of man that certain truths which exceed human reason should be made known to him by divine revelation."[9]

This was put very clearly by a Dominican of the last century in his commentary on questions 1–7 of the treatise on faith in the *Summa*.[10] Revelation and the faith that believes and accepts the revelation are not ends in themselves.[11] Faith, some theologians postulate, will pass away when the vision of God is attained, and the purpose of revelation is to make possible the attainment of this vision. "The God of faith is a God who has spoken. He has spoken to tell us who he is. He has spoken to tell us the truth and to have it become a part of us."[12]

---

[9] 1a pars, 1,1, STD 1:1.

[10] R. Bernard, O.P., *La Foi* (Paris: Desclée, 1963), vol. 1.

[11] "L'objet de la foi n'est pas que je puisse acquérir des vérités sur Dieu, c'est que Dieu fasse pénétrer en moi sa vérité à lui, c'est qu'il fasse chez-nous lui-même oeuvre de vérité" (ibid., p. 316).

[12] "Le Dieu de la foi est un Dieu qui a parlé. Il a parlé pour dire ce qui est. Il a parlé pour nous dire le vrai et pour nous le faire passer dans l'esprit" (ibid., p. 328). In the *Summa Contra Gentiles*, St. Thomas says that man can know divine things in three ways. In the first place, man can, by the light of human reason, rise to the knowledge of God from the world of creation. In the second, divine truth comes down to us by way of revelation, not like a proof to be analyzed, but like a truth to be believed. In the third way, the mind is raised to a perfect vision of what has been revealed. Revelation then was instituted to lead us to the blessed vision of God where our eyes shall see him and be satisfied (*Summa Contra Gentiles* IV, 1).

God's revelation of himself in Jesus Christ is given to us so that we might inherit eternal life. But this revelation is presented to us through *enuntiabilia*, or propositions. It is by means of these propositions that we are enabled to put our faith in Christ Jesus and him crucified. It is in the Bible and the Creeds that we find what God wished to communicate to us. Kierkegaard put what I take to be the Christian position on this question very clearly. He wrote in one of his efforts "to seek out experimentally an interpretation of existence":[13] "I scarcely suppose that anyone will deny that it is the Christian teaching in the New Testament that the eternal happiness of the individual is decided in time, and is decided through the relationship to Christianity as something historical."[14]

Latitudinarians find this position to be naïve and, as Cardinal de Bernis suggested, in bad taste, even if it is true that a great many people in the eighteenth century, and today as well, did not come out and say it very directly. Often enough the dismissal of the Christian concept of revelation was put forward by those who presented themselves as friends of Christianity; their purpose, they argued, was to present a purified and rational religion that would be worthy of a free and enlightened humanity. Kierkegaard's clear vision, for whatever reason, was certainly not shared by these well wishers of Christianity.

John Toland, for example, in his book *Christianity Not Mysterious* (1689), a precursor of the full-blown Enlightenment, argued that the true religion must necessarily be reasonable and intelligible. What he means by this can be learned

---

[13] Søren Kierkegaard, *Concluding Unscientific Postscript*, trans. David F. Swenson and Walter Lowrie (Princeton, N.J.: Princeton University Press, 1943), p. 322.

[14] Ibid., p. 330.

from the subtitle of his book: *A Treatise Showing that There Is Nothing in the Gospel Contrary to Reason; Not Above It; and That No Christian Doctrine Can Be Properly Called a Mystery.*[15] The guarantee of what he continues to call revelation becomes, on this view, the reasonableness of the content of what is revealed. The belief that God is supposed to have revealed this or that doctrine is dismissed as at best irrelevant. The test used to evaluate the content of anything that claims to be a revelation is internal to the putative revelation: Do we see in the supposed revelation "the indisputable character of Divine Wisdom and Sound Reason; which are the only Marks we have to distinguish the Oracles and Will of God, from the Impostures and Traditions of Men"?[16]

From this standpoint a religion that claims to have its origin in certain historical events may still have value. The essential point, however, is that it ceases to be authoritative because of its origins, and its value is to be determined solely in terms of the dictates of natural morality. In the final analysis, it has to be said about any revelation that if it is in accord with natural morality, then it is superfluous; if, on the other hand, its dictates contradict natural morality, it is not only false but also often harmful.

It follows from these principles that any notion of redemption or salvation as a particular action, or set of actions, on the part of God becomes not only superfluous but harmful as well. The Church believes that Christ took upon himself our sins and died upon the Cross. St. Peter writes of the redemption in the following words: "[Christ] himself bore our sins in his body on the tree, that we might die to sin

---

[15] Quoted in Henry E. Allison, *Lessing and the Enlightenment* (Ann Arbor: University of Michigan Press, 1966), p. 12.

[16] Ibid., p. 13.

and live to righteousness. By his wounds you have been healed" (1 Pet 2:24). St. Paul says: "For I delivered to you as of the first importance what I also received, that Christ died for our sins in accordance with the scriptures" (1 Cor 15:3). These texts state the mystery that it was through Christ's death on the Cross that our sins are forgiven and that we are given the grace to live a new life in God. Furthermore, this saving death was a sacrifice Christ made of himself for us. In the Letter to the Hebrews, Christ is depicted as the great high priest offering his blood in atoning sacrifice:

> But when Christ appeared as a high priest of the good things that have come, then through the greater and more perfect tent (not made with hands, that is, not of this creation) he entered once for all into the Holy Place, taking not the blood of goats and calves but his own blood, thus securing an eternal redemption (Heb 9:11).

There is no doubt as to how the Church understands these texts: "[Christ], our Lord and God, was once and for all to offer himself to God the Father by his death on the altar of the cross, to accomplish there an everlasting redemption." [17] Then, finally, the Church links the sacrifice on the Cross to the sacrifice of the Mass: "The sacrifice of Christ and the sacrifice of the Eucharist are *one single sacrifice*." [18] In the chapter on the *Paschal Mystery* we will examine this teaching in more detail. Here I want only to point out that

[17] Council of Trent, cited in CCC 1366.

[18] CCC 1367. The *Catechism* then goes on to cite the famous words of the Council of Trent: "In this divine sacrifice which is celebrated in the Mass, the same Christ who offered himself once in a bloody manner on the altar of the cross is contained and offered in an unbloody manner" (Council of Trent [1562]: *Doctrina de ss. Missae sacrificio*, c. 2:1743; cf. Heb 9:14, 27).

the notion of Christ's sacrifice for sin and its connection to the Eucharist is in fact Catholic teaching.

The Enlightenment would respond to the texts I have just cited either by emptying them of their particular content or by saying that they represented an objectionable moral position. The words of St. Peter might be said to represent Christ's life and death as merely an example of generous human living and a noble human dying, while the words of St. Paul might be understood as showing the regrettable consequence of immoral behavior—the death of a good man. Such interpretations turn the words of St. Peter and of St. Paul into statements about human behavior that anyone in any culture or with any belief could in fact accept. If, though, we think St. Peter is saying there was something particularly efficacious in Christ's death as a particular death, then we are propounding something immoral. It is immoral because it adds something particular and arbitrary to the reasonable world of natural justice. It is not fair that one man's death should have this particular power; nor is it fair that only those who stand in some sort of special relationship to it should be particularly privileged.

One of the main objections the Enlightenment had to revelation was that it was *unfair* that salvation should be connected with the particular events and the particular teachings of Jesus Christ. From this they went on to argue that to live seriously as a Christian was to act according to a natural law that all men shared in virtue of their humanity, and any law in addition to this was superfluous and often harmful. If we view matters in this way, it follows that ethical considerations become the test of religious principles. It is the universal moral character of Christian teaching that should be of primary concern, and this universal character of Christian morality is based on reason and not on the fact that it was said to have been taught by Jesus Christ. If this is true, then any particular religious law or practice has to be judged by the standards of a morality that everyone shares as a human being.

This turning away from Christian revelation was thought to be one more example of progress and the triumph of rationality over superstition. But it was not intended to be a rejection of Christian morality; rather, it was often presented as a purification of morality by placing it on a firm rational foundation and removing what the Enlightenment would have regarded as its contingent, haphazard, and untrustworthy historical foundations. The result of this detachment from Christianity leaves a morality that they, the enlightened, thought retained the kernel of Christian living without the unnecessary scaffolding provided in the Gospels. The consequences of this view for the liturgy are easy to see. Catholic liturgy is based firmly and squarely on the conviction that Christ's death on the Cross reconciled us to God and to each other and that in the liturgy we find this saving death perpetuated through time. If the death of Christ has no more than a moral significance, then the Mass becomes only the celebration of the memory of a good man's death. But if, to use Newman's words, we think that Christianity has the power to staunch "the one deep wound of human nature" [19] and that this power comes from the

---

[19] "[The] remedy for both guilt and for moral impotence, is found in the central doctrine of Revelation, the Mediation of Christ.... This is the secret of its sustained energy, and its never-flagging martyrdoms; this is how at present it is so mysteriously potent, in spite of the new and fearful adversaries which beset its path. It has with it that gift of staunching and healing the one deep wound of human nature, which avails more for its success than a full encyclopedia of scientific knowledge and a whole library of controversy" (*Grammar of Assent*, with an introduction by Étienne Gilson [New York: Doubleday, Image Books, 1958], p. 376.)

death on the Cross, then in the Eucharist we have come into contact with something greater than ourselves; we have come into contact with the sacrifice of Christ, who for our sake was made "to be sin who knew no sin, so that in him we might become the righteousness of God" (2 Cor 5:21).

The men of the Enlightenment replaced these central Christian doctrines, doctrines that are central to both tradition and the Bible, with a natural religion. This natural religion they identified with the proper use of reason. The most sure and effective way of determining the nature of this religion of reason was to forget about churches, Scripture, and creeds and to look within. Lord Herbert of Cherbury, for example, wrote:

"To state the whole in a few words, every divine and happy sentiment that we feel within our conscience is a revelation, although properly speaking there are no other revelations than those which the inner sense knows to be above the ordinary providence of things."[20] On this view, revelation, in any acceptable use of the term, becomes our understanding of the principles of religion that is available to us on the basis of our common humanity: "Retire into yourself and enter into your own faculties; you will find there God, virtue and the other universal and eternal truths."[21] Furthermore, because these interior principles are universal and eternal, they are common to all religions:

Thus it appears that the common notions which recognize a sovereign Author of all things, which bid us honour him, lead holy lives, and repent of our crimes, and expect reward

[20] Lord Herbert of Cherbury, quoted in Basil Wiley, *The Seventeenth-Century Background* (Garden City, N.Y.: Doubleday Anchor Books, 1953), p. 137.

[21] Ibid., p. 131.

or punishment after death, come from God, are imprinted in the whole human race. . . . We gladly believe that in every religion, and even in each conscience, whether by grace or by nature, a man has means sufficient to render himself acceptable to God.[22]

This sapping away of belief in revelation has created a climate of opinion in which the liturgy as the celebration of the central mysteries of revelation is becoming less and less meaningful to most people. That does not mean the mysteries are no longer true, but it does mean they have to be taught more clearly, and practiced more faithfully. Radically to restructure the Christian message by succumbing to the temptation to re-present the Enlightenment ideals of a free and autonomous subject using a Christian vocabulary helps our understanding neither of Christianity nor of the world to which we are supposed to be witnessing. Kierkegaard would certainly not have been surprised that people were continuing to tell us what Christianity was really all about; but he would have treated these efforts with derision:

> For a man to prefer paganism to Christianity is by no means confusing, but to discover paganism as a highest development within Christianity is to work injustice both to paganism and to Christianity; to Christianity, because it becomes something other than it is, and to paganism, which doesn't become anything at all, though it really was something.[23]

---

[22] Ibid., p. 135.
[23] Kierkegaard, *Concluding Unscientific Postscript*, p. 333.

CHAPTER THREE

KANT AND MORAL RELIGION: GIVING UP ON THE CHURCH AND THE SACRAMENTS

There is only *one* true *religion*; but there can be *faiths* of several kinds. We can say further that even in the various churches, severed from one another by reason of the diversity of their modes of belief, one and the same true religion can yet be found.

—Immanuel Kant, *Religion within the Limits of Reason Alone*

It would be a mistake to think of deism as merely the product of ecclesiastical trimmers. At its best, deism was the product of men who really did believe that they were purifying religion and, so, laying the foundations for peace in society and for moral improvement. The Enlightenment was dominated by the idea of freedom and an overwhelming belief in the power of human reason, especially as displayed in the natural sciences. We have seen how this conviction that reason was the final court of appeal resulted in the condemnation of revelation. Now, we should look at how Christianity fared in a world whose intellectual leaders had done away with revelation.

At the close of the Enlightenment period there stands the austere and unbending figure of Kant,[1] and Kant presents us with a perfect example of what happens to Christianity when we begin to discount the Bible and the Creeds. We are left with a moral religion that leaves room for God but does not leave room for much else in the way of religion. For all its strength and attractiveness, Kant's religion based on morality is destructive of Catholic Christianity.

Kant is the philosopher, par excellence, of human freedom and human rights, and he teaches the unconditioned obligation to treat others as possessing absolute value as members of a "kingdom of ends". Yet he ends up by condemning prayer, sacraments, and the Church in the name of human freedom and human dignity. It is not merely that prayer, sacraments, and the Church are harmless (if irrelevant); they are actually pernicious, and to take prayer, sacraments, and the Church as a visible structure seriously is immoral.

How did Kant arrive at this position?

Kant's philosophy was an effort to answer three fundamental questions. How is metaphysics possible? How is physics possible? And how is morality possible? His analysis of religion depends on his answer to these three questions.

His response to the first question, how is metaphysics possible, was that if we think of metaphysics as knowledge of the ultimate reality, what he calls "transcendent

---

[1] "Kant inspires our awe as a representative of the spirit of the eighteenth century. We cannot help feeling that in him this spirit has not only reached maturity and beyond. In him, we feel this spirit is not merely at loggerheads with itself in a riotous way; it does not merely strive beyond itself in enthusiastic if poetic fervour and it does not become a prey to Mephistophelean self-mockery. It has quite simply come to terms with itself; it therefore knows where it stands and it has thus acquired humility" (Karl Barth, *From Rousseau to Ritschl*, trans. Brian Cozens [London: S.C.M. Press, 1959], p. 152).

metaphysics", or "dogmatic metaphysics", we are doomed
to failure. The human intellect is just not capable of undertaking that sort of inquiry, and if we develop our natural
propensity to ask general questions about such matters as
the eternity of the world or the immortality of the soul we
will end in scepticism.[2] Instead, he replaced the view that
metaphysics has to do with being as such, or with the way
things really are, with a new kind of metaphysics modeled
on how he himself understood the advances in natural
science.

The triumph of science, and especially of Newtonian physics, he thought, had been made possible by a new understanding of how reason and experience worked together to
discover truth. This model of scientific investigation is neither empiricist nor rationalist; rather (according to Kant), it
consists of understanding nature in terms of the demands
of reason. Theoretical reason is equipped to deal with nature
but not with what is beyond nature; and nature is receptive
to being understood in terms of the demands of reason.[3]
Reason, as he puts it, without experience is empty, and
experience without reason is blind. Metaphysics, in an acceptable sense (what he calls "immanent" metaphysics), is based
on this model.

The reader is asked to consider, or reconsider, Kant's position and intention in regard to metaphysics. His position

---

[2] "The critique of reason, in the end, necessarily leads to scientific knowledge; while its dogmatic employment, on the other hand, lands us in dogmatic assertions to which other assertions, equally specious, can always be
opposed—that is, in *skepticism*" (*Immanuel Kant's Critique of Pure Reason*, trans.
Norman Kemp Smith [London: Macmillan, 1950], B 23, p. 57).

[3] "From this new standpoint Kant develops phenomenalism on rationalist
lines. He professes to prove that though our knowledge is only of appearances, it is conditioned by *a priori* principles" (Norman Kemp Smith, *A Commentary on Kant's "Critique of Pure Reason"* [London: Macmillan, 1930], p. 18).

was that the desire for ultimate explanations or descriptions of the nature of reality was a fundamental and almost ineradicable temptation of the human mind. Yes, Kant says, it is quite true we do want to reason about the nature of things beyond appearances; yes, he says, we do want to speculate about the nature of the human soul and about its fate after death; yes, he says, we do want to ponder the question of whether or not God exists; nonetheless, the human intellect has no capacity to deal meaningfully with these questions. That is his position about metaphysics.

Kant's intention in regard to metaphysics was to replace it with a new doctrine whose subject matter was to establish the foundations of science and morality. This chapter of *The Mass and Modernity* shows how religion fared at the hands of this new doctrine that Kant calls an immanent metaphysics.

In spite of the heavy verbal reliance on Kant's thought, the extraordinary familiarity with the absolute reality displayed by many modern Catholic theologians cannot be justified on Kantian principles. These thinkers use Kant to support their arguments on one side, while contradicting him on the other. That is, they claim to accept Kant's attack on metaphysics and so are able to dismiss most of traditional Catholic theology; but these same thinkers also make claims about the capacity of the human mind that Kant would have rejected. Thomas Sheehan has written: "Unlike generations of Catholic philosophers who had studied Kant the way anti-aircraft gunners study enemy planes, Rahner in large measure *presumed* Kant's devastating critique of metaphysics and argued that what little we know of the divine we know by being irreversibly turned toward the world." [4]

[4] Thomas Sheehan, "The Dream of Karl Rahner", *The New York Review of Books*, vol. 29, no. 1 (February 4, 1982).

This is unacceptable on two counts. First of all, what does "in large measure *presumed*" mean? In practice it seems to mean that Kant is useful as a weapon against tradition, but that does not stop Rahner from employing a discourse that is clearly metaphysical in the sense that Kant thought was reprehensible. Secondly, on Kantian principles, we do not know a "little . . . of the divine" by "being irreversibly turned toward the world"; this is so, because on the same Kantian principles, we know absolutely nothing at all about the divine by "being irreversibly turned towards the world".

In considering Kant's response to the second question, that is, the answer concerning the foundations of physics, it should be noted that Kant began his academic career as a teacher of science, and his first published work, which he had actually written while still a university student, was on the controversial concept of force.[5] Kant's contribution to the debate is of interest to us because it shows that we cannot understand Kant or his influence unless we take into account his early, and abiding, interest in science.

Natural science, Kant thought, was the effort to discover universal and necessary laws that govern all experience. The very possibility of anyone undertaking this search implies the conviction that nature is governed by patterns of events that are constituted by cause and effect. To find these causal patterns is the aim of natural science.

Hume had attacked the theoretical foundation of the causal axiom; that is, Hume did not deny we have to use the prin-

---

[5] *Thoughts on the True Estimation of Living Forces*, begun in 1746 (when Kant was twenty-three), was finished three years later. His work was not in the class of the work of Euler or d'Alembert. Lessing famously remarked that Kant in the estimation of living forces neglected the estimation of his own forces. See Ernst Cassirer, *Kant's Life and Thought*, trans. James Haden (New Haven and London: Yale University Press, 1981), p. 30.

ciple of cause and effect, but he did maintain there was no ground in reason for its use. It was a custom or habit based on the observation of our own intellects that prompted the idea that two events are causally connected. Kant was under no illusion as to the challenge Hume posed for the theoretical basis of natural science. Kant understood both the importance of the causal axiom and the force of Hume's criticism. The *Critique of Pure Reason* is primarily an effort to refute Hume and put the causal axiom on what he regarded as a sound footing. He attempted to do this by what he called a transcendental argument. Beginning with the fact that physics is possible, because after all we in fact do it, he then asks what the necessary conditions for the possibility of physics are. He then argues that among these conditions is the truth of the proposition that every event has a cause; and, if every event has a cause, then this establishes the reign of law in nature. The reality of this reign of law is what makes it possible for us to do physics. His position is that natural necessity constitutes the objective world we all experience, but we have no way of knowing whether or not this necessity also characterizes the world lying behind the objective world of appearances.

Finally, there is the question about the possibility of morality. Morality requires the possibility of freedom and responsibility for what we do. If nature is causally determined, then it is difficult to see how we can be either free or responsible. Kant's answer to this difficulty is to say that in our experience of obligation we come into contact with a realm of freedom that is not determined by natural necessity. Through our involvement with this world of freedom, we find the fulfillment of our nature as rational beings by freely legislating a moral law that is valid for all rational beings. We escape the causal necessity of nature, but our freedom consists in the capacity to follow a moral law that binds us absolutely in terms of our common rationality as human beings.

In *Religion within the Limits of Reason Alone*,[6] Kant insists that reason and morality are the test of true religion. Revelation, properly conceived, may be useful for some people, but it must submit to the test of morality, and by morality he understands an exercise of a practical reason common to all mankind. This practical reason is motivated only by the intention of acting according to the moral law; and a genuinely moral act can have no other intention than to be law-abiding.

Kant was determined to establish morality on a firm foundation. The morality he tried to vindicate was an ethics of duty. According to him, the only thing that can be called good without qualification, either in this world or out of it, is a good will. Any personal good that we can think of, such as intelligence, wit, health, or strength, becomes actively harmful if the will is bad. On the other hand, even without intelligence, wit, health, or strength, a good will is of absolute and intrinsic value whether or not it ever accomplishes anything practical.

Kant's ethics is thus an ethics of intention. The consequences of what I might do have no part in determining the rightness or wrongness of my proposed course of action. What, then, determines the rightness or wrongness of an action? A good action is one that is the result of my free adhesion to the law my reason imposes on me in virtue of its own reasonableness. "Morality", he says in the *Groundwork*,[7] "is based upon the conception of man as a free agent who, just because he is free, binds himself through his reason

---

[6] Immanuel Kant, *Religion within the Limits of Reason Alone*, trans. Theodore M. Greene and Hoyt H. Hudson (New York: Harper & Row, 1934).

[7] The full title of the book is *The Groundwork of the Metaphysic of Morals*, trans. H. J. Paton (London: Hutchinson's University Library, n.d.).

to unconditioned laws." These laws, though, are the laws of his own reason. Furthermore, because reason is the defining characteristic of all reasonable beings, it follows that the law freely imposed on the self is a law common to all. The law that we freely impose upon ourselves is called by Kant the *Categorical Imperative*. It is categorical because what it prescribes is not a means to anything else but is an end in itself. It is imperative because it commands, and it does so whether or not it is obeyed. In the *Groundwork*, Kant gives several formulations of this law and argues that we have to treat other people as ends in themselves because they, too, are autonomous legislators of the moral law. "Morality", he says in his usual uncompromising fashion, "is the only condition under which a rational being can be an end in himself: for only through this is it possible to be a law-making member of a kingdom of ends." [8]

In acting morally, I become associated with all those who also act morally and whom I treat, even as they treat me, as ends in themselves. This moral way of acting is the foundation of human dignity. The human person, as an end in himself, is never to be used as a means for any purpose, no matter how apparently noble. Man's dignity is beyond price, and its foundation is his membership in the kingdom of ends, a kingdom made up of all those who freely impose upon themselves the law of man's own reason.

In the *Critique of Practical Reason*, Kant sets out to show how the moral agent escapes the world of natural necessity, a necessity he was at such labor to establish in the *Critique of Pure Reason*. His question now becomes: How is it that natural necessity can be a real aspect of the world of nature, and how at the same time can man be free? His answer

---

[8] Ibid., no. 76.

rests on the distinction between the objective world we all experience and the noumenal world of reality with which we come into contact through our experience of obligation. Nature really is determined in terms of the a priori relation of cause and effect, while in our experience of duty we encounter the real world of freedom. This distinction rests on a prior analysis of the human intellect into *understanding*, on the one hand, and *reason*, on the other.

With this background in mind, we can now approach what Kant had to say specifically about religion. Here it is appropriate to remind the reader that I am presenting a standard interpretation of the various thinkers I deal with. It is this standard interpretation that has had the greatest influence on the general consciousness. *Religion within the Limits of Reason Alone* is a strange and difficult work even by Kantian standards, and there are parts of it that are difficult to reconcile with the rest of Kant's philosophy. Karl Barth, the great Protestant theologian who has been called the St. Thomas Aquinas of Protestantism, was so concerned about these elements that by an extraordinary feat of intellectual brilliance, he thought they could only lead to Rome![9] Let us be content, however, with a more usual understanding of the book.

Mankind, Kant thinks, is impelled to believe "in the co-operation or management of a moral Ruler of the world".[10] This moral ruler is going to ensure that the morality of duty will somehow find its completion in what Kant

---

[9] "Where else is a doctrine of salvation to end, which is intended to be an anthropology and nothing but anthropology, even if it does have as its background a metaphysics with an ethical foundation—where else could it end, but in the twofold possibility of the Roman Catholic doctrine of salvation?" Barth, *From Rousseau to Ritschl*, p. 186.

[10] Kant, *Religion within the Limits*, p. 130.

calls "the idea of the highest good", an idea of a condition in which happiness will find its proper place. The
search for happiness does not enter into the intention to
be law-abiding, and it is this intention that constitutes the
essence of morality. If we start considering the consequences of what we believe in terms of happiness or of
any other good, then we have given up on real morality.
On the other hand, justice seems to maintain that there
ought to be a connection between duty and happiness. It
is clear that all too often doing the right thing does not
bring happiness in any obvious sense, but this seems wrong.
Yet, for a variety of complex reasons, Kant held that we
cannot in practice live a moral life unless we postulate, or
accept, the existence of God as "unchangeably omni-
scient, omnipotent," and so on, but as possessing these
characteristics insofar as, and only insofar as, he under-
writes morality. Apart from moral activity, we know nothing at all about him in any metaphysical, theoretical, or
religious way. We *have* to believe in God if we are going
to lead moral lives, and we have to lead moral lives because
living such a life is an aspect of our rationality. To fail to
be rational is to be less than human, less than ourselves. It
is to live in a way determined inexorably by a universe
ruled by the cause and effect that operates everywhere in
the world of experience. So to escape determinism, and
to live as a free, rational, and moral human being, requires
a belief in the "moral Ruler of the world". Belief in Kant's
God is required for morality, and our only awareness of
him is in our effort to lead moral lives. Furthermore, what
we know of God is exclusively concerned with his function as a prop for morality. (Strictly speaking, we do not
even know if he exists, but we are forced to act as though
we knew he did.)

Now the universal true religious belief conformable to this requirement of practical reason is belief in God "(1) as the omnipotent Creator of heaven and earth, i.e., morally as *holy* Legislator, (2) as preserver of the human race, its *benevolent* ruler and moral Guardian, (3) as Administrator of His own holy laws, i.e., as *righteous* Judge".[11]

Our awareness of God, then, is totally bound up with our moral experience, and our only knowledge of God has to be described in terms of moral experience. We know God only as a "holy Legislator", "moral Guardian", and "righteous Judge". Is there a God? To ask that, Kant would say, is to ask the wrong sort of question. It is the wrong sort of question because it shows a belief in the possibility of doing metaphysics understood as a science of being that provides answers about the way things really are, and the human intellect is incapable of knowing or describing this reality. On the other hand, living as a human being forces you to acknowledge the reality of the God you cannot know or describe metaphysically.

The consequences of this position for institutional Christianity are spelled out in *Religion within the Limits of Reason Alone* and illustrate that, however important and attractive it may be to argue for the primacy of morality, it has also to be understood that morality, at least as understood by Kant, leaves no room for a church founded on anything specifically Christian.

The church is one because although "divided and at variance in unessential opinions", nevertheless the fundamental thrust of those who belong to it is toward "a general unification in a single church".[12] The nature of this thrust

[11] Ibid., p. 131.
[12] Ibid., p. 93.

toward unity is a moral one: "union under no motivating forces other than moral ones". The members of this church are free both as regards the political power of the state and in relation to each other. It is a sort of republic in which there is no hierarchy and no democracy, understood as the imposition of other people's arbitrary opinions on the other members of the church.

This church is invisible because it is the union of free moral agents, and their ethical commonwealth has no essential relation to either the state or other members who are, all of them, autonomous legislators of the same moral law. Any visible structure is concerned only with "incidental regulations, concerning merely its administration", and these "may be changed according to time and circumstance". So, I take it, even under an oppressive state the church would still be free, because its essential nature has nothing to do with the visible aspects that the state could touch.

The church, then, is one and invisible, and its unity is based on the fact that we all share a common rational nature, which displays itself as every individual legislating for himself the same moral law. Kant spells out what this position entails for the idea of revelation and then applies his analysis to specifically Christian practices such as prayer and sacraments. Revelation, he says, does not necessarily mean an activity that is unreasonable or arbitrary. This is so because revelation can be understood as a sharing in the moral requirements necessary for leading a moral and therefore human life. Revelation properly understood "can certainly embrace the pure religion of reason".[13] On the other hand, if we think revelation necessarily has anything to do with the historical and particular, such as, for example, the life

[13] Ibid., p. 11.

of Jesus Christ, then we are including what is unessential in our view of revelation. Kant likens the pure religion of reason to the smaller of two concentric circles, while anything historical and particular is like the larger of the two circles. The truth of a revelation such as Christianity is to be found only insofar as it coincides with the smaller of the two circles. "The Philosopher, as a teacher of pure reason, must confine himself within the narrower circle, and, in so doing, must waive consideration of all experience." [14]

But what, then, of the larger circle, that is, the one containing various historical and doctrinal statements such as those found in the Gospels? Kant does not dismiss these out of hand and tries to show that if the positive aspects are properly understood, they will be seen as having value as a means toward the practice of the one, true, pure moral religion. Yet there is nothing important or necessary about the relation of this religion with anything historical. The historical elements in any religion may be necessary for a time, and in certain places, as a means to teach the fundamental truths of all religion, but this is to say they have value only as means, and not in themselves. The positive elements, as he puts it, "would often have to be shaken up together that they might, for a short while, be united". This union, though, is like a mixture of oil and water; it is fortuitous or accidental, and there is no real connection between the two: "Like oil and water, they must needs separate from one another, and the purely moral (the religion of reason) be allowed to float to the top." [15]

Kant is perfectly clear that the oil of true religion contains no elements of anything other than the moral law.

[14] Ibid.
[15] Ibid., p. 12.

"The one true religion comprises nothing but laws, that is, those practical principles of whose unconditioned necessity we can become aware, and which we therefore recognize as revealed through pure reason (not empirically)." [16] He then spells out the various consequences of this in no uncertain terms. First of all: "Whatever, over and above good life-conduct, man fancies that he can do to become well-pleasing to God is mere religious illusion and pseudo-service of God." [17]

Nonetheless, as we have seen, for the sake of a church, "of which there can be different forms, all equally good", there can be various statutory rules, which are shaken up with the pure oil of moral faith. The only way most people find religion, and are thus in a position to find true religion, is through a church that instructs them in the rudiments of the moral life. These statutory rules are the water of religion, but if they are viewed as divine by those who adhere to them, they are suffering from an illusion:

> To deem this statutory faith (which in any case is restricted to one people and cannot comprise the universal world-religion) as essential to the service of God generally, and to make it the highest condition of the divine approval of man, is *religious illusion* whose consequence is a *pseudo-service*, that is pretended honoring of God through which we work directly counter to the service demanded by God Himself. [18]

With this perspective on the true nature of every religion, including Christianity, the following dismemberment of religious practices should come as no surprise.

[16] Ibid., p. 156.
[17] Ibid., p. 158.
[18] Ibid., p. 156.

1. *Praying.* If we think of praying as a means of grace, it is "a superstitious illusion (a fetish-making)".[19] God needs no such information regarding "the inner dispositions of the wisher; and so nothing is accomplished by it, and it discharges none of the duties to which, as commands of God, we are obligated".[20] It is not wrong to pray, Kant is telling us, so long as you realize it is a way of reminding yourself of how far you fall from the perfect observance of the moral law and so has to do with your own moral improvement. Unfortunately, in his eyes we tend to transfer what really has reference solely to our own moral improvement "into a courtly service, wherein the humiliations and glorifications usually are the less felt in a moral way the more volubly they are expressed". This Kant thinks is to get everything wrong: prayer as intercession has no value in itself "but may be used merely to quicken the disposition to a course of life well-pleasing to God".[21]

2. *Churchgoing.* Churchgoing is a good thing *in general*, he insists, so long as it is realized that the practice can have two good results. First of all, it may serve as a reminder to each worshipper that he is bound to pursue the moral life. Secondly, churchgoing can be looked on as directly obligating him as a member of the universal ethical church. Churchgoing reminds us that we have to try to obey the categorical imperative in our own lives, but we must do this as a member of the kingdom of ends. This church worship, however, must have nothing in it incompatible with the true religion of duty:

[19] Ibid., p. 183.
[20] Ibid.
[21] Ibid., p. 186.

> [This church must contain] no formalities which might lead
> to idolatry and so burden the conscience, e.g., certain prayers
> to God, with His infinite mercy personified under the name
> of a man—for such sensuous representation of God is con-
> trary to the command of reason: "Thou shalt not make unto
> thee any graven image, etc." [22]

Churchgoing, then, becomes a bad thing when the worshipper begins to think he is doing something acceptable to
God merely through his acts of worship in common with
other people. Thinking like this debases the character of a
man "and serves, by means of a deceptive veneer, to con-
ceal the bad moral content of his disposition from the eyes
of others, and even from his own eyes".

3. *The Sacraments.* Kant's treatment of the sacraments is
only an application of the above. If we look on baptism,
for example, as an initiation into the ethical Christian community, then it is a significant and appropriate ceremony:

> The ceremonial *initiation*, taking place but once, into the
> church-community, that is, one's first acceptance *as a mem-
> ber of a church* (in the Christian church through *baptism*) is a
> highly significant ceremony which lays a grave obligation
> either upon the initiate, if he is in a position himself to
> confess his faith, or upon the witnesses who pledge them-
> selves to take care of his education in this faith.[23]

When we look on baptism from this perspective, it has a
holy aim, because it has to do with the development of a
man into a citizen in a divine community. On the other
hand, if we think the act itself has anything to do with

[22] Ibid., p. 187.
[23] Ibid.

growth in the spiritual life, we are deluding ourselves, and
Kant is blunt enough for anyone to take the point:

> This act performed by others is not in itself holy or pro-
> ductive of holiness and receptivity for the divine grace in
> this individual; hence it is no *means of grace*, however exag-
> gerated the esteem in which it was held in the early Greek
> church, where it was believed capable, in an instant, of wash-
> ing away all sins—and here this illusion publicly revealed its
> affinity to an almost more than heathenish superstition.[24]

The other sacraments are treated no better, and it is difficult to see how Kant could do otherwise. At best the sacraments are reminders of our duty to obey the moral law,
and the church that brings them to us is a visible reminder
of an invisible kingdom of ends that is the true church of
all believers. In a passage that Hegel was later to use,[25] Kant
sums up once again his basic position. He says that while
there is a tremendous difference in *manner* between a *sha-
man* of the Tunguses and a European *prelate* ruling over
church and state alike, there is no difference in principle in
what they believe. This applies as well to those who are
merely adherents of the faith, whether they be "the wholly
sensuous *Wogulite*" or "the sublimated *Puritan* and Independent in Connecticut". All these unfortunates belong to the
same class in principle, "namely the class of those who let
their worship of God consist in what in itself can never
make men better (in faith in certain statutory dogmas or
celebration of certain arbitrary observances)."[26]

---

[24] Ibid.

[25] "The Spirit of Christianity", in *Early Theological Writings*, trans. T. M.
Knox (Chicago: University of Chicago Press, 1948), p. 211.

[26] Kant, *Religion within the Limits*, p. 164.

If, however, we accept Kant's teaching, then we will now know that all religion is fundamentally a moral matter and that our membership in an invisible kingdom of ends is what constitutes the true church. Unlike those who cling to their outmoded view that Christianity has a link with the life and teaching of Jesus Christ that cannot be dissolved, the followers of Kant will be distinguished from most religious people by a "far nobler principle": "the principle, namely, whereby they confess themselves members of an (invisible) church that includes within itself all right-thinking people and, by its essential nature, can alone be the true church universal." [27]

Here we should remind ourselves of just how far Kant's moral religion is from Catholicism. Catholicism is a sacramental religion, and the practice of Catholicism is based on the sacramental principle. By the sacramental principle, I mean the Catholic teaching that God uses ordinary material things such as water, oil, bread, and wine as a means for communicating himself to us. This communicating is not primarily intellectual or verbal; rather, it is a giving, in love, by one person of himself, that is, God, to other persons, that is, to his people. In the sacraments, then, we are dealing, not merely with the speaking of a message through words, but with the God of love giving himself to us, and he gives himself to us so that we can become more like him. Christ came to share in our humanity so that every one of us could become partakers of his divinity.[28]

The Church at her deepest, truest level is the living presence of Christ working among us, and in us, through his

[27] Ibid.

[28] "... and become partakers of the divine nature" (2 Pet 1:4). See below, pt. 3, "The Lamb's High Feast".

sacraments. We may not always sense his presence; there will be times of obscurity and darkness; but in a faithful and serious sacramental life, we know that God is gradually remaking us into the image of his beloved Son. And, just as the Father was well pleased with the Son, so he will be well pleased with us—if we remain in the Son.

If we take the sacraments seriously, then we have to take the importance of the visible Church seriously. The Church is more than a society for the promotion of an ethics of duty; she is Christ's Mystical Body here on earth where the mercy of God is found in the sacraments.[29]

It is Christ who instituted the sacraments, and it is Christ's power that is at work in the sacraments. In an extended sense Christ himself can be called a sacrament. This is so because he is the outward and visible sign of the presence of God's love among us. Christ is a sacrament because he is not just a sign, but a sign that brings about what he signifies. What Christ signifies and brings about is our redemption through his Passion, death, and Resurrection. We do not just learn about our redemption like a lesson in the catechism, because at Holy Mass we share in Christ's suffering, his death, his Resurrection, and his glorious Ascension into heaven. And, this Paschal Mystery, Christ's Passion, death, Resurrection, and Ascension, is the efficacious sign of God's love for each one of us.

---

[29] "Celebrated worthily in faith, the sacraments confer the grace that they signify [cf. Council of Trent (1547): DS 1605; DS 1606]. They are *efficacious* because in them Christ himself is at work: it is he who baptizes, he who acts in his sacraments in order to communicate the grace that each sacrament signifies. The Father always hears the prayer of his Son's Church which, in the epiclesis of each sacrament, expresses her faith in the power of the Spirit. As fire transforms into itself everything that it touches, so the Holy Spirit transforms into the divine life whatever is subjected to his power" (CCC 1127).

Vatican II says that the Church is the "universal sacrament of salvation".[30] The Church is the visible sign of the hidden reality of salvation; she is the sign and the sacrament of the communion of God and men. Cardinal de Lubac had earlier given a notable expression to this idea:

> The Church is a mystery; that is to say that she is also a sacrament. She is "the total *locus* of the Christian sacraments", and she is herself the great sacrament that contains and vitalizes all the others. In this world she is the sacrament of Christ, as Christ himself, in his humanity, is for us the sacrament of God.[31]

We love the Church, and we try to be faithful to the Church, not primarily because of structure or good works, but because she is the living reality whereby God's grace is conveyed to a suffering humanity through the sacraments. But the sacraments are the sacraments of the Church, not merely in the sense that the Church, as it were, owns them, but in the deeper sense that they require the Church for their existence. The sacraments are "of the Church" as the *Catechism of the Catholic Church* puts it,[32] and although the Church does not create them, she brings them from out of her being in time and in history to help reintegrate a wounded and flawed humanity into the unity of the Mystical Body of Jesus Christ.

---

[30] *Lumen Gentium* 48 (A 79).

[31] Henri de Lubac, *The Splendor of the Church*, trans. Michael Mason (San Francisco: Ignatius Press, 1999), p. 202.

[32] CCC 1118: "The sacraments are 'of the Church' in the double sense that they are 'by her' and 'for her.' They are 'by the Church,' for she is the sacrament of Christ's action at work in her through the mission of the Holy Spirit. They are 'for the Church' in the sense that 'the sacraments make the Church' [St. Augustine, *De civ. Dei*, 22, 17: PL 41, 779; cf. St. Thomas Aquinas, *STh* III, 64, 2*ad*3], since they manifest and communicate to men, above all in the Eucharist, the mystery of communion with the God who is love, One in three persons."

CHAPTER FOUR

HUME AND ATHEISM: GIVING UP ON GOD AND EVERLASTING LIFE

William Cullen, one of a battery of distinguished phy-
sicians attending Hume in his last illness, reported that
Hume jovially found only one regret at leaving this world:
he "thought he might say he had been very busily
employed in making his countrymen wiser and particularly in delivering them from Christian superstition, but
that he had not yet completed that great work".

—Peter Gay, *The Enlightenment: An Interpretation*

The deism of the Enlightenment led inevitably to an out-
right denial of the existence of God. Christ's life and his
teaching are historical; Christians claim, that is, that Christ
lived and taught at a particular time and place, and to be a
Christian necessitates a connection with this life and with
this teaching. We have already seen what this denial of particularity did to Christianity. Now we have to see what it
did to God. Simply put, if God has nothing to do with
human living, and if God has nothing to do with how the
creation develops, then he has become a useless entity.
Human history, human morality, and human ideas are just
that: they are human. As a result, God becomes, at best, an
enormous irrelevance, but, in the opinion of many, even to
believe in him is a moral evil.

Intellectual positions, and the debates through which they crystallize and begin to dominate, are important if we are going to understand how human consciousness changes and develops. On the other hand, neither the positions themselves nor the debates that brought them about are immediately effective in bringing about change, and so we have to add two other factors if we are to understand the triumph of Enlightenment thought. The first of these, which fueled the missionary zeal of the *philosophes* in their efforts to dismember Christianity, was a heightened awareness of the existence of physical and moral evil in a world that was supposed to have been created by an all-powerful and loving God; the second was a widespread sense that to be really free meant giving up on the existence of God.

The difficulties of believing in an all-powerful God who was at the same time a loving and good God did not have to wait until the eighteenth century to be voiced. St. Augustine thirteen hundred years earlier had agonized over the question and was tempted to conclude that either God was not all-powerful or else he was not really good. It seemed impossible for him to reconcile his Christian belief that God had really created the universe and was in charge of his universe on a day-to-day, hour-to-hour, and minute-to-minute basis with history and experience.

> Augustine not only wanted to follow the Christian (and Platonist) view that God is good, but the Christian view that he is all-powerful. He wanted to argue, in fact, that everything bad is either caused by a soul other than God, and is permitted by God for His "Good" reasons, or is inflicted by God for reasons of Justice.[1]

---

[1] John M. Rist, *Augustine* (Cambridge: Cambridge University Press, 1996), p. 262.

There is no obvious evidence of a loving providence in the dreary tale of man's inhumanity to man, the wars, the concentration camps, and the murder of the innocent that is history's tale; and it is not surprising that many have been tempted to conclude that God is at best incompetent or perhaps even evil. On the other hand, if he is good, then he cannot really be a creator who is in complete charge of his creation.[2] St. Thomas rather takes the bull by the horns in dealing with this and uses the difficulty to argue for the omnipotence and goodness of God: "As Augustine says, *Since God is supremely good, he would not permit any evil at all in his works, unless he were sufficiently almighty and good to bring good even from evil.* It is therefore a mark of the limitless goodness of God that he permits evils to exist, and draws from them good." [3]

The most vocal and effective exponent of the failure of God in modern times was Nietzsche. He certainly added powerful advocacy to the positions worked out by eighteenth-century thinkers, but he was building on positions already well established. Regarding nature as though it were proof of God's goodness and providence;

> interpreting history in honour of divine reason; as a constant testimonial to an ethical world order and ethical ultimate purpose; explaining all one's experience in the way pious folk have for long enough, as though everything were providence, a sign, intended, and sent for the salvation of the soul: now all that is *over*, it has conscience *against* it, every sensitive conscience sees it as indecent, dishonest, a pack of lies, feminism, weakness, cowardice—this severity makes us *good* Europeans if any-

<hr />

[2] Augustine even uses the phrase "cruelly weak" (ibid., p. 262).
[3] STB Ia, 2, 3 ad 1.

thing does, and heir to Europe's most protracted and brav-
est self-overcoming![4]

The second factor fueling the atheism of the eighteenth
century was a sense that to be free meant not only to be
rid of God, but also to live without anxiety about God and
human destiny. It is possible for someone to declare himself
a nonbeliever, and even to produce arguments against the
existence of God, and yet to be tortured with guilt about
this unbelief. No one has ever argued with more clarity
against the cogency of natural religion than did Hume, but
that was not enough. He wanted to show that even thinking, much less worrying, about God and eternal life was a
waste of time, and sensible people would not bother themselves with these sorts of subjects.

"The *imagination* of man is naturally sublime, delighted
with whatever is remote and extraordinary, and running
without control, into the most distant parts of space and
time in order to avoid the objects, which custom has ren-
dered too familiar to it."[5] A correct judgment on this
propensity of the imagination to wander into areas incapable of any sort of demonstration is to show by an
examination of human reason that it has not got the power

---

[4] This passage from *On the Genealogy of Morals* is cited by Susan Neiman
in *Evil in Modern Thought* (Princeton, N.J.: Princeton University Press, 2002),
p. 113. In this book Neiman gives us an extended and powerful treatment of
how the question of evil has altered, or should have altered, the history of
philosophy. In keeping with my purpose in this book, I have not even tried
to provide a response to what she says. My interest, rather, is in showing
how accommodation with that history, in the interests of comprehensiveness
or learning from the world, has helped to destroy the liturgical dimension of
traditional Catholicism.

[5] David Hume, *Enquiries concerning Human Understanding*, ed. L. A. Selby-
Bigge, 2nd ed. (1777; Oxford: Clarendon Press, 1953), p. 162.

to follow the imagination into "whatever is remote and extraordinary". Kant was to say the same thing in more measured tones about this incapacity of the human mind to do metaphysics, but Hume's way of dealing with this hankering after ultimate explanations is very different from Kant's. Kant produces an "immanent metaphysics" as complex as anything ever written, but Hume's tactic is to show the reader that he can live happily ever after without bothering himself with questions about our final destiny or the existence of God. First we must labor to destroy the pretensions of metaphysics, and then we will be free. "We must submit to this fatigue (that is, of enquiring about the limits of the human understanding), in order to live at ease ever after." [6]

"In order to live at ease ever after"—there we have the goal. We are here a world away from Kant's determined effort to reconcile the claims of duty with natural necessity and with his various lessons that the key to understanding our existence is through a strenuous moral life and through striving to realize a kingdom of ends. The message from Hume is very different. We have to do philosophy to show there is no place for metaphysics and then enjoy the freedom this realization will bring. Lord Melbourne, Queen Victoria's first Prime Minister, said to Professor Hampden: "Be easy, Doctor, I like an easy man." [7] There we have the ideal: no fuss, no straining after any sort of absolutes either

---

[6] Ibid., p. 12.

[7] Cited in Sheridan Gilley, *Newman and His Age* (London: Darton, Longman and Todd, 1990), p. 147. Melbourne lived well into the nineteenth century, but in temper and outlook he was pure Enlightenment. He is reported to have remarked after hearing an evangelical sermon, "Things have come to a pretty pass when religion is allowed to invade the sphere of private life" (ibid., p. 117).

moral or metaphysical. If we want to do philosophy, well and good, but keep it at a low pitch.[8]

Much of what I have just said is captured in an existential sort of way by a famous death-bed scene. On a Sunday morning in July 1776, James Boswell, "being too late for Church", went to visit David Hume, "who was returned from London and Bath, just a-dying",[9] and so achieved what has been referred to as the "journalistic scoop of the eighteenth century".[10] Hume was one of the most important intellectual architects of the Enlightenment as well as one of the best advertisements known to us for the secularized consciousness. Hume was dying; he knew he was dying; yet he received his inquisitive visitor with great courtesy and patience. Hume, about to die, said clearly and imperturbably that he did not believe in an after-life. "I asked him if the thought of annihilation never gave him any uneasiness. He said not the least; not more than the thought that he had not been, as Lucretius observes."[11] Hume also made it clear that he detested religion: "He said flatly that the morality of every religion was bad, and, I really thought was not jocular when he said that when he heard a man was religious, he concluded he was a rascal though he had known some instance of very good men being religious."[12]

Hume was courteous but self-assured and unyielding in the face of Boswell's rather bumbling and unsuccessful efforts

---

[8] "Those who have a propensity to philosophy, will still continue their researches; because they reflect, that, besides the immediate pleasure, attending such an occupation, philosophical decisions are nothing but the reflections of common life, methodized and corrected" (Hume, *Enquiries* p. 162).

[9] James Boswell, *The Journals, 1761–1795*, selected and introduced by John Wain (London: Heinemann, 1990), p. 247.

[10] Ibid.

[11] Ibid., p. 249.

[12] Ibid., p. 248.

to present a Christian view of life and eternity. The death-bed scene encapsulates and displays the Enlightenment when in the face of what it regards as unreconstructed faith: good manners, good taste, good education, and a certain bland assumption of superiority, on the one hand, and, on the other, all too often, a confused, overly emotional, and unsuccessful effort to put even a dint in the carapace of the enlightened. What poor Boswell was up against was one of the most sophisticated thinkers of his own, or of any other, time, who had a clear and well thought out intellectual position. The bland self-assurance and well-mannered contempt displayed by Hume were not the mood of a passing moment but the settled convictions of a powerful and innovative intelligence. It is these attitudes, as well as Hume's intellectual stance, that we have to contend with today.

Hume thought that superstition and fanaticism (or what he sometimes called *enthusiasm*) were the twin diseases from which all religions, but especially Christianity, suffered. Furthermore, if he had to choose, he preferred the superstitious, as they tended to be more easygoing than the enthusiastic. He also thought that paganism was preferable to Christianity: "The pagan religions, as more purely ceremonial, and therefore also more tolerant and sociable, 'sit easy and light on men's minds', and 'make no such deep impression on the affections and understanding'." [13]

Superstition, then, is tolerant and sociable, but religions that maintain the unity of God are, he holds, just the opposite: "The implacable narrow spirit of the Jews is well known. Mohometanism set out with still more bloody princi-

[13] From Hume's *The Natural History of Religion*, cited in *Hume's Dialogues concerning Natural Religion*, ed. Norman Kemp Smith (Oxford: Clarendon Press, 1935), editor's introduction, p. 16.

ple.... The human sacrifices of the Carthaginians, Mexicans, and many barbarous nations, scarcely exceed the inquisition and persecution of Rome and Madrid."[14]

Hume's hatred of religion, and of Christianity in particular, colors all his work. He wrote that religion was "fanatical", "intolerant", "grotesque"; it was "scholasticism" (these are all Hume's words), and he argued with elegance and with a great deal of success that there was no good reason to accept either the existence of God or eternal life. His arguments against the existence of God are to be found in an explicit way in his *Dialogues concerning Natural Religion*, but the whole of his work is an implicit and sometimes very explicit rejection of God's existence. He did not like Christianity, and he did not think a rational man could be a believer. His role in the development of atheism was enormous, and so he had a major influence on the environment in which the Church had to live.

The influence of his work on Catholics about the question of God, however, was indirect and through the intellectual environment. That is, I suppose most Catholic thinkers would hold that God exists even if one might wonder how they understood this belief; but the "death of God" theology has not been a major concern in Catholic circles. What he said about miracles, however, has had a very profound and long-term impact on the way some Catholics nowadays approach the question of the miraculous and, especially, the Resurrection of Jesus Christ. If we are to put the Paschal Mystery at the center of our thinking about liturgy, it would be a good idea to see what really is intended when we say we believe in Christ's triumph over sin and death.

[14] Ibid., p. 19.

In the First Letter to the Corinthians St. Paul wrote: "For I delivered to you as of first importance what I also received, that Christ died for our sins in accordance with the Scriptures, that he was buried, that he was raised on the third day in accordance with the Scriptures, and that he appeared to Cephas, then to the Twelve" (1 Cor 15:3).

This text from St. Paul was written many years before the accounts of the Resurrection found in the Gospels. It states plainly that St. Paul received his knowledge from those who had been most closely connected with Christ having been raised from the dead. That is to say, he received the message he was to proclaim from the apostles themselves, those apostles who were the witnesses to the risen Christ.

This unemotional, almost dry recounting of the facts of the case, the facts as they had been related to St. Paul by those closest to our Lord, is in itself a suasion to the truth of what St. Paul has to tell us. There is no appeal to sentiment or to the desire to provide a plausible or pleasing story. This, St. Paul tells us, is the way it happened; here is the plain, unvarnished truth.

The world to which St. Paul was writing was all too familiar with vague, unsubstantiated stories and mythical happenings; and one of the dominant themes of the cults of his day was the myth of the dying and rising God. But we should not imagine that everyone in the ancient world was ready to believe these stories; or, indeed, that anyone believed them except as stories that made no claim to objective truth. When St. Paul went to Athens and spoke to the cultivated descendants of the great Greek philosophers about the Resurrection as something that had really happened, they began to make fun of him. The Greeks to whom St. Paul preached were an urbane, sceptical, and hard-headed lot, and even if their preferred categories were not *empirical* and *scientific*, they had no intention of accepting what this new teacher was trying to get across. And what was he trying to get across? He was trying to convey the enormous, outrageous, appalling truth that Christ died for our sins in accordance with the Scriptures, that he was buried, that he was raised from the dead, according to the Scriptures, that he appeared to Cephas and then to the Twelve.

You do not have to be David Hume to see that there is something very strange about all this, because, in fact, it is all, obviously, very strange. St. Paul knew his message would provoke intellectual scepticism among the intelligentsia and religious outrage among the Jews. "We preach Christ crucified", St Paul said, "a stumbling block to Jews and folly to Gentiles" (1 Cor 1:24), and that is what Christianity still is to the nonbeliever: a stumbling block to the vaguely pious and foolishness to enlightened, right-thinking, cultivated modern man.

Christ was crucified in the reign of Emperor Tiberius, when Pontius Pilate was governor of Judea. These are people we know quite a lot about from ordinary nonreligious history. Christ was crucified; he died. He was really dead, and the body was buried at Jerusalem. Sometime, in the historical order, during the second night after his death, his body was restored to life. At one moment it was dead, and in another it began to live again. At Easter, in the special *communicantes* of the First Eucharistic Prayer, the Church affirms that Christ "rose from the dead in his human body", and that is what we mean by Christ's Resurrection.

Many New Testament scholars do not accept this position,[15] but the basis of a good deal of this unwillingness to

---

[15] "It has become accepted within much New Testament scholarship that the earliest Christians did not think of Jesus as having been bodily raised from the dead; Paul is regularly cited as the chief witness for what people

accept the traditional view seems to me to stem from philosophical rather than biblical evidence. Hume in his essay
on miracles taught that the evidence of any miracle is always
less than the general presumption that miracles cannot happen. It follows from this that no particular miracle, including the Resurrection, ever really happened. "A miracle is a
violation of the laws of nature; and as a firm and unalter-
able experience has established these laws, the proof against
a miracle, from the very nature of the fact, is as entire as
any argument from experience can possibly be imagined." [16]

Of course there is a lot more to Hume's argument than
this, but even the short excerpt should strike the reader as
familiar. "We all know nowadays that miracles cannot happen, so they don't." It is powerful, and it is pervasive. The
sort of thinking represented in Hume's rejection of miracles is alive and well today in the Catholic Church. Edward
Schillebeeckx, O.P., summed up his view on the Resurrection in this way:

> A Jesus experience is not the object of neutral observation;
> it is a faith-motivated experience in response to an escha-
> tological disclosure, expressed as a Christological affirma-
> tion of Jesus as the risen One, that is, disclosure of and
> faith in Jesus in his eschatological, Christological signifi-
> cance. This was again the sole essence of all other Christ
> manifestations, which have subsequently been filled out either

---

routinely call a more 'spiritual' point of view" (N. T. Wright, *The Resurrection of the Son of God* [Minneapolis: Fortress Press, 2003], p. xvii).

[16] *Enquiries*, p. 114. This, at least, is the usual understanding of Hume's
argument. Robert J. Fogelin, in *A Defense of Hume on Miracles* (Princeton,
N.J.: Princeton University Press, 2003), argues that Hume's argument does
not really take the a priori form I have outlined above. This may be so, but
it does not alter the effect of the argument (that is, that miracles just do not
happen, and so neither did the Resurrection) on the development of modernity.

with the theology of the communities represented by Matthew, Luke and John or with the concrete career of the apostle Paul himself.[17]

In other words, the Resurrection is not something that happened first to Jesus, and then the disciples believed in it; on the contrary, belief in Christ leads to what these followers of Hume (and that is what they are, whether they know it or not) look on as a coarse and spiritually unrefined belief in the Resurrection as an event that took place in space and time.[18] The view of many modern scholars seems to be that the early Christians felt that God must have the last word, and so they postulated (in Kant's sense), or affirmed, the Resurrection of Christ as a necessary belief. In spite of the "historical fiasco"[19] of Jesus' life, they expressed their belief in the victory of God by affirming the Resurrection in a way that leads one toward what modern scholars of Schillebeeckx's way of thinking consider "a crude and naïve realism".[20] In their misguided efforts to vindicate their faith in God, the Christians developed the unfortunate belief that

[17] Cited in Wright, *Resurrection,* p. 703.

[18] Consider, for example, the following excerpt by Thomas Sheehan, who, as we saw in pt. I, p. 47, has written extensively on Karl Rahner. "The Easter victory of Jesus was not a historical event—it did not take place in space and time—... the appearances of Jesus did not entail the sighting of Jesus' risen body in either a physical or a spiritual form" (Thomas Sheehan, "The Resurrection: An Obstacle to Faith?" *The Fourth R*, vol. 8, no. 2 [March/April, 1995]): 3. Again, "The 'resurrection' of Jesus was an eschatological occurrence, beyond space and time—a meta-historical act of God that took place 'in heaven' when the crucified Jesus dies on earth. And it could not more be observed by human beings within history than one could observe Lucifer's fall from grace or the entrance of one's great-grandmother into heaven" (ibid., p. 8).

[19] The phrase is from Albert Schweitzer, cited in Wright, p. 705.

[20] The phrase is from Schillebeeckx, cited in ibid.

something actually happened at Easter. The Resurrection, if we understand it properly, is, according to this theory, a new experience of grace. Nothing really changed on the first Easter, but it does not really matter. N. T. Wright comments ironically: "But . . . the historical study of early Christian practice and hope leaves us no choice but to conclude that this unfortunate belief was what all early Christians held. Indeed they professed that it was the very centre of their life." [21]

There is another theory, in addition to this one, that is sometimes called the theory of "cognitive dissonance". Wright characterizes this as "the hypothetical state, studied within social psychology, in which individuals or groups fail to come to terms with reality, but live instead in a fantasy which corresponds to their own deep longings." [22]

In other words, the disciples so badly wanted the Resurrection to happen that they performed some sort of corporate act of wish fulfillment and created the belief in the Resurrection. No doubt, this was a community activity. This theory has even less to commend it than the one that says that the construction of belief in the Resurrection was a grace-filled event.

The reaction of those closest to our Lord when they were faced with the empty tomb and his appearances ranged from the downright disbelief of Thomas, to the confusion of the women, to the slowness of the Emmaus-bound disciples to understand the Scriptures. The reactions in all three cases are unmistakably the reactions of ordinary human

---

[21] Ibid. When Wright writes here of "this unfortunate belief", he is, of course, being ironical. He has written an 800-page book to defend "this unfortunate belief".

[22] Ibid., p. 697.

beings in the face of the most extraordinary event in all history. Their reactions show they were not victims of wish fulfillment. Their reactions also show they were not cunning manipulators of the truth; on the contrary, their reactions, when presented with the Resurrection, show they neither expected it beforehand nor believed it very easily afterward.

To believe or not to believe in the Resurrection is to take sides. To adopt a stance of neutrality is to show you do not really grasp what is at stake. Hume at least understood some of the major affirmations of Christianity. He hated them and did his best to show why no reasonable person could accept them; he knew precisely what he was doing. At least Boswell did not capitulate to unbelief, and in this we should try to follow him; he made something of a fool of himself, not because what he stood for was foolish, no matter how badly he may have expressed it, but because he was faced with more than he could handle. It is a constant theme of St. Paul's that "it pleased God through the folly of what we preach to save those who believe" (1 Cor 1:21). St. Paul knew to his pain and sorrow that speaking the truth is no guarantee it will be heard and that sometimes witnessing to the gospel may seem foolishness even to the one who tries to do the preaching and teaching. And, after all, the Resurrection really is a challenge to the unbelief of the world, perhaps even to our own; it is, as John Updike wrote, "a monstrous" event.

> Let us not mock God with metaphor,
> Analogy, sidestepping, transcendence;
> Making of the event a parable, a sign painted in the
>   faded credulity of earlier ages;
> let us walk through the door.

Let us not seek to make it less monstrous,
For our own convenience, our own sense of beauty,
lest, awakened in one unthinkable hour, we are
    embarrassed by the miracle,
and crushed by remonstrance.[23]

Even though Hume's dismissal of the Resurrection of Christ and of eternal life have not often been taken up explicitly by Catholics, the atmosphere his work engendered has had a profound influence on Catholic worship, and this can be seen from the way the funeral Mass is often celebrated today.

What goes on at funerals shows what is really believed about the passage from this life. If the rite of Christian burial does not clearly show that funerals are in the first place intimately connected with the state of the person who has died, then it fails to be Catholic. What I am objecting to is the all too common conviction that funerals are a sort of instant canonization of the dead person in the interests of the community left behind; or, as an even stronger version of this goes, "funerals have nothing to do with the dead person."

It is true, first of all, that death does affect those left behind. Death always presents us with a mystery, and all the old, bitter questions so often seem to surface when we come to bury our dead. The whys and the wherefores of life, the losses we have suffered in the past are all born again with each new death. And this is especially the case when the dead person is someone we have known well and loved. At times like this it often seems as though silence would be the best policy. Fr. Frederick Faber of the Oratory wrote in one of his hymns:

---

[23] John Updike, from "Seven Stanzas at Easter", quoted by N. T. Wright, ibid., p. 684.

O that they would not comfort me!
Deep grief cannot be reached;
Wisdom, to cure a broken heart,
Must not be wisdom preached.[24]

Death strips away so much artificiality and false reticence, and we feel the grief of others. We do not want to intrude, but we do want, somehow, to show our sense of solidarity, to bear witness that all of us share the same human nature, a human nature that is under sentence of death. Our presence at funerals just as human beings is a sign of love and support, not only for those nearest to the dead person, but for each one of us, each one of us as human beings confronted, once again, with the mystery of our human existence and the certainty of our own death. We come together to lend each other what support and help we can at a purely human and natural level.

And secondly, it is true that at the burial of the dead we ought to reaffirm our belief in Christ's own death and Resurrection; there is more to our presence at funerals than a manifesting of our human solidarity. We are also Christian people. We know that in the end our only real and lasting support is our Lord Jesus Christ, who suffered not only for us, but with us, and then went to death as we all must do; or, as Fr. Faber wrote in another hymn:

Ah! death is very, very wide
A land terrible and dry;
If Thou, Sweet Saviour! hadst not died,
Who would have dared to die?[25]

---

[24] From "Deep Grief", cited in Ronald Chapman, *Father Faber* (Westminster Md.: Newman Press, 1961), p. 319.
[25] From "The Length of Death", ibid., p. 321.

In each other's presence we renew our faith in Christ's redeeming death and Resurrection. At funerals we light the Paschal candle that was first lit on the great Vigil of Easter in order to symbolize, and remind us of, Christ's victory over death. In our baptism we were baptized into Christ's death so that we could share in his Resurrection. We come together to renew our faith in the promises of our Lord concerning everlasting life. But this is not all there is to the Catholic response in the face of death. We also come together to pray for the souls of those who have gone before us.

Belief in Purgatory is still part of authentic Catholicism. The *Catechism of the Catholic Church* repeats the age-long tradition of the Church and the solemn teaching of many councils—including that of Vatican II—when it states: "All who die in God's grace and friendship, but still imperfectly purified, are indeed assured of their eternal salvation; but after death they undergo purification, so as to achieve the holiness necessary to enter the joy of heaven."[26]

The *Catechism* goes on to say that the Church calls this final purification Purgatory. From the earliest days of the Church the memory of the dead has been held in honor, and prayers, especially the Eucharistic Sacrifice, have been offered for the holy souls in Purgatory, so that they may speedily come to the beatific vision of God. The *Catechism* reminds us that the giving of alms, the obtaining of indulgences, and works of penitence are also practices recommended by the Church to help our dead.

While it is true that belief in Purgatory is still part of an authentic Catholicism, it is also true that we do not hear much about it any more. We do not hear much about it because there is a new attitude in the air that owes little to

[26] CCC 1030.

either Scripture or the teaching of the Church. This attitude is largely due to the followers of Karl Rahner.

> What, then, happens in the afterlife? For Rahner, precisely nothing—for there is no afterlife, no duration beyond experienced time. We may choose to speak of man's salvation by talking about eternity, Rahner says, but that "does not mean that things continue on after death as though, as Feuerbach put it, we only change horses and then ride on." Death *is* the end of man, but as fulfillment, the "self-realization which embodies the result of what a man has made for himself during life" and which "comes to be *through* death and not *after* it."[27]

This probably sounds clearer and more exciting than it is, but it is the received doctrine of many theologians of great influence on the day-to-day life of the Church. Such a view, whatever it means exactly, effectively removes the need for a belief in Purgatory. It should be pointed out that, as one might expect, Rahner's own discussion is more complex, but Sheehan has certainly brilliantly encapsulated the actual influence of Rahner's thinking on contemporary Catholic attitudes. Rahner explicitly affirms the existence of Purgatory and even describes it as "real penal suffering".[28] However this strain in his thought comes packaged with his theory that eschatology, that is, the doctrine of the

[27] Thomas Sheehan, "Resurrection", p. 3. This is just the sort of thinking that Kant considered completely vacuous. See above pp. 77–80.

[28] [Purgatory is] ... that process of integration whereby after death the totality of the human person is enlisted against the resistance arising from and built up by his own sins, is real penal suffering, but suffering radically supported by the grace accepted in the basic decision, and thus issues necessarily and without fail in the perfection of man, that is, the ultimate vision of God" (Karl Rahner and Herbert Vorgrimler, *Theological Dictionary* [New York: Herder and Herder, 1965], *Purgatory*, p. 391).

last things, has to be understood "as a projection by the Christian community about its own future".[29] This theory has led to the view often expressed today that funerals are for the benefit of the community, and not for the person who has died.

If Sheehan is right about Rahner, and I think he is, then it does seem that there is an exoteric and an esoteric Rahnerian doctrine. The exoteric doctrine, that is, what Rahner actually says, can, with a little effort, be squared with the teaching of the Church, while the esoteric teaching, that is, what his teaching really seems to have meant in the life of the Church, has caused a radical revision in the presentation and understanding of Catholicism. This esoteric teaching has in fact replaced what the tradition of the Church has taught about praying for the dead and the conduct of funerals.

The doctrine of Purgatory is not a harsh or a gloomy doctrine, but it is certainly a realistic one. Purgatory reminds us that few of us leave this world in a fit state to meet God.

Let us look at this a bit more carefully. We pray, and we try to live so that we may die in a state of grace, with our sins forgiven. But while sin, as an offense against God, may be forgiven, forgiveness in itself does not alter the truth that we have *in fact* both done what we should not have done and not done what we should have done. Sin leaves a mark on the soul. Wrongdoing defaces the image of our Creator and causes it to take on the image of the world and its false values. Sin strengthens all those tendencies in man that pull him away from God and true happiness and so make him, in part, the slave of the flesh. The Christian has

---

[29] Karl Rahner, *Foundations of the Christian Faith*, chap. 9, "Eschatology", p. 1, paraphrased by Mark E. Fischer.

not always said no to the devil, the devil who has tried to turn him, as he is himself, into a rebel against God and has often partially succeeded. The Catholic may die free from mortal sins; but few die a saint. The world, the flesh, and the devil have left the traces of their dealings upon souls, and most go to their Maker, their Redeemer, and their Judge bearing the wounds, the tendencies, and the scars of a lifetime. It is only by a real and painful cleansing and realigning of his nature that the individual will be capable of sustaining the beatific vision when it has not been completed in this life. It is in Purgatory that this cleansing and realigning take place.

Purgatory has not disappeared. And the very good reasons that led the Church, guided by the Holy Spirit, to expound infallibly the tradition given to her by Christ himself about Purgatory have not disappeared, either. Our Lord has taught us to pray for those we love. In the mystery of the inscrutable will of God, there is his request for prayer, and the Church has always taught that as prayer for those we love and see is part of our loyalty to our family and friends, so prayer for those we see no longer is also part of our loyalty to our family and friends.

It seems to me obvious in the light of what I have written that wearing white vestments for funerals ought to be the exception and not the norm. Funerals are about, and for, the person who has died. The comfort of the bereaved and all the other important community aspects of death must be recognized, but they must not determine the rite of Christian burial.

CHAPTER FIVE

HEGEL: GOD BECOMES THE COMMUNITY

> Rightly understood ... [Hegel] was the true philosopher of the modern consciousness, and those who, like Russell, see only the pretentious exterior of his thinking, show themselves to be blind to the profound spiritual crisis that Hegel was striving to describe—the crisis of a civilization that has discovered the God upon whom it depended to be also its own creation.
>
> —Roger Scruton,
> *A Short History of Modern Philosophy*

In *The Mass and Modernity* I am discussing the impact different thinkers and movements have had on the life of the Church, not trying to provide a sketch of the history of modern philosophy. It is especially important to remember this as we come to discuss Hegel. Hegel wrote about religion in general and Christianity in particular, and although this interest is essential to understanding the development of his thought, it is not central to his mature work. It is not central because faith for the mature Hegel has been transfigured into philosophy,[1] and while religion (along with art) is said to be absolute, it has become the doorway to

---

[1] See Emil L. Fackenheim, *The Religious Dimension in Hegel's Thought* (Bloomington: Indiana University Press, 1967), chap. 6, "The Transfiguration of Faith into Philosophy".

philosophy. Doorways are important—you cannot get into the house without them—but they are not the house. It follows from this that an account of Hegel's thought that deals exclusively with his religious concerns, and this is what the reader will find in this chapter of *The Mass and Modernity*, leaves aside much of his work and influence.

While Hegel was prepared to argue for the necessity and value of the work of the Enlightenment, he was also cruel about its weaknesses. He thought that as an attitude toward our existence it is completely inadequate, and he traced its breakdown in both the political and spiritual world. In the political world, the Enlightenment led to the French Revolution and the Terror. In the spiritual order, it ended in the moral philosophy of Kant. This philosophy, Hegel argued, destroyed man's humanity just as effectively as the guillotine put an end to his physical existence. He was certainly right about that.

Hegel's thought has been enormously influential in forming the way we think about ourselves and our world. His views on philosophy, politics, history, art, community, and religion are still a vital aspect of contemporary writing on who we are and how we fit into the scheme of things. When this influence is understood in conjunction with that of Marx, we have one of the main architects of modernity. I have already made it clear that, insofar as Christianity is concerned, Hegel and Marx are an insalubrious and indistinguishable duo.[2] A good deal of their writing has influenced thinkers in the Church.[3] It is not always very clear

---

[2] See above, p. 39.

[3] John Milbank writes: "In recent Catholic theology, the Hegelian and Marxist traditions have acquired an unprecedented degree of influence" (*Theology and Social Theory beyond Secular Reason* [Oxford, U.K.; Cambridge, Mass.: B. Blackwell, 1990], p. 206).

whether those who write theology are aware of the source
of their ideas or, if they are aware, just how frank they are
prepared to be about the real foundations of their thought.
This is especially true of liberation theology and those who
write in the same mold without being very explicit about
what lies behind what they write. For example, when a
contemporary theologian writes that "the old theological
formulations based on abstract and metaphysical categories
are inadequate" because (among other reasons) *they are alien
to modern religious consciousness. Contemporary experience of the
world has shifted that consciousness*,[4] we are being told that
the modern experience has *shifted* the religious consciousness from the "abstract and metaphysical categories" of an
older theology to a newer, modern one. Well, what is this
newer basis of the religious consciousness? It is said to be
found in the idea of "transformation", which includes the
idea of freedom but is in some ways a broader notion.

> [Transformation] represents an essential dimension of con-
> temporary cultural experience. Transformation presumes
> other concepts, such as the human quest for meaning and
> freedom. It can apply in different ways to the person, to
> the community, and to the world in general. Transforma-
> tion, therefore, constitutes an important hermeneutic tool
> for opening the Eucharistic mystery to contemporary reli-
> gious consciousness. *It is also more in tune with a modern-day
> dynamic interpretation of the person as part of the creative process
> at the heart of humanity itself and of human history.*[5]

I contend that such passages are based on a philosophical
view that owes more to Hegel and to Marx than it does to

---

[4] German Martinez, *Signs of Freedom: Theology of the Christian Sacraments*
(New York: Paulist Press, 2003), p. 178 (my emphasis).
[5] Ibid., p. 170 (my emphasis).

Christianity. I will return to this point below when I come to discuss the Paschal Mystery,[6] but for the time being I want only to emphasize that the Hegel-Marx syndrome is still very much with us. "Man", said Marx, "should revolve about himself as his own true sun." [7] This absorption of man with himself was not new to Hegel and Marx; what was new, as has often been said, was putting the observation forward as precept, or counsel, for reinterpreting experience:

> Man his own maker, man the discoverer of himself, who in discovering also creates: the beginning of such ideas as these go back a long way. But what used to be buried in metaphor, in verbal gestures whose implications were not clear to those who made them, emerged in the light of day as the hold of religion grew weaker.[8]

We cannot understand modernity without understanding the pervasive influence of Hegel and Marx. This has not always been clearly recognized because until recently Hegel has been looked on primarily as a great metaphysician who claimed to understand all reality as the dialectical self-manifestation of an absolute Spirit, while Marx was regarded as the architect of economic determinism and not much else. Both views are inadequate, but since the source of the ideas that have done most damage to the Church is Hegel, I want to continue to put him in first place in this chapter.

---

[6] See below, pt. 3, chap. 1, "The Paschal Mystery".

[7] Cited in John Plamenatz, *Karl Marx's Philosophy of Man* (Oxford: Clarendon Press, 1975), p. 322.

[8] Ibid.

The perception of Hegel as a metaphysician has resulted in a great deal of work devoted to his thought and influence from the perspective of his dialectical and metaphysical concerns. Recently this has begun to change, and the focus now is more on Hegel as a philosopher of politics, religion, and even more generally of the spiritual and social problems of our age.[9] It is the religious and political thought and influence of Hegel that now attract attention in scholarly circles, and it is quite possible to admit this influence without tackling the further question of how exactly this influence finds its source in *das System* or whether or not Hegelian metaphysics is a credible enterprise.[10] But, even

[9] "Like no one before, and perhaps no one since, Hegel's thought explores the self-conception of modern human beings, the ambivalent relation of modern European culture to its Hebraic-Hellenic heritage, its quest in the modern world for a new image of nature and society, its hopes and self-doubts, its needs and aspirations" (Allen W. Wood, *Hegel's Ethical Thought* (Cambridge: Cambridge University Press, 1990), p. 5.

[10] Charles Taylor, in his magisterial *Hegel*, traces the rise of Hegel's influence in the late nineteenth and twentieth centuries and writes: "This renewed interest continues unabated to this day. Interrupted on the Anglo-Saxon scene by the reaction against the British 'Hegelians', it is nevertheless returning. But with all the attention focused on Hegel, his actual synthesis is quite dead. That is, no one actually believes his central ontological thesis, that the universe is posited by a Spirit whose essence is rational necessity" (*Hegel* [Cambridge: Cambridge University Press, 1975], p. 538).

This, I think, has become the standard way of looking at Hegel's work today, although John Milbank, in *Theology and Social Theory beyond Secular Reason*, has some technical difficulties with Taylor's desire to use Hegel's *Phenomenology* as an "immanent critique". "If one calls into question Hegelian logic and the principle of determinate negation, then one must also call into question the idea of 'immanent critique'" (p. 156).

Wood expresses the scholarly consensus when he writes: "The Hegel who still lives and speaks to us is not a speculative logician and idealist metaphysician but a philosophical historian, a political and social theorist, a philosopher of our ethical concerns and cultural identity crises" (Wood, *Hegel's Ethical Thought*, pp. 5–6).

with the less ambitious Hegel in vogue today, his thought is still immensely comprehensive and fertile, and so to discuss one or two themes is inevitably so selective that it fails to give an adequate picture of the whole. It has also to be remembered that although modern scholarship has less time than it used to for Hegel the metaphysician, it is still the *System* that knits the different strands together and that (in Hegel's mind, anyway) gives to these different strands their meaning and value.

In this chapter I take four themes from Hegel's work, themes which have clearly influenced our understanding of faith and our perceptions of the meaning of life. In part this influence and these perceptions have spread by means of Marx's use of his ideas, by the various reactions to Marxism, both positive and negative, that Hegel's thought has provoked, as well as by many currents of existentialism.[11] But even without Marx and existentialism, Hegel's views continue to influence contemporary writing on who we are and how we fit into the scheme of things.

First of all, I emphasize that in spite of what might at first appear, Hegel accepted and reinforced the rejection of the particular character, what he calls the *positivity*, of revelation. Although his relationship to the thought of the Enlightenment and particularly to Kant is ambiguous in many respects, Hegel held that it was irrational to accept the belief that Christian revelation is tied essentially to particularity and history. His influence here is, from the Christian point of view, particularly baleful, as he consistently uses Christian

---

[11] "The religious thought of classical German idealism has long vanished into the past. Yet it is not of concern to historians only, but still speaks to present philosophers and theologians. It speaks indirectly, mainly through the mediation of existentialism. It also speaks directly, by virtue of its own profundity" (Fackenheim, *Religious Dimension*, p. xi).

themes and terminology, and this effectively disguises the
fact that he rejected the historical nature of Christianity.
The second part of this chapter looks at Hegel's theory of
the community and shows that, while his thinking here represents a real advance on the views of the Enlightenment,
it cannot be accepted as a basis for a Catholic theory of
community. Thirdly, I point out that, from the beginning,
Hegel's thinking about religion had a political component,
and I look at Hegel's theory of civil society. It is true that
the Church has to live in the modern world as it is, but
Hegel is teaching more than that; he wants us to understand that we will not even understand what religion really
is without an awareness of social and economic developments. Finally, I draw the conclusion that Hegel's view of
the community in civil society necessitates giving up on
the transcendence of God.

1. "Positivity"

[T]he Hegelian ontology itself in which everything is founded
on rational necessity is ultimately incompatible with Christian faith. Hegel's philosophy is an extraordinary transposi-
tion which "saves the phenomena" (that is, the dogmas) of
Christianity, while abandoning its essence. It is not a theism,
but it is not an atheistic doctrine either, in which man as a
natural being is at the spiritual summit of things. It is a genuine third position, which is why it is easy to misinterpret.[12]

In ordinary English, "positive" means "formally laid down
or imposed; arbitrarily or artificially instituted; conventional opp. to *natural*";[13] in legal theory, law is said to be

---

[12] Taylor, *Hegel*, p. 494.
[13] *Oxford English Dictionary*.

positive when it is established and maintained by a sovereign authority. Hegel uses the word *positive* to describe any religion that is grounded on authority, and Judaism and Christianity are usually represented as being *positive* religions.[14] A positive religion, he says, is "a religion which is grounded in authority, and puts man's worth not at all, or at least not wholly, in morals".[15] Hegel was at one with the Enlightenment in rejecting this positivity of the Christian religion, but he also thought the Enlightenment had misunderstood the importance of religion for the education of the human spirit. This has resulted in an impression that Hegel's work is much more benevolent to Christianity than in fact it is.

Kant, Hegel maintained, left us with ways of understanding reality that resulted in an alienated world. That is, Kant left us with a world that is harshly divided into broken, unrelated realities that are not fit for men to live in. For example, the world of natural science, causally determined, is one such reality, and the world of freedom is another; and this division plays itself out in each one of us by an inexorable moral law of reason set over against the affective, passionate side of human nature. Hegel wanted to find a way of healing these divisions while at the same time holding on to what he regarded as the real advances made by the Enlightenment. Given our purpose in this book, it

---

[14] "Hegel sometimes uses the word 'positive' in a quite neutral, descriptive way. But in connection with 'religion' or 'faith' it always retains something of the force that it has in legal theory.... As such, 'positive faith' and 'positive religion' are always regarded by Hegel as evils" (H. H. Harris, *Hegel's Development*, vol. 1, *Toward the Sunlight, 1770–1801* [Oxford: Clarendon Press, 1972], p. 225n).

[15] "The Positivity of Christian Religion", in *Early Theological Writings*, trans. T. M. Knox (Chicago: University of Chicago Press, 1948), p. 71.

is especially important to see that among these advances, as Hegel saw it, was the elimination of the particularity of revelation. There is a good deal of Christian language in Hegel's philosophy, but as Kierkegaard saw clearly, the Christian language no longer tells the story of Jesus of Nazareth as the incarnate Son of God, nor does it recount the mysteries of creation and redemption as being the foundations of our existence. It is rather the case that these truths of faith are understood as and become illustrations of something even more fundamental. And this something more fundamental than faith is, for Hegel, philosophy itself. Hegel thought that Christianity was the absolute religion. But its characteristic of being absolute depends, not on the fact that it is the religion of Jesus Christ, but on the fact that it represents in a pictorial and imaginative (if necessary) way the absolute philosophy of Georg Wilhelm Friedrich Hegel. The claim is so astonishing that its implications seem, often enough, not to be understood. Hegel wanted to repair some of the damage created by the Enlightenment, but the repairs provide little comfort for the Christian.

How did Hegel arrive at this very singular position? Hegel began his university life as a student for the Lutheran ministry. He was, it seems, forced into this course of studies by his father. At the same time, he wanted to be more than an academic and aspired after influencing the public life of his own time; he wanted to be a *Volkserzieher*, an effective educator of the people. He thought at the beginning of his intellectual life that religion was the best vehicle to get his ideas across, although that does not mean his interest in religion was anything but genuine. His earliest works, unpublished in his lifetime, were written under the impetus of this desire to help bring about a regeneration of the society of his age. These works, published in English with the title

Early Theological Writings, are a series of intellectual experiments in which he tried to reconcile the Enlightenment, Christianity, and a political vision based on his reading of the politics of ancient Greece.

What is required, then, is a new religion rooted in the actual life of the people, but not based on superstition. Furthermore, it will not be a Kantian sort of religion, with its harsh divisions, but will be a religion that incorporates the affective and passionate sides of our nature into a harmonious whole.

> I. Its doctrines must be grounded on universal reason.
> II. Fancy, heart and sensibility must not thereby go empty away.
> III. It must be so constituted that all the needs of life and the public affairs of the state are tied in with it.[16]

The first requirement shows Hegel's fundamental adherence to the Enlightenment. Later, in the *Phenomenology of Mind*, he made clear that he accepted the destructive side of the Enlightenment, insofar as it concerned the idea of a particular revelation in history, and accepted the attack on what he called the positivity of the Christian religion. He contended that the negative and destructive aspects of the work of the Enlightenment represent a necessary phase in the education of the human spirit, and, as such, they must be appreciated as valuable steps in the process that leads to freedom.

His own "genuine third position", which appears to "save the phenomena", as Taylor so accurately puts it, consists either in reinterpreting Christian dogma so that any important element of particularity (positivity) is removed, or else

---

[16] "Religion ist eine" (Harris, *Hegel's Development*, p. 499).

in simply ignoring those elements of the Creeds that do not interest him. Hegel, for example, insists on the historicity of the Incarnation, but he alters its meaning in a way that any *Aufklärer* could accept. He thinks that Jesus Christ was a real historical person, but he could not be said to be God in any sense other than we are all identical with God. When it comes to doctrines such as the Resurrection and Ascension, he just seems to ignore them.[17]

So, in a heavily disguised way, Hegel continued the attack of the Enlightenment on the particularity of revelation, or on what he himself called the positivity of the Christian religion. His analysis of the Enlightenment ended in a new religious settlement. He taught the world it could have reconciliation without the blood of Christ; he told us there could be a Christian community without a transcendent God. But all this had to be paid for by giving up the historical and positive dimensions of Christianity.[18]

2. The Community

Hegel's deepest concern was the coherence of all of European man's experience—intellectual, religious, moral, social and political—which had been undermined by the ideas of

[17] "As for the Resurrection and Ascension, although Hegel never states anything one way or the other, the impression one gathers is that he really did not consider them as historical events" (Taylor, *Hegel*, p. 495).

[18] "Against scepticism, against materialism, against Spinozistic Pantheism, against Deism or Arianism—nothing is easier to prove by the aid of Hegel than wherever such creeds differ from orthodox Christianity, they are in the wrong. But this is not the end. The ally who has been called in proves to be an enemy in disguise—the least evident but the more dangerous. The doctrines which have been protected from external refutation are found to be transforming themselves till they are on the point of melting away, and orthodoxy finds it necessary to separate itself from its insidious ally" (John McTaggart Ellis, *Studies in Hegelian Cosmology* [New York: Garland, 1984], p. 264).

the Enlightenment and the forces released by the French Revolution and the industrial revolution typified by Britain. His philosophy was the result of a search for community in the culture of society of the modern world.[19]

We can discuss the idea of community from either an internal or an external point of view. That is, we can outline what we mean by a community, say why it is important, or even essential, for human living. Or, we can discuss how different sorts of community are related to each other and what part communities play within larger groupings, such as the state or the Church. Hegel had a lot to say about both the internal and external aspects of community. In this section I am mainly concerned with the first question, that is, what does Hegel mean by a community, and why is it important.

Hegel's own views on community were elaborated initially in the *Phenomenology*, and they are directed in the first place against the view that individuals are so many self-formed units who come together to constitute society.[20] Such a theory is what is called social contract, but the focus of Hegel's argument is not directed against social contract theory but against any theory that teaches that man can exist in isolation from a community. He is not merely making the obvious point that in fact we depend on other people for goods and services and that in even the most primitive community there must be some division of labor if anyone at all is to survive. He argued for something much more profound, and this is that you cannot even begin to be a human being without a community.

---

[19] *Hegel's Political Philosophy: Problems and Perspectives*, ed. Z. A. Pelczynski (Cambridge: Cambridge University Press, 1971), p. 12.

[20] When I say "initially", I am talking about works published in his lifetime. As we saw in section 1 of this chapter, he was interested in the question from the start.

Common sense would seem to dictate that there is some sort of real distinction between the individual and the community. Individuals are obviously real in a way that even the family, and much more any other sort of community, is not real. After all, it seems to be obvious[21] that you can see and touch other people in a way that you cannot see or touch either *family* or *community*. But this does not get us very far, because we have not done much more than draw attention to the fact that individuals have bodies and exist in space and time; and do we really want to argue that bodies in space and time are all we mean by *individual*? Hegel says we mean a great deal more than this by using the word, and surely he is right.

The community is required for an individual to be a human being, just as it is required if the child is to survive after birth. Hegel argues in the *Phenomenology* that this necessity is based, first of all, on the fact that we cannot think without language. Most of us seem to be wedded to the idea that there can be private languages to which only the individual who creates them has any access. But Hegel did not have to wait for Wittgenstein with his beetle in the box[22] to think this idea was fundamentally incoherent. We do, of course, have private experiences, but even the experience itself is conditioned by the use of language,[23] and

[21] Although, according to Hegel, this is not really all that obvious and is in fact mistaken. This is the burden of his argument in the first chapter of the *Phenomenology of Spirit*, "Sense-Certainty".

[22] Ludwig Wittgenstein, *Philosophical Investigations* (Oxford: Blackwell, 1958), section 288. There is a very clear exposition of Wittgenstein's argument about private languages in Roger Scruton, *Modern Philosophy* (New York: Allen Lane, Penguin Press, 1995), pp. 50–54.

[23] Charles Taylor, *Human Agency and Language* (Cambridge: Cambridge University Press, 1985), chap. 9, "Language and Human Nature". Taylor has developed a theory, based on Herder, which he calls *Expressivism*, and he

any description of the experience (even to ourselves) requires the use of language.

Language, however, requires participation in a linguistic community. This is perhaps easier to see than the first point. Someone has to teach us our language, and we have to learn it. Teaching and learning, however, only take place in a community. Even "teach yourself" books already presuppose an elaborate structure of shared concepts, not to mention the cooperative process of publishing and distributing the books.

Lastly, if thinking presupposes language, and language presupposes a community, it follows that a community is required for an individual to be a thinking being. If you say that an individual is more than a thinking being, then Hegel would be the first to agree with you. There is a sustained polemic through his work against a rationalist or Kantian view that sees the individual as essentially a rational being who is distracted by feeling and the passions from the pursuit of truth and from fulfilling the moral law. Nature must be integrated into individuality, not only because unless we do so it will become a distraction, but also because it is only through the harmonizing of what nature teaches us with what reason thinks that we will be able both to think properly and to answer to the legitimate claims of morality.[24]

---

wants to maintain that: "The revolutionary idea of expressivism was that the development of new modes of expression enables us to have new feelings, more powerful or more refined, and certainly more self-aware. In being able to express our feelings, we give them a reflective dimension which transforms them. The language user can feel not only anger but indignation, not only love but admiration" (p. 233).

[24] There is an excellent outline of this argument in Michael N. Forster, *Hegel's Idea of a Phenomenology of Spirit* (Chicago and London: University of Chicago Press, 1989), pp. 82–86.

Human beings require other human beings to be human. The necessity for others is built into what is involved in being human. That is Hegel's first lesson about community, but there is something else to be learned from his work. A community can go badly wrong, and this happens when it becomes a mirror in which its members see themselves as idealistically pursuing noble and unselfish purposes. When this happens, the community becomes nothing more than egoism writ large. There is, in the *Phenomenology*, an acid account of this process. In their effort to organize themselves around a goal, a goal that may be praiseworthy in itself, the members all too quickly begin to see themselves both as embodying and reflecting that goal and as superior to those outside their group.

> The spirit and the substance of their community are ... the mutual assurance of their conscientiousness, of their good intentions, the rejoicing over this reciprocal purity of purpose, the quickening and refreshment received from the glorious privilege of knowing and expressing, of fostering and cherishing, a state so altogether admirable.[25]

That spirit is still with us, but it does not find its source in what Hegel intended to teach. Because we might think that some sort of vindication of the idea of community is required, it does not follow that everything we read in contemporary theories finds its source in Hegel. He thought that each culture is a self-contained whole and has to be understood in terms of its own goals and its own internal laws. But he did not think that every social order and every example of a community was just what it was and, so, beyond

---

[25] G. W. F. Hegel, *The Phenomenology of Mind*, trans. J. B. Baillie, 2nd ed. (New York: Humanities Press, 1964), p. 664.

criticism.[26] That is a mistake that is often made, and it results in attributing to Hegel a theory of multi-culturalism in which no society, or grouping within society, can be criticized except in terms of its own goals or practices. Hegel has no use for this sort of thinking.[27] In the *Philosophy of Right*, there is a painstaking effort to show how different societies and institutions have grasped and made real the standards he sets forth in his own book. This effort on Hegel's part may be dismissed as misguided, but it is certainly not relativistic or pluralistic.

But nothing ever stays put in Hegel, and there are further questions to be asked. These questions are about what I called the external view of community, that is, how communities fit into larger wholes. This leads us to his theory of civil society.

3. Civil Society

The dialectics of civil society create a universal dependence of man on man. No man is an island any more, and each finds himself irretrievably interwoven into the texture of production, exchange and consumption.[28]

---

[26] "Hegel prefers organism over mechanism as the metaphor for a society. Like Herder before him, Hegel infers from this metaphor that each culture is a self-contained whole that must be understood and appreciated in terms of its own internal laws, and not measured by a rigid standard foreign to it" (Wood, *Hegel's Ethical Thought*, p. 202).

[27] "The term 'ethical' for Hegel does not signify adherence to a Romantic pluralism or relativism, but instead is being used to articulate some sort of standard for ethical conceptions and the social orders that embody them" (ibid., p. 203).

[28] Shlomo Avineri, *Hegel's Theory of the Modern State* (Cambridge: Cambridge University Press, 1972), p. 126.

Hegel developed the idea that, in addition to government and the extended family, there was a structure in human living called *civil society*.[29] He thought that civil society was the sphere of modern economic activity, and it was in civil society that the associations created by economic activity were given room to develop and flourish. We are so used to thinking of Hegel as a rather abstract metaphysician, or as a cultural critic, that it is easy to overlook his profound interest in the economic realities of life. Yet from his early twenties, when he was a tutor in Berne, he began to think about the role of economic life in society, and he was especially influenced by Sir James Steuart's *An Enquiry into the Principles of Political Economy*. "It is from this description of the activity and analysis of the market mechanism by Adam Smith's mentor and contemporary that Hegel derived from that time onwards his awareness of the place of labour, industry and production in human affairs."[30]

Civil society is a translation of *bürgerliche Gesellschaft*, and as a member of this society, a *Bürger* sees himself, not primarily as a citizen of the state, but, to use the French word, as a *bourgeois*. We do not use the word *Burgher* in ordinary English, and *the bourgeois* indicates pretty well what Hegel meant. We often use the word in English to mean middle class, but it can also be used to refer to society itself in a way that shows what Hegel meant. When the nineteenth century opened, France was a republic, then a dictatorship under Napoleon. This was followed by a restored monarchy, and this in turn by another republic. Then there was another session of the Bonaparte family under Napoleon III,

[29] The actual term *civil society* has had a long history and has been used by such writers as Locke and Hume as well as by Hegel's French contemporaries, whom he had read.
[30] Avineri, *Hegel's Theory*, p. 4.

and finally the century ended with another republic. Throughout all these changes in the arrangement of the government of the state, French life continued; and it was the existence of civil society as distinct from the state that made this possible.

The theory that civil society is an aspect of modern life that is distinct both from the state and from the life of the family was taken over by Marx and the Marxists and has had a long and fiercely contested history of interpretation.[31] This history is not itself our concern, but what does matter for us is to realize that the foundations of the modern rhetoric about community can be found in Hegel and Marx. This is not to say that everyone who starts talking about community is thereby shown to be a Hegelian or a Marxist. What I do want to claim, though, is that when we talk about community today, we are using ideas that come from Hegel and Marx and do not have their source in the thought of the direct heirs of the Enlightenment.

The theme goes something like this. The claims for the complete triumph of the Enlightenment are often exaggerated, and opposition to its claims and to its spirit was not exclusively on the part of the stupid, the unlettered, and the people with a vested interest in the status quo. The reaction to the Enlightenment is usually called the Romantic Movement. Cultural phenomena are notoriously difficult

[31] "The selective Marxian appropriation of 'civil society' and the state/civil society distinction has added a large element of contestability to the two concepts. It has forced writers sympathetic to Hegel to question Marxian interpretations, while writers who are Marxist or sympathetic to Marx's standpoint have felt it necessary to repeat his criticisms in order to distance themselves from Hegel. The aura of contestability around the state/civil distinction is still further enhanced by divisions within the Marxist camp itself" (Z. A. Pelczynski, ed., *The State and Civil Society* [Cambridge, England: Cambridge University Press, 1984], p. 2).

to describe accurately, and this is certainly true about romanticism. That does not mean, however, that the term is meaningless, and there are two of its aspects that are important to us. In the first place, there is a new emphasis on the importance of the self and its feeling; and secondly, this self requires other selves if it is to become fully human. Hegel taught that prior to the development of the modern world there were two elements in society, taken in a broad or nontechnical sense, that had to be taken into account: these two elements were the family and the city state. The life of the family he called ethical life, and he described it as being unreflective, or immediate. Family life was the basis of society and was lived within the larger whole of the state, which dealt with the good of the entire community. The life of the city, the *polis*, in ancient Greece, is the exemplar of this arrangement. Family life, with its unreflective, powerful norms, is in the hands of the women, and public life, and its law, is in the control of the men. Ideally, the norms of family life and the laws of public life should harmonize, and tragedy results when they do not.

Hegel uses Sophocles' play *Antigone* to illustrate and discuss this tragedy. Antigone gives the funeral rites to her dead brother, but in doing so she breaks the law of the state, which, in a particular set of circumstances, forbade this to be done. She owes obedience to two laws, but here and now she cannot fulfill her obligations to both. She chooses to obey the law of the family and pays with her life for disobeying the law of the state. There is no possibility of reconciliation between the two sets of duties.

In the modern world, Hegel says, a new order has come into existence, and this he calls *civil society*. Civil society provides a necessary element in harmonizing the unresolved conflicts of pre-modern life. Civil society grew out of the family and is the sphere where family members work with members of other families to pursue ends that are directly related neither to the family, on the one hand, nor to the state, on the other. In civil society the individual becomes more than a member of the family and participates in a system of social relationships that are largely economic. Through this system he becomes an individual person who is neither only a member of a family nor a citizen of the state. He now pursues his own particular aims, and he does this in union with other individuals who are also doing the same thing.

> The concrete person, who is himself the object of his particular aims, is, as a totality of wants and a mixture of caprice and physical necessity, one principle of civil society. But the particular person is essentially so related to other particular persons that each establishes himself and finds satisfaction by means of the others, and at the same time purely and simply by means of the form of universality, the second principle here.[32]

Hegel thought that this civil society was not merely a description of how history actually developed when the complexities of ordinary life forced a division of labor into social life. Even fairly primitive societies soon discovered that life required specialization and cooperation on a much larger scale than even an extended family could provide, but Hegel is talking about more than this. His interest in political economy was awakened (as we have seen) by reading Steuart, and his analysis of economic life is based on the work of eighteenth-century economists such as Smith, Say, and

[32] G. F. W. Hegel, *Hegel's Philosophy of Right*, trans. with notes by T. M. Knox (Oxford: Clarendon Press, 1949), p. 122.

Ricardo, and he acknowledges his debt to them.[33] His contribution, as has often been pointed out, was to see civil society as a distinctive modern form of human community, and this new and distinctive form of the human community has been essential for the development of the modern self. Modern man cannot be properly understood either as a member of the family or as a citizen of the state;[34] rather, he must also be understood as a member of civil society, and this understanding provides the basis for a complex and rich idea of community and society.

Once again, however, we have to be careful. Hegel is not talking about what people seem to intend today by such expressions as "the Christian community" or "the parish community" of such and such a place. This is because for him associations are largely developed to further economic life. Civil society provides the individual with associations that are more complex than those of the family and that nurture the development of the human person through his interaction with others in a complex of economic activity based on need. It is true that Hegel argued that this interaction, and even competition, did not mean giving up on ethical life; that is, he did not think economic life had to

[33] "Political economy is the science which starts from [this] view of needs and labour but then has the task of explaining mass-relationships and mass-movements in their complexity and their qualitative and quantitative character. This is one of the sciences which have arisen out of the conditions of the modern world" (ibid., p. 126).

[34] "Civil society is a social institution, a form of ethical life, grounded on the self-image of modern individuals, on a far richer and more complex image of the individual self than that which grounds the family. It is only within civil society that the self as person gains concreteness, through the economic relation of private property owners recognized by the system, of legal justice. It is also chiefly in the contingent interactions of private persons afforded by civil society that moral subjectivity finds free scope for its activity" (Wood, *Hegel's Ethical Thought*, p. 26).

be destructive (and Marx thought he was wrong here) of human values. The satisfaction of needs is in itself legitimate, and, whether it is through cooperation or competition, the actual living of the life of society begins to build communities and develop the human person.

> In a rational civil society, economic relationships are not merely instrumental to personal satisfaction; they also express, and are mediated by, the individual's sense of community and identity with others. In this respect the corporations perform the important function of engendering recognitive social value.[35]

Nonetheless, to repeat the point, civil society is the arena of economic life, and economic life is not supposed to be the mother of the Christian community. However we understand the place of the Church in modern society, it would not be adequate to view her as only one more grouping of people pursuing economic goals. The associations of civil society are semi-public, and they grow and flourish only within a state that provides a stable legal system of property rights. The state also has the power both to enforce its own laws and to oversee the development of the rules and regulations of the particular associations within its boundaries. There may be Catholics today who find this an acceptable model for the role of the Church in society, but these people turn their backs on the traditional conviction that there are areas of life that are not Caesar's.

4. God and the Community

If orthodox Christianity, while incompatible with Hegelianism, is nevertheless closer to it than any other religion,

---

[35] A. S. Watson, "Economy, Utility and Community", in Pelczynski, *Hegel's Political Philosophy*, p. 260

it is natural that Hegelianism should support Christianity
against all attacks but its own, and should then reveal itself
as an antagonist—an antagonist all the more deadly because
it works not by denial but by completion.[36]

We saw in the chapter on the Enlightenment that while
such men as Hume directly attacked the existence of God,
there were also a larger number who wanted to preserve
the Deity but to remove him from any real involvement
with the universe except as a kind of underwriter for what
order in fact exists in creation. Much of this talk was produced by people who thought of themselves as believers,
but believers who were trying to purify religion. In this
sense, those who made the observations did not view themselves as hostile to religion; they looked on what they were
doing as a tidying-up operation. Gradually, however, the
rational, unemotional religion of deism was replaced by views
that more and more explicitly rejected the idea of a transcendent God. It was not that God became an unimportant
theme and disappeared from the intellectual and cultural
horizon in the way that Hume wanted. What happened,
though, was that God began living somewhere else. For
Hegel, the existence of God is necessary if we are going to
understand the world we live in, but, and this is the crucial
matter, the world we live in is necessary if God is to be
truly God. We can see Hegel working himself toward this
position in the *Phenomenology*, which traces the cultural history of mankind and culminates in what he calls *Absolute
Knowledge*. Absolute knowledge is not only our knowledge
of the Absolute; it is also the way that Spirit comes into
being through knowing itself. Spirit, *Geist*, or God puts

---

[36] McTaggart, *Studies in Hegelian Cosmology*, p. 264.

itself forth both as nature and as history and knows itself
finally for what it truly is.

Large tracts of nineteenth-century philosophy were influenced by this thrust in Hegel's thinking. God did not disappear, but the God who remained was a God who had
been recast in the light of the needs of the community. For
God to be really himself he must make himself real, or actu-
alize himself in nature, time, and history. Protestant theology was particularly influenced by this sort of talk, and it
was the work of the neo-Orthodox, especially Barth, to try
to put forward again a biblical idea of God, a God who was
not dependent on his creation and who was, to put it simply, in control of history.

Catholic theology has always been wary of this rewriting
of the idea of God, but Catholics do live in the world the
new mentality has created, and this new mentality has certainly affected the way people think about God and the
world. The point of entry of this influence on the Catholic
consciousness has been a growing awareness of the importance of the social sciences. Even when there is no explicit
acceptance of Hegel's sort of view that God becomes ever
more completely himself in nature and history, there has
been a shift in the relative importance given to theology,
on the one hand, and history, psychology, and sociology,
on the other. The subject of sociology is society, and where
you find God is in society.

Hegel had no use for positivism and what later came to
be called scientism. He thought that an adequate view of
modern-day living required that attention be given to what
he called civil society. It was within civil society that a community living that was neither purely familial nor govern-
mental was developed. Many people have thought that
Hegel's view of modernity provides an escape from scientism

and the rule of the social sciences, and in this they may be correct. For the Catholic, however, it is a case of *caveat emptor*—let the buyer beware. Let the buyer beware because buying into Hegel means overextending the community and destroying the transcendence of God.

There is no confusion about this in Hegel himself. The confusion seems to be with Christians who think Hegel provides a way around the Enlightenment of Kant and Hume. Hegel defines religion "as being in the stricter sense the self-consciousness of God".[37] For self-consciousness there has to be an object. We become aware of ourselves as a subject in an experience that involves more than ourselves—it is not really a difficult idea. We are conscious of a tree, and at the same time we are aware of ourselves as perceiving the tree; but without the tree to act as a sort of foil or mirror, we lack consciousness of our self as a definite entity. It is the same, Hegel thinks, with God. Until he has an object other than himself—in the case of God, this is the world and history—then he is not aware of himself: "Self-consciousness in its character as consciousness has an object, and it is conscious of itself in this object; this object is also consciousness, but it is consciousness as object, and is consequently finite consciousness, *a consciousness which is distinct from God, from the Absolute.*"[38]

Whatever we may think of the tortured prose or the argument itself, the conclusion is clear: God needs finitude to be God. But Hegel's story does not end here, because, while God needs finitude to be himself, he also reconciles this object with himself by reuniting it to himself through the

---

[37] *Lectures on the Philosophy of Religion*, trans. E. B. Speirs and J. Burdon Sanderson (1962; reprinted, New York: Humanities Press, 1974), 2:327.

[38] Ibid. (my emphasis).

Spirit, that is "movement and life". "God is love; i.e. He represents the distinction referred to, and the nullity of this distinction, the sort of play of this act of distinction which is not to be taken seriously, and which is therefore posited as something abolished, i.e. as the eternal, simple idea." [39]

On the face of it, this might seem to be a harmless reformulation of the doctrine of the Trinity, and this is what Hegel intends it to be. "This eternal Idea, accordingly, finds expression in the Christian religion under the name of the Holy Trinity, and this is God himself, the eternal Triune God." [40] But this is clearly not what Catholicism means by the Trinity: God does not need the world to be himself. Nor does Catholicism affirm Hegel's further contention that God only becomes "really real" when, as Spirit, he reconciles the world to himself. We are much safer with a thinker like Hume; at least we know what we are up against. [41]

It is not difficult to see the influence of Hegel's thinking on the liturgical life of the Church. We have seen in this chapter that he denied the historical nature of Christianity; then, that while his theory of the community was an advance on those of the Enlightenment, this advance was bought at the price of introducing an inescapably political and social

[39] Ibid., 3:11.

[40] Ibid.

[41] The Christian doctrine of the Trinity is set out in CCC 234: "The mystery of the Most Holy Trinity is the central mystery of Christian faith and life. It is the mystery of God in himself. It is therefore the source of all the other mysteries of faith, the light that enlightens them. It is the most fundamental and essential teaching in the 'hierarchy of the truths of faith' [General Catechetical Directory 43]. The whole history of salvation is identical with the history of the way and the means by which the one true God, Father, Son, and Holy Spirit, reveals himself to men 'and reconciles and unites with himself those who turn away from sin' [General Catechetical Directory 47]."

element into the practice of the faith; and, finally, that all this necessitated abandoning any idea of the transcendence of God. It is the constant theme of critics of the present liturgical arrangements that these arrangements leave little room for adoration and contemplation and that they are almost exclusively concerned with the needs and aspirations of the community. I am not maintaining that the liturgists under attack have read Hegel, but I am saying that his ideas have so colored our ways of looking at things that they have entered into liturgical practice in a pervasive and harmful way.

The liturgy and especially that of the Eucharist is supposed to express the nature of the true Church. But, with the new emphasis on community, the sense of the true Church as the sacramental presence of God among us is in danger of being lost. Bishop Garriga[42] has put this in a way few of us would have dared to write and has emphasized that the liturgy has become "desacralized", or "secularized",[43] and that the center of interest of the liturgy, which ought to be the mystery of Christ and the adoration of the living God, has been shifted into a forum for ideological or sociological reflection. He describes several views of the Church and of the liturgy and homily each one tends to produce.

We can go, in fact from a model of the Church as a "perfect society" in which the liturgical celebrations become official ceremonial acts which are the responsibility, fundamentally, of the master of ceremonies; to another model of

---

[42] Bishop Garriga was one of the writers who contributed to *Il Concilio Vaticano II*, ed. Rino Fisilchella (Cinisello Balsamo [Milan]: San Paolo, 2000); see above, p. 33.

[43] Ibid., p. 52.

the Church, namely one made up of a group of well-known and close friends, who share their faith as well as their tastes and ideals; this setting seeks above all else that the participants are made to feel comfortable in the liturgy, and for this to succeed, a group animator or leader is required who will maintain the tone, who will find hymns and symbols adapted for every occasion.... There are also other models of the Church, more or less behind other liturgical ideas, and which result in other kinds of liturgy: the notion of the Church as a *movement*, with its own group of members, who value the celebration insofar as it strengthens the commitment (of its members) or it moves (others) to make such commitment, and calls for reflection and revisions, and which does not know quite how to deal with (the elements of) sacramentality and thanksgiving (in the liturgy). Something similar happens with the notion of the Church as an ideological group or party, and here what counts before everything else is the message of the leader—that is of the homilist—and the mutual encouragement of the leader and the group.[44]

We might characterize these as:

1. the "perfect society" view;
2. the "all pals together" view;
3. the "movement" view;
4. the "political party or ideology" view.

1. *The "Perfect Society" View.* This holds that the liturgy is the reflection of the Church understood as a perfect society. That is, a society that has all the means necessary for the attainment of its purposes.[45] I think the Bishop is

[44] In ibid., p. 55.

[45] For example, after discussing the family and civil society, Pius XI continues: "the third society, in which man by the waters of baptism enters a life of divine grace, is the Church, surely a supernatural society embracing the

referring here to some celebrations of the Old Rite that reflect a deliberate attempt to ignore the temporal and historical aspects of the tradition of the Church. I will discuss this view in the chapter on the Old Rite.[46] Whatever drawbacks there may be with this sort of celebration, they are not obviously concerned with overemphasis on the community, so they can be left for the time being.

2. *The "All Pals Together" View.* This "groupie" view of liturgy is at the other end of the scale from the first. What unites the group is friendship, or at least like-mindedness about what they consider important. These people are not crusaders, but they want a liturgy that helps to bind them together and affirm them in their unity. Along with the faith, as the Bishop says, they share the same tastes and ideals, and they want this reflected in the liturgy.

The malice of this sort of celebration may not be immediately obvious. What, after all, is wrong, it will be asked, about a special Mass for the bird-watchers society of St. Francis Parish? There are two things that can go wrong with such celebrations. In the first place, the celebration very quickly becomes an adjunct to the purely social dimension of the group. The liturgy becomes one more means, even if an important one, to strengthen and solidify the interests and ideals of the group. Secondly, if you do not happen to share the tastes and interests of the group, you will feel out of place at the Mass, and that is pernicious and shows that the focus of the group's worship really has become its own interests and its own members.

---

whole human race; perfect in herself, since all things are at her disposal for attaining her end, namely, the eternal salvation of man and thus supreme in her own order" (DS 2203).

[46] See below, pt. 3, chap. 4, "Mr. Ryder Comes to Town", pp. 297–313.

I am not talking about the celebration of Mass in a hospital or an old people's home, where the inhabitants are more or less confined to the house. That is a different sort of need from providing social glue for a group of like-minded and perhaps cliquey people.

3. *The "Movement" View.* This approach overidentifies a particular movement within the Church and sees the liturgy as essentially an activity that will help the movement along. The goals themselves may be admirable, but there is an ever-present danger of a reversal of means and ends. A deeper communion with each other and spiritual liberation are good in themselves and encouraged by the Church, but the liturgy does not exist in order to further the purposes of the movement. When this begins to happen, then, as the Bishop points out, the liturgy is valued insofar as it captures the thrust of the movement itself and not because it is the worship of God through Christ. The homilies at such liturgies show that the purpose of the celebration is reflection on the purposes of the group, not the Gospel.

4. *The "Political Party or Ideology" View.* Finally, the political and ideological slant on the liturgy inevitably turns away from God to the *cause*, and it does this in a way that focuses the attention of the worshippers on what is to be done. What really counts in this sort of celebration is the words of the leader who is pointing the way forward toward attaining the goals of the cause, which are, as often as not, of a political nature. Once again, the worship of God takes a back seat.

The Second Vatican Council developed and put in the forefront the vision of the Church as "a people made one with the unity of the Father, the Son, and the Holy Spirit".[47]

---

[47] *Lumen Gentium* 4 (A 17).

It was this teaching that was supposed to revivify all aspects of the Church's life, including, or even especially, the liturgical life of the Church. It is the liturgy itself, and especially the Eucharist, which is meant to express the nature of the true Church as the unity of all Christians in a communion of love and service. But this communion, to repeat the point, is not a community founded on the nature and aspirations of mankind; rather, it is brought into existence, and sustained in its life, through the operation of God himself, Father, Son, and Holy Spirit.

The concentration on the community has meant in fact that the focus of the liturgy as God-directed has been displaced, and any sense of mystery and awe at being in the presence of God has disappeared. Behind this, whether it is recognized or not, is the philosophical belief that the community is necessary for God to be totally real. The dynamic of this new emphasis on the community has led to a total exclusion of any reference to God as transcendent and as having a being that is other than, and not dependent on, his creation. In fact the community from having first of all displaced the focus of divine worship is in danger of becoming itself the object of worship.

This focus on the community has not resulted in a more effective evangelization or in an increased influence of the Church in the modern world. Like a self-preoccupied adolescent who sees the world completely in terms of his own standpoint, the interest in the domestic concerns of the community has led to an increasing ineffectiveness of the Church, at least in the West. The Letter to the Hebrews says that through suffering Christ brings "many sons to glory" (Heb 2:10), and it is the Lord of Glory who should be the focus of our worship.

CHAPTER SIX

COMTE: "POLICING THE SUBLIME"

(THE EXPRESSION IS JOHN MILBANK'S)

In the name of the Past and of the Future, the servants
of Humanity—both its philosophical and practical
servants—come forward to claim as their due the general direction of the world. Their object is to constitute
at length a real Providence in all departments—moral,
intellectual, and material. Consequently they exclude, once
and for all, from political supremacy all the different servants of God—Catholic, Protestant, or Deist—as being
at once outdated and a cause of disturbance.

—Auguste Comte, *The Catechism of Positivism*

Sociology is the discipline that claims to be scientific and
that deals with society. The Enlightenment was sure that
science held the key to a humane and rational future, and
the sort of thinking required for doing science was one of
its major preoccupations. Then, Hegel developed the idea
of civil society and said that we could have no adequate
understanding of ethical life without a serious study of what
this society was actually like. Insofar as sociology claims to
examine society in a scientific way, it is clearly the grandchild of the Enlightenment, but in the importance it ascribes
to society itself, it is clearly the child of the counter-
Enlightenment themes of the Romantic Movement and of

Hegel's teaching about the centrality of life in society and the state.[1]

We have, then, two things to look at. The first of these is the conviction that science holds the key to understanding the good life. The second is the growing certainty that it was the science of society that would actually provide this good life for us. The first conviction (that science holds the key to understanding the good life) is the beginning of what is usually called *scientism*. Scientism, as Habermas puts it, means "science's belief in itself: that is, the conviction that we can no longer understand science as one form of possible knowledge, but rather must identify knowledge with science".[2] The second requires we understand that, as society is the fundamental reality, then the science that deals with society will be the most important scientific discipline.

The origins of scientism are closely connected with the development of sociology. The term *sociology* was coined by Auguste Comte, and a modern editor of his work has written that "the work of this thinker is, for better or for worse, essential to an understanding of the modern period."[3] This might seem to be an astonishing claim to make about any sociologist, no matter how famous he might be. But the editor is making the claim about Comte, not merely as a sociologist, but as someone who claimed to be the founder of a system designed to bring order and harmony into soci-

[1] "In recent years there has been considerable discussion as to whether sociology, especially in its French guise, is to be considered a child of Counter-Enlightenment, or a grandchild of Enlightenment" (John Milbank, *Theology and Social Theory beyond Secular Reason* [Oxford, U.K., and Cambridge, Mass.: B. Blackwell, 1990], p. 52).

[2] Jürgen Habermas, *Knowledge and Human Interests*, trans. Jeremy J. Shapiro (Boston: Beacon Press, 1971), p. 4.

[3] Gertrud Lenzer, *Auguste Comte and Positivism* (New York: Harper & Row, 1975), p. xiv.

ety.[4] This system Comte called *positivism*, and it had a two-fold thrust. First of all, it taught a theory of scientific knowledge, and this theory, he maintained, was based on a philosophy of history. This philosophy of history he called the law of the three stages. Secondly, he tried to use this theory of knowledge to create a new sort of religion that would help to stabilize society, as Catholicism did, but without the supernatural, nonscientific elements of Catholicism. God was replaced by an object of worship that was a single corporate being—in fact, God had become society itself writ large.[5] The enduring influence of Comte's work is not in what T. H. Huxley called this "incongruous mixture of bad science and eviscerated papistry, out of which Comte manufactured the positive religion";[6] but he is remembered today as the founder of sociology and a purveyor of scientism.

Comte's positivism claimed to recognize only positive facts and observable phenomena, the objective relations of these facts and phenomena, and the laws that determine these relations. This thesis, that all knowledge consists in a description of the coexistence and succession of phenomena, is to be found in other thinkers both before and after him. The novelty of his position is that he grounded this belief in a historical hypothesis that, he claimed, explained the development both of society and of the human mind. This hypothesis, or law of the three stages, as he called it, showed that history is divided into three periods: the religious, the metaphysical, and the positive.

---

[4] "Comte's major concern was with the re-organization of modern society and within it the establishment of a lasting order" (ibid.).

[5] See Pierre Arnaud, *Le "Nouveau Dieu": Préliminaires à la politique positive* (Paris: J. Vrin, 1973).

[6] Cited in Antony Flew, *The Presumption of Atheism* (London: Elek Books, 1976), p. 33.

The law had already been articulated by French thinkers such as Condorcet and Turgot, but Comte saw its importance for science and extended it to cover the whole of the evolution of humanity. He also thought that the law could be shown to be true both from history and from the psychology of the human being. In 1822 he formulated the law in this way: "From the nature of the human intellect, each branch of our knowledge, in its development, is necessarily obliged to pass through three different theoretical states: the theological or fictitious state; the metaphysical or abstract state; finally the scientific or positive state." [7]

As history has now reached the positive stage, it follows that explanations must be grounded on observable facts and the laws governing their interaction. This leads him to conclude that from now on there will be no room in the modern scientific mentality for a religious or metaphysical inquiry into the causes or ultimate origins of phenomena. He spells this out by claiming that the establishment of sociology is both a terminus and a starting point. It is terminus because history has been directed toward the establishment of the rule of the science of society (which is the most noble and complicated of all phenomena), and, now that it reigns supreme, there is no need or possibility for the existence of anything other than scientific explanations. But sociology is also a starting point for the future of morality and politics, and this is so because sociology and those who practice it are in possession of what we could call the master plan for the establishment of the positivist society.

Comte had no doubts as to the importance of what he was doing:

---

[7] From "Plan of the Scientific Operations Necessary for Reorganizing Society" of 1822, cited in Lenzer, *Auguste Comte*, p. 29.

On the one hand, positive sociology mutually connects all the sciences, and, on the other, it adds to all resources for investigation a new and higher method. While, from its nature, dependent on all that went before, social physics repays as much as it receives by its two kinds of service towards all other knowledge. *We can already perceive that such a science must form the principal band of the scientific sheaf, from its various relations, both of the subordination and of direction to all the rest.*[8]

Theology and metaphysics still have their supporters because only they can provide universal explanations such as the mind craves to have; but once sociology has been put on a proper footing and has begun to generate universal and necessary law, then the supposed necessity for theology and metaphysics will quickly disappear, and sociology will direct society on "scientific principles".

There is no doubt that Comte's program has been enormously important at the level of both practice and influence. In his own country, France, his thought was the avowed foundation of the educational policies of various anticlerical governments at the end of the nineteenth and the beginning of the twentieth centuries. At the same time, it also provided the intellectual structure of the extreme right-wing reaction to these policies in the royalist movement of Action Française led by Charles Maurras.[9] His influence in the English-speaking world was through the work of John Stuart Mill. Mill was an enthusiastic supporter of much of Comte's doctrine until he broke with him over the question

[8] Comte, from "Sociology and Other Departments of Knowledge", in ibid., p. 261 (my emphasis).

[9] See Francesca Aran Murphy, *Art and Intellect in the Philosophy of Etienne Gilson* (Columbia and London: University of Missouri Press, 2004), especially p. 130.

of Comte's Positive Religion; nonetheless, the orientation of Mill's thought cannot be understood without taking into account Comte's work.[10]

In spite of this influence, both practical and theoretical, Comte's work is obviously based on a law that cannot meet his own requirements for genuine knowledge. There is no way, that is, that the law of the three stages can be verified within the system of the empirical sciences.

> This developmental law obviously has a logical form that does not correspond to the status of lawlike hypotheses in the empirical sciences. The knowledge that Comte invokes in order to interpret the meaning of positive knowledge does not itself meet the standards of the positive spirit.[11]

It is said that you cannot argue with success. But you can, I think, analyze whether the success has been brought about by the means its agents claim. Habermas says that we can understand why Comte was not bothered by the apparent irrationality in the foundations of his system by underlining the fact that Comte was involved in an ambitious program to reorganize society, and this required putting science at the center of things. If we take into account that the law was merely a tool he used to further his own fundamental conviction that scientific knowledge was the only

---

[10] "[Mill's] essays on Comte are important because although Mill rejected Comte's elaborate attempts to provide the Religion of Humanity with a ritual, they reveal the permanence of the debt Mill owed to Comte: his belief that a new doctrine was necessary in the scientific age in which he was living and his attempt—by taking the best out of all existing religions—to provide one. However much Mill reacted against Comte's ritualistic excesses, one center of Mill's doctrine is Comtean" (*Selected Writings of John Stuart Mill*), edited with an introduction by Maurice Cowling [New York and Toronto: New American Library, 1968], p. 14).

[11] Habermas, *Knowledge*, p. 71.

sort of knowledge there really was, then we can understand his cavalier attitude toward the foundations of his astonishing claims. "The paradox of a thinker using a clearly metaphysical law to establish that only empirical science gives us knowledge disappears as soon as we discern the intention of early positivism: the pseudo-scientific propagation of the cognitive monopoly of science." [12] Well, the paradox disappears with respect to why Comte used the law, but the fundamental incoherence of basing science on a law that is unverifiable, on Comte's own terms, does not disappear.

Sociology was the means by which Comte established his scientism, and it was sociology conceived on a grand scale. His new science was not going to be content to describe what is found in any existing society; it was also going to be a super-science that was to organize all the other sciences and oversee their application to society.

> It must be the end of the work that I must treat of sociology as completing the whole body of philosophy, and showing that the various sciences are branches from a single trunk, and thereby giving a character of unity to the variety of special studies that are now scattered abroad in a fatal dispersion. [13]

The principle behind this claim is the law of the three stages. Comte's positive social doctrine has elaborated the law, and "all scientific speculations whatever, insofar as they are human labours, must necessarily be subordinated to the true general theory of human evolution." [14]

We are not interested in this book in trying to assess Comte's achievement as the founder of an academic discipline

[12] Ibid.
[13] "Sociology and Other Departments", p. 259
[14] Ibid., p. 261.

called sociology. It is his fundamental convictions, which are still floating around in today's intellectual atmosphere, that are important for us; and we can summarize these fundamental convictions in four points:

First of all, Comte viewed sociology as a positive science, that is, as we saw, an empirical science based on facts and the laws that connect these facts.

Secondly, he thought that the only true model for any sort of knowledge was this scientific one, and this has been called *scientism*. Scientism, he held, was proved to be true by the law of the three stages.

Thirdly, he thought that when sociology had been properly developed, it would be a sort of super-science that would establish harmony as well as direct all other scientific pursuits, including, of course, the application of positive science to the direction of society itself.

Finally, Comte believed that society itself was the ultimate reality of human existence. This belief is the direct heir of Hegel's views. Hegel, as we have seen, had no time for the liberal view of things that held that society was made up of individual units, called human beings, who were the only real aspects of society and the state.[15] For there to be individual human beings, there had first to be a community of some sort, and so it was essential to understand the community if we were going to obtain a true view of the good life. But, furthermore, the community was also necessary as a kind of field of operations for God, a field of

---

[15] "Liberal discourse presupposed only the isolated, self-conserving individual. From the interrelationships of such individuals, the political and the economic had to be deduced as an artificial construct, or else as the 'cunning' operation of providence. In either case, the collective order was related to the individual in a negative and indirect fashion" (Milbank, *Theology and Social Theory*, p. 51).

operations where God, as the ultimate reality, became ever more himself in history. These two convictions, that community is required for our existence as human beings and that this community is also the locale where the ultimate reality develops itself, ushered in a new way of looking at society and an increasing awareness of its importance.

> In the nineteenth century, initially in France, a different [that is, different from the liberal, "positive"] discourse arose. This presupposed, as an irreducible "fact", not only the individual but also the "social whole" or the "social organism". Unlike the political and the economic the "social" did not have to be deduced; instead it was merely given, in all its unfathomable finitude.[16]

Comte, for all his oddness, put the idea of society at the center of his system and was the first to use the word *sociology* for the study of society. In doing this, he both expressed and helped to develop a modern concern with the community as distinct from the state. He also thought the study of sociology was a science with all the attributes of the hard sciences, such as physics or chemistry. There was also the further and sinister conviction that there is no reality beyond society itself; society had become *le nouveau Dieu*—the new god.[17]

It is not too hard to expose the flaws in Comte's system. We have already seen that the foundation of his science is the law of the three stages, and this law—even if it were true—cannot be proved by anything Comte himself would call science. Again, there is his contention that sociologists ought to rule society. His argument for this unlikely position is quite simple: sociology stands at the head of all other

[16] Ibid.

[17] There is a helpful account of the relation of Comte's new religion to political life in Arnaud, *"Nouveau Dieu"*.

sciences, and its role is to coordinate and direct their activities in the best interests of society. Obviously, however, sociology requires sociologists who will do this coordinating and directing, and so it follows that sociologists should be in control of society.

Comte thought, however, that most people are not clever enough and well educated enough to understand and benefit from the wise directions of the sociologists and, if left to themselves, might be restless and unwilling to accept the hegemony of the sociologists. This is where Comte's *positive religion* comes into play. The function of this religion is to present the truths and plans of the new directors of society in a mystical or symbolic guise that ordinary people will be able to identify with. Mankind's need for worship will be used to habituate the citizens of the new order to obeying what the new science tells them is really in their own best interests and most conducive to their own development. Comte openly acknowledged his debt to the Catholic system, but he invented a new Church out of his head, which he then tried to have put into practice.[18] This new "religion of humanity", as he called it, was not an outstanding success compared with Catholicism, but it represents a frightening example of the mind-set of a social scientist who is out of control.[19]

Comte's system as he himself presents it is certainly not very credible, but it is not difficult to see that his ideas are

[18] See, Comte, *Catéchisme positiviste*, ed. Pierre Arnaud (Paris: Garnier-Flammarion, 1966). It has everything: elaborate instructions for worship (*le culte*), a new calendar, a list of books to be read by the proletariat, and even new saints' days.

[19] Fr. Frederick Copleston discusses Comte's "Religion of Humanity" in his usual even-handed and fair way in *History of Philosophy* (New York: Image Books, 1977), 8:113.

still alive and in good health and that they have created an atmosphere easier to recognize than to deal with. Karl Stern in a book that still bears rereading wrote in the 1950s:

> Apart from the danger of a tool for mass manipulation and social engineering, there is the general climate which these sciences create. They work more or less on the basis of a creed, which is this: values, particularly moral ones, are non-transcendental, and lie on the same plane as the social, economic, and psychological function investigated; they are contingent on, and a product of, social, economic, and psychological data which themselves are arbitrary and shifting.[20]

There is no reference beyond society that we can use to discuss and evaluate human values, especially moral ones. It follows from this that anyone involved in the social sciences considers himself, and is considered by others, to be entitled not only to pronounce on the good life, but also to take it in hand actually to enforce his views. Mass manipulation and social engineering have gone hand in hand toward the realization of Comte's dream of the social sciences as top dog, with the sociologists themselves as the ultimate managers of every sort of "resource", and that includes human resources. Comte's project has not been entirely realized, but we are on the way to making his dreams come true.

We can see this by considering again the question of revelation. The Catholic view of revelation clearly has a transcendental reference. If we affirm, for example, that God is a Trinity of Persons in one God, we claim that our belief is based on God speaking to us through his Son; and, furthermore, we hold that this belief is not the result of any sort of empirical survey. The social scientist can survey to

---

[20] Karl Stern, *The Third Revolution* (New York: Image Books, 1961), p. 93.

his heart's content as to who believes what, but belief in the Trinity is not based on any sort of experience that could be examined by a social scientist. Once, however, you admit that there is nothing beyond ordinary experience, then you leave yourself open to being told, not only what everyone else believes, but what it is reasonable for you to believe. "Objective" surveys about what Catholics "really" think about the Eucharist show this clearly enough. The aim of such surveys is to promote change—"look", they say to those in charge, "look here, no one believes that any more, so adapt before it is too late."

The attitude manifests itself in an off-handed dismissal of the mysteries of faith, a dismissal that nowadays is more and more openly expressed and has been well summed up by Karl Stern:

> The element which is perhaps more than anything else reminiscent of the hatching period of nihilism is that ubiquitousness, certainty, and peculiar touch of banality which is so difficult to define—a characteristic sort of *petit bourgeois* mediocrity associated with a contempt for the spirit.[21]

One of the most baleful consequences of this "mediocrity associated with a contempt for the spirit" is the sociological dismissal of history and tradition. The attitude is not new, and it is found very clearly in Descartes, who is usually, and correctly, identified with providing the original philosophical foundations of modernity. It was from physics, mathematics, and perhaps metaphysics that Descartes hoped to find secure and certain knowledge. History was interesting and even useful toward the formation of a practical attitude, but indulged in for too long, it was harm-

---

[21] Ibid.

ful.[22] But, even more important than this was the fact that history was incapable of providing us with true knowledge:

> The most faithful historians, even if they do not alter or exaggerate the importance of matters to make them more readable, at any rate almost always leave out the meaner and less striking circumstances of the events; consequently, the remainder has a false appearance.[23]

This attitude toward history clearly has unhappy consequences for a religion like Catholicism, which is based on history and which maintains that its historical revelation is to be found not only in written documents but in tradition as well. The historical dimension of Catholicism led Newman to say there was "an utter incongruity" between Protestantism and historical Christianity. "To be deep in history", he said, "is to cease to be a Protestant." [24] One could turn this aphorism around and say that to try to do without history is to cease to be a Catholic. Nowhere is this more evident than in the liturgy. Liturgical worship until after the Second Vatican Council developed over time, that is to say, through history. In the aftermath of the Council, however, a rite was imposed that broke with the organic

[22] "For it is almost the same thing to hold converse with men of other centuries as to travel. It is well to know something about the manners of different peoples, in order to form a sounder judgment of our own, and not to think everything contrary to our own ways absurd and irrational, as people usually do when they have never seen anything else. But a man who spends too much time traveling becomes a foreigner in his own country; and too much curiosity about the customs of past centuries goes as a rule with great ignorance of present customs" (*Discourse on Method*, in *Philosophical Writings: A Selection*, trans. and ed. Elizabeth Anscombe and Peter Thomas Geach [Edinburgh: Thomas Nelson, 1966], 10).

[23] Ibid., p. 11.

[24] John Henry Newman, *An Essay on the Development of Christian Doctrine* (New York: Image Books, 1960), p. 35.

development of the liturgical life of the Church. There are
many studies about the way this organic development of
the Roman liturgy was set aside and about how a new liturgy devised by experts was put in its place.[25] Let one citation from Fr. Nichols suffice to point to what I am talking
about: "Church authority gave the professionals what almost
amounted to a blank check, enabling them to redesign the
Liturgy in just that inorganic way against which such reflective commentators ... as Bishop Sailer had warned."[26]

The only brake on ecclesiastical authority is tradition, and
this was clearly recognized by those who enforced the new
liturgical arrangements. The seeds of revolution are sown by
those who believe that ideas matter and that truth is not nego-
tiable in the interests of political concerns. That does not mean
that revolutionaries are always right; nor does it mean their
motives are necessarily any purer than anyone else's. What it
does mean is that there exists a dynamic of distrust engendered by a heavy-handed use of authority about things that
people think matter. This has nothing to do with who is right
or wrong in some absolute sense, but it is important to make
the obvious point that something more than talking about obedience is required for the "peace, order, and good government"[27] of any sort of social organism.

The Church is a social organism. She is a lot more than
that, but she is that. Criticism of the liturgy, and it does
exist, often has a shrill ring about it, because the critics

[25] There is an exhaustive and authoritative survey of this question in Alcuin
Reid, O.S.B., *The Organic Development of the Liturgy* (Farnborough: Saint
Michael's Abbey Press, 2004).
[26] Aidan Nichols, O.P., *Looking at the Liturgy* (San Francisco: Ignatius Press,
1996), p. 48.
[27] This phrase is from the *British North America Act* of 1867, describing the
overall powers of the Federal Government of Canada.

have a deep sense that to those in authority it does not matter very much what is said or what arguments are adduced. There is a feeling that authority just continues to demand obedience, not only to particular liturgical practices, but even to the arguments justifying those practices. One is told to obey because authority knows best, and authority knows best because its arguments are sound. To criticize the arguments, or to adduce facts that seem to cast doubt on the arguments, is dismissed as indicating that one is disrespectful of authority or not thinking with the Church; and yet, at the same time, the arguments are presented as something compelling in themselves and as proofs that any well-intentioned person would automatically accept.

The pattern for this type of thinking was set by Archbishop Bugnini, who was the architect of the way the document on the liturgy of Vatican II was interpreted and enforced. This can be seen in his own account of how he dealt with opposition to his views. Professor Hubert Jedin was one of the great German historians of the Counter-Reformation, but he had criticized the Archbishop's work. In Bugnini's own words: "Instead of helping to throw water on the fire, some reputable students of the liturgy and the sacred sciences fanned the flames, showing that they did not understand either the tact required by the situation or the pastoral goals of the reform." The Archbishop then goes on to summarize Jedin's argument:

> The liturgy is here listed first among the causes of the present crisis and depicted as responsible for "violent opposition", "chaos", and dangerous experimentation. Here was a primarily negative vision of the reform, with nostalgic regrets for the lost Latin language, which had been a "bond of unity", and for the "immortal creations of our sacred music".

Jedin also pointed out the defects of the translations, especially those in German.[28]

Perhaps some of us might be tempted to think that Jedin was correct in his observations and was certainly a prophet of future developments, but it is the response of the Archbishop that is so revealing. Jedin was told that his intervention was mischievous because the reform of the liturgy was for the people's good, and Jedin, according to the Vatican official, took no account of this central point.

> As a good historian who knows how to weigh both sides and reach a balanced judgement, why did you not mention the millions and hundreds of millions of the faithful who have at last achieved worship in spirit and in truth? Who can at last pray to God in their own languages and not in meaningless sounds, and are happy that henceforth they know what they are saying? Are they not the Church?[29]

But the point at issue was whether the results were positive or negative. It is not necessary to think Jedin was in fact correct in his assessment of the reforms for us to appreciate that he was not in fact answered. It is conceivable, for example, that Bugnini was correct about the importance of the vernacular, although, as the Archbishop understood the use of the vernacular, that is by no means clear. The point here is that Jedin's criticism was ruled out of order because

---

[28] Annibale Bugnini, *The Reform of the Liturgy, 1948–1975* (Collegeville, Minn.: Liturgical Press, 1990), p. 283.

[29] Ibid. Fr. Louis Bouyer, whose patient work over the years on the liturgy and especially on the Paschal Mystery did so much to prepare the foundations for the Council's work, also fell under the Archbishop's censure. To anathematize both Jedin and Bouyer in the same paragraph for lack of both tact and interest in "the pastoral goals" of the reform is a breathtaking example of the Enlightment mind with its contempt for history and tradition in full flight.

the reforms had been instituted by the Archbishop in the light of ends Jedin was said not to share, and the Archbishop was right in instituting the reforms because the changes were in fact successful in bringing about these ends. The judgment that these reforms were in fact successful was made by the Archbishop himself. But, even supposing that Bugnini's aims are accepted, the point at issue was the success of putting of these ideas into practice and the cost sustained by the Church in the new order of things; and for all of this we have nothing but the judgment of the man who created the changes.

It is hardly surprising that lesser men than Professor Jedin have despaired of making any impact on local and national liturgical commissions. Nor is it surprising that they have become bitter and at times incoherent. Nor, finally, should anyone be surprised that the intransigence and unwillingness even to consider the experience of those who deal week in and week out with ordinary people's needs should finally have resulted in the schism of Archbishop Lefèbvre, which is said to number a million adherents.

The sad conclusion of the whole matter is this. Just at the moment the Church was trying to open herself to the world, she destroyed one of the strongest instruments she had for presenting the truth of Christ to a world that desperately needed it.

PART TWO

THE NIGHT BATTLE

Controversy, at least in this age, does not lie between the hosts of heaven, Michael and his Angels on the one side, and the powers of evil on the other; but it is a sort of night battle, where each fights for himself, and friend and foe stand together. When men understand each other's meaning, they see, for the most part, that controversy is either superfluous or hopeless.

—J. H. Newman, *University Sermons*

In part 1 we had a look at many of the ideas that have formed the way we all look at the world. The modern world is the world created by the Enlightenment and the rise of science, by Hegel and his followers, and by the social sciences. These forces have not faded away and died. It is rather the case that they have become a part of our common consciousness and of our deepest reactions to the world in which we live. But the ideas that helped make the modern world come to us like tangled-up fishing lines. We think we have one thread unwound, and then we find its ends are knotted up with several others. In part 2, I am engaged in trying to do some untangling, to assess what has really gone on and how in fact various strands of the Enlightenment and of its heritage still affect the practice of the Church.

In the first chapter I look at the idea that the modern world created by the Enlightenment no longer exists and that we live in a postmodern age. Because, so it is argued, we live in a postmodern age, it follows that the ideas that have gone to make up what I have been calling modernity, or the world we live in, are no longer greatly relevant to understanding our existence. They are no longer relevant, because there is no single reality, no single history, no single one "out there" or "other than I am" that can be even partially understood in terms of such leading ideas as objectivity or universal human rights or freedom in its many forms.

Postmodernism has been welcomed by many who are troubled by the darker sides of the Enlightenment project, and they view postmodernism as a liberating solvent of the political, moral, and social structures that continue to bind the human spirit in today's world. But this promise of liberation has to be balanced by the constant theme, often voiced in terms of sweet reason and the well-bred voices from the Academy, that we really all know that the negative destructive sides of the Enlightenment are an effaceable accomplishment and are to be accepted without argument. They must be accepted, that is, if we do not want to be looked on as backward and out of step. At the same time, however, those in control of the universities, the media, and the courts operate in a way that demonstrates, sometimes explicitly, that the modernist values and presuppositions of the world described in the first part of this book are still in practice dominant in contemporary society. Postmodernism has been adopted by modernism as one more weapon in its battle against any sort of transcendental reference; and any effort to establish traditional morality or human rights on a religious or metaphysical basis is held to be vulnerable to postmodernist criticism. It is evidently bad form not to accept postmodernist criticism when applied to religion. However, postmodernist arguments against the main thrust of Enlightenment thinking cut no ice in the practice of those who actually control society.

In the second chapter, I examine the dominance of the principles of modernity by considering the question of secularization. One of the constant themes of those in charge of liturgical reform is that the worship of God must be radically altered because the liturgy does not relate to the secularized consciousness of modern man. But the idea of secularization is not an easy one to get hold of, and very different things are meant by those who use the word. As a result of these differences in usage, there are totally different evaluations of the state of Catholicism in the world today. It follows from this that there is no obvious formula that would justify the radical changes that have been imposed.

In the third chapter I look at what Iris Murdoch has to say about an escape from both modernism and postmodernism, and I examine her belief that we must find our way back to a view of existence that anchors human values in a realm of being that is beyond, or transcends, the world we live in. In the end, she fails, but her work is a lesson to Catholics that it is possible to argue with modernity in a fruitful and illuminating way without capitulating either to scientism or sociology, on the one hand, or to postmodernism, on the other. Her clearheadedness and courage in seeing through the false promises of modernity, as well as her refusal to take refuge in a postmodernism that has little reference to the world in which we actually have to live, is an example Catholics ought to follow. Unhappily, in Newman's "Night Battle" she is not to be counted on.

CHAPTER ONE

Postmodernism—Blowing It All Up

Derrida says that Heidegger is the last metaphysician, but structuralism does look like another not uninteresting, not uninfluential metaphysic.

—Iris Murdoch, *Metaphysics as a Guide to Morals*

Things have moved on since Flannery O'Connor was writing about wingless chickens in the fifties and sixties of the last century. After modernism we now have postmodernism. This is an expression that has become so common that we find it in the daily papers and hear it on the radio and television. What it seems to mean at this level is that everything is in flux, and this includes the person who experiences a world in which there are no stable centers or fixed meanings. Everything has been shaken up, and nothing much has been put together again. Or, so it is claimed.

It has been argued that postmodernity is merely a continuation and sharpening of themes we associate with modernity, and I think this is correct. This seems to be Charles Taylor's basic position. For him, modernity is all pervasive, and he does not think that any important questions can be raised that are not questions within or about modernity. However, with characteristic subtlety, he also seems to hold that insofar as the postmodernist impulse can be treated (contrary to its own intentions) as having to do with moral intentions and how to ground them, then he will entertain the possibility of a genuinely postmodernist position. Taylor appears to want to argue that there is a moral escape from the negative aspects of modernity.[1]

Others claim that postmodernity has all along accompanied modernity as a somber realization that the world pictured by modernity is never realized.[2] For still others, it seems to mean little more than a free-for-all in which there are no standards, no fixed meaning, and no self and has given rise to what, I suppose, is the most common impression of postmodernism "as the death of meaning and the triumph of wild and unregulated interpretation".[3]

The trouble with many discussions about postmodernism, and even more with its common use, is that no one seems to be very clear as to what is being talked about. For its partisans, it is clearly very unsophisticated to ask what the phrase might mean. It is unsophisticated because language for postmodernists is not something used by autonomous individuals to arrive at truth; it is rather the case that the individual is submerged in language. The individual does not control language; it is language that controls

[1] See below, chap. 3, "Swimming against the Tide". I owe much of the understanding of Taylor's attitude to Fr. Philip Cleevely.

[2] After saying that modernity is constituted by "grand narrative", Andrew Shanks continues: "Postmodernity, on this understanding, is not a period coming after modernity. Rather, it is a counter-current of disillusionment with those narratives—almost as old as modernity itself" (*God and Modernity: A New and Better Way to Do Theology* [London and New York: Routledge, 2000], p. 18).

[3] Frederick Christian Bauerschmidt, "Aesthetics: The Theological Sublime", in *Radical Orthodoxy*, ed. John Milbank, Catherine Pickstock, and Graham Ward (London and New York: Routledge, 1999) p. 201.

the individual.[4] All this is very strange, which does not mean it should not be looked at. The inspection process, however, would be long and difficult because the territory is so vast, and, whatever the merits of the movement might be, clear writing is not among them.

In her very even-handed and informative book, *The Postmodern and the Post-industrial*, Margaret A. Rose has laid out the need for some clarity about this pervasive pathology of our times.

> Because many of the theories using the terms post-modern or post-industrial have been developed in different decades and on the basis of a variety of understandings of the terms modern, modernism, modernization, modernity, industrial and post, there is ... a real need for those theories to be clearly and critically delineated and analyzed if we are to be able to assess the usefulness—or potential dangers—of their various examples for either the present decade [the nineties] or future century.[5]

The result of her labors is a fascinating portrait of a world in which Christianity seems to have little relevance; in fact she says very little about it. That, surely, shows how far things have moved along. Catholicism is concerned with the truth of its message as it touches both faith and morals; but there is no place for such an objective reference in the world of postmodernism. Furthermore, there does not seem to be even an interest in the claims of Christianity to be true and important.

---

[4] "As a doctrine [postmodernism] might be called Linguistic Idealism, Linguistic Monism, or Linguistic Determinism, since it presents a picture of the individual as submerged in language, rather than as an autonomous user of language" (Iris Murdoch, *Metaphysics as a Guide to Morals* [London: Penguin Books, 1992], p. 185).

[5] Margaret A. Rose, *The Post-Modern and the Post-Industrial* (Cambridge: Cambridge University Press, 1991), p. xi.

There are two things we can take away from this pre-liminary discussion of postmodernism. First of all, it can be understood as very much a world view or a metaphysics. We can call this *hard-line postmodernism*. Secondly, though, it can be understood in a much more restricted sense as a rejection of the world whose creation began with the Enlightenment and was finished up by the sociologists, that is, the world we have been talking about in the first part of this book. This *soft-line postmodernism* is in fact used by Christians in an interesting and helpful way.

First of all, there is the hard-line version of the phenomenon. Iris Murdoch, who did not like postmodernism and was not afraid to say it out loud, thought that it was a movement populated by and large by the semi-literate and totally barbarous. Of course, it was not without interest, and her first novel, *Under the Net*, was written about the not so brave new world of the postmodernists. In her Gifford Lectures she described the origins of the phenomenon:

> The origins of structuralism (post-structuralism, deconstruction, modernism, post-modernism) are to be found in anthropology (Lévi-Strauss) and in linguistics (Saussure), but (as it has affected the second half of the twentieth century) the doctrine is mainly the property or creation of Jacques Derrida, and its influence and effects are to be understood through his ideas. It has been widely dispersed (often in simplified and cruder versions) among literary critics, and to a lesser extent among historians and sociologists.[6]

To this description of the origins and extent of postmodernism, she then goes on to add her laconic and damning judgment: "It does not seem in general to be using

[6] *Metaphysics as a Guide to Morals*, p. 185.

philosophical arguments. Derrida, who calls Heidegger the last metaphysician, is declaring the end of philosophy as we know it and the beginning of *a new thinking.*" [7]

Jacques Derrida may have the property rights, but he has been aided and abetted by many others. In fact the semi-popular vocabulary for much of this thinking is to be found in the work of Jean-François Lyotard. Since, however, he is writing about a world—to use an old-fashioned word—in which there is no fixed reference, it is hardly surprising that his message has been variously understood. There is, however, one theme that usually surfaces, and that is "incredulity towards grand narrative";[8] or perhaps "master" or "overall" accounts of reality puts it better.[9]

> Simplifying to the extreme, I define *postmodern* as incredulity toward metanarratives. This incredulity is undoubtedly a product of progress in the sciences: but that progress in turn presupposes it. To the obsolescence of the metanarrative apparatus of legitimation corresponds, most notably, the crisis of metaphysical philosophy and of the university institution which in the past relied on it. The narrative function is losing its functors, its great hero, its great dangers, its great voyages, its great goal.[10]

[7] Ibid.

[8] "Postmodernism, according to Lyotard's definition, is a species of solidarity-project founded on 'incredulity towards grand narratives'. Modernity is that which is constituted by 'grand narratives', as a basis for solidarity" (Shanks, *God and Modernity*, p. 18).

[9] "In perhaps its most common usage, associated with Jean-François Lyotard's *The Postmodern Condition*, the 'postmodern' marks the end of the master narratives of modernity, indeed the end of *all* grand narratives" (Bauer-schmidt, "Aesthetics", p. 201).

[10] Jean-François Lyotard, *The Postmodern Condition: A Report on Knowledge*, trans. G. Bennington and Brian Massumi (Minneapolis: University of Minnesota Press, 2002), p. xxiv.

Metaphysics is in trouble because it looked for overall accounts of reality, but such accounts cannot in fact be had. Now Christianity is "a master" or "overall" narrative, and believers think this master narrative is the key to understanding their existence. But, if we know that the very idea of a general understanding of reality is impossible and realize that Christianity is just such a general scheme, then clearly the effort even to understand, much less to evaluate, our faith is ruled out of court before we even start.

There are Christians today who seem prepared to accept postmodernism in the strong sense and to embrace the fact that Christian theology is no *grand-discours*. The Gospel for them is just one more tale among many others—a *petit-discours*, a sort of semi-private story, we might say, but only one more story among many others with no roots in reality. An example of this can be found in Andrew Shanks, who has written on Hegel, is interested in literature and poetry, and so manifests many of the typical concerns of the postmodernist, although, it has to be said, he is very much his own man. Look for a moment at what he says about faith. Faith, he says, "in the true theological sense, is not a metaphysical opinion". Shanks means, I take it, that when someone says: "I believe in God" or "I believe in Jesus Christ, his only Son our Lord", he is not making any claim about reality; he is not saying, "Look here, this is what I believe to be true." Those kinds of statements have no place in a discourse about faith, because, Shanks says, "Faith is what saves." He then goes on to say that "no metaphysical option, not even the most orthodox or the most enlightened, can ever save." [11] In itself, this last sentence is

---

[11] Andrew Shanks, *What Is Truth? Towards a Theological Poetics* (London and New York: Routledge, 2001), p. 5.

unexceptionable, but I do not think anyone ever seriously thought that the words themselves did the saving. It is not sentences or propositions that save; rather, it is whatever they refer to that matters most. Catholics, and I would have thought most Christians, believe it is Jesus Christ who does the saving. No matter what theory we might have as to how we are made aware of this truth,[12] we think it is true.

We are, however, confused, according to Shanks, although we must be shown patience, as the confusion is "quite easily understandable". The confusion of thinking that statements in the Creed, for example, have any reference to truth has arisen because faith, in every culture, is always found associated with "certain opinions", and it is the opinions themselves that make truth claims. For example, that Baal wants the sacrifice of children; that Jehovah wants circumcision; that Allah wants total abstinence; that Jesus wants chastity, and so on, are all opinions *associated* with faith, but they have no intrinsic connection with faith. In itself, faith contains no elements of opinions at all.[13]

"Thus, what is faith? I go back to what I said above: faith, surely, is *a community-building or community-transformative appropriation of the very deepest poetic truth.*"[14] So poetry through the good offices of the community provides us with the content of faith. The picture presented by Shanks, and many like him, of a constant in human experience, called faith, that is without a fixed content is a response to the

---

[12] See, for example, John Montag, S.J., "Revelation, The False Legacy of Suárez", in *Radical Orthodoxy*, pp. 38–63, who ably shows how complex this subject is.

[13] "The confusion is, to be sure, quite readily understandable: faith is always conventionally *associated with* certain opinions; in each religious culture, a different set" (Shanks, *What Is Truth*, p. 5).

[14] Ibid.

attack by the Enlightenment on Christianity and then on God, as well as to Hegel's reconstruction of the Deity as a necessary component of the development of the world spirit.

Karen Armstrong, the author of *A History of God*,[15] is one of the foremost British commentators on religious affairs. She takes a line similar to that of Shanks, but from a different perspective, and links her criticism of modernity to a vindication of the importance of the symbolic. In arguing for a return to the appreciation of symbols, she provides the basis for a central role for liturgy. On the one hand, she has little use for the view that "accepting certain creedal propositions was the prime religious activity",[16] but, on the other hand, she thinks that our modern Western society has lost the sense of the symbolic that "lay at the heart of all pre-modern faith". "For traditional faith, Christ was present ... in the eucharistic symbols of bread and wine. Once the Protestant reformers stated that the eucharist was *only* a symbol, and essentially separate from Christ, the modern spirit had declared itself." [17]

Armstrong says that in the premodern world there were two recognized ways of "thinking, speaking and acquiring knowledge", and these were *mythos* and *logos*. "Myth was not concerned with practical matters, but with meaning. Unless we find some significance in our lives, human beings fall very easily into despair. The *mythos* of a society provided people with a context that made sense of their day-to-day existence." [18] She then goes on to argue that myth

---

[15] Karen Armstrong, *A History of God* (New York: Alfred A. Knopf, 1993).

[16] Karen Armstrong, "Faith and Modernity", in *The Betrayal of Tradition: Essays on the Spiritual Crisis of Modernity*, ed. Harry Oldmeadow (Bloomington, Ind.: World Wisdom, 2005), p. 76.

[17] Ibid., p. 74.

[18] Ibid.

only became "a reality" when it was embodied in "cult, rituals and ceremonies which worked on the worshippers esthetically".

> Without a cult or mystical practice, the truths of mythology make no sense, and seem arbitrary and incredible. In rather the same way, a musical score remains opaque to most of us and needs to be interpreted instrumentally before we can appreciate its beauty and intuit "the truth" that the music is trying to convey.[19]

The valid and important criticisms of modernity by Shanks' as well as Armstrong's attempt to establish the foundations of liturgy on a vindication of the importance of non-conceptual ways of experience, ways she calls the experience of myth, are bought at too high a price. It is the truth that will make us free (see Jn 8:32), and truth is more than an experience of authenticity or an awareness of aesthetic values. I suppose that Aquinas for these people is a modernist before his time. After all, they might say, he taught that belief involved the use of propositions or sentences he thought were true; and he thought they were true in the strong sense that they referred to reality. But Aquinas did not think God himself was a proposition; nor did he teach that the human mind had any direct contact with the formal object of faith, which was not a proposition but God himself.[20] God, as the first truth, is, Aquinas maintained, unknowable by the human mind; nonetheless, because of God's revelation in Jesus Christ, we can worship the Father "in spirit and truth" (Jn 4:21). If the best the critics of modernity can produce is a poetic way of experiencing whatever it is we find important as an escape from meaninglessness

[19] Ibid., p. 75.
[20] See above, pp. 66–68.

and despair, then objectivity in both worship and morals has become a lost cause. The human situation will then be nothing more than "one man's meat is another man's poison".

Both Shanks and Armstrong in their different ways echo Wittgenstein, who wrote that faith is related, not to "abstract mind", but to "my soul with its passions".[21] Religious belief acts as a framework for what will satisfy "my soul with its passions". Different things satisfy different people's hearts, and so consequently religious belief expresses itself in an apparently endless diversity. But it is not the framework that matters. In relation to Catholicism, for example, Wittgenstein wrote:

> The symbolisms of Catholicism are wonderful beyond words. But any attempt to make it into a philosophical system is offensive. All religions are wonderful, even those of the most primitive tribes. The way in which people express their religious feelings differ enormously.[22]

This is important. Catholics cannot just shrug their shoulders and comfort themselves with the reflection that the world is full of crazy people, and postmodernism proves the point. Postmodernism is alive and well and carries with it the message of the Enlightenment pushed to extremes, even if this is only by way of reaction.[23] Furthermore, this message, as we have seen, has a missionary and destructive

---

[21] "[F]aith is faith in what is needed for my *heart* and *soul*, not my speculative intelligence. For it is my soul with its passions, as were with its flesh and blood, that has to be saved, not my abstract mind." Cited in Ray Monk, *Ludwig Wittgenstein: The Duty of Genius* (London: Vintage, 1991), p. 383.

[22] Cited in Norman Malcolm, *Wittgenstein: A Religious Point of View?* (Ithaca, N.Y.: Cornell University Press, 1994), p. 11.

[23] "Postmodernity is too easily identified with nihilistic accounts of the truth, for such an association presumes an identification of modernity with truth and reason" (Bauerschmidt, "Aesthetics", p. 201).

side to it. There is no way that a shrug of the shoulders is an adequate response.

One of the happy hunting grounds for postmodernism is theology. Faith for St. Thomas and the Catholic tradition is a response to a God who is. There is a good deal of interesting discussion as to how this is to be understood in a postmodernist world, but that is not to accept the principal postmodernist contention that there are no *grands-discours*. The writers of *Radical Orthodoxy* are very aware of the world we live in, and they do not like it much.

> For several centuries now, secularism has been defining and constructing the world. It is a world in which the theological is either discredited or turned into a harmless leisure-time activity of private commitment.... Today the logic of secularism is imploding. Speaking with a microphoned and digitally simulated voice, it proclaims—uneasily, or else unashamedly—its own lack of values and lack of meaning. In its cyberspaces and theme-parks it promotes a materialism which is soulless, aggressive, nonchalant and nihilistic.[24]

Radical Orthodoxy uses the analysis and criticism of modernity that postmodernism has put forward, but it does not accept the hard-line "metaphysical" account, for example of Derrida, of what really constitutes postmodernism. There was little that was distinctively Christian by the time modernity had done its work; deism was the best that could be hoped for, and the sociologists who were "policing the sublime" were in control of the expression of religion in society. Postmodernism for the writers of *Radical Orthodoxy* creates a space in which theology can once again become a meditation on God's revelation; a meditation that is not based

---

[24] Milbank, Ward, and Pickstock, "Introduction: Suspending the Material: The Turn of Radical Orthodoxy", in *Radical Orthodoxy*, p. 1.

on the scraps of religiosity that the modern world is willing to accord to religion and theology.

At first sight the position of *Radical Orthodoxy* has much to commend it precisely because it points up clearly the constricting and anti-religious aspects of modernity. On the other hand, what it is not clear about is the truth of Christianity with regard to both faith and morals. Unless Catholics think there is more to their beliefs than an attitude of "this is my opinion, and I am entitled to it, just as you are entitled to yours", then it is hard to see how Christianity is to be preached both as a saving doctrine and as a way of life.

It is not postmodernism itself that provides the material for the *grand-discours* that is Christianity; that comes from God's revelation.[25] Karl Barth and Hans Urs von Balthasar both share in this desire to liberate theology from being the handmaid of the philosophy of the Enlightenment and the modern world in general. Central to the work of all these thinkers, in spite of the differences, is the proclamation of God's revelation; and this proclamation is not required to authenticate itself[26] either by referring to modern canons of rationality or by taking refuge in a universe of discourse that may be coherent but that makes no claims on everyday existence.

It is important to hold on to the truth that postmodernism as it is usually presented is a metaphysics, that is, it is a statement about what things are really like. Iris Murdoch is correct to question the postmodernists' claim that they write

[25] "Postmodernity in no way constitutes the condition for the possibility of theology; the possibility of speech about God can be founded on nothing less than God's own speaking" (Bauerschmidt, "Aesthetics", p. 201).

[26] The pros and, of course, the cons of Barth's and von Balthasar's stance can be found in Fergus Kerr's *Immortal Longings* (London: SPCK, 1997), in chap. 2, on Barth, and in chap. 7, on the natural desire for God.

in a postmetaphysical age. On the other hand, the various positions of postmodernist writers are often presented with imagination and power: this movement certainly cannot be ignored.

> It claims a break with traditional philosophy, and is certainly unlike philosophy in that it is short of philosophical arguments and of their kind of extended careful lucid explanatory talk and use of relevant examples which good philosophy, however systematic, includes and consists in. But it has rhetorical power which depends on an impressive image or set of images, "language" as fundamental system, written not spoken, a totality to be enjoyed without external verification, etc.; and may, like other metaphysics, be treated as a kind of pragmatism or aesthetic guide. It looks more like traditional metaphysics than like science.[27]

In the place of this powerful and pervasive metaphysics, we have to remind ourselves of an older and saner view of the world. Postmodernism may bring with it the promise of freedom. In fact, though, it opens the way to the reinforcing of the principles and attitudes of modernity, and this will deliver us all into the hands of those who are actually in control of society.

[27] Murdoch, *Metaphysics as a Guide to Morals*, p. 197.

CHAPTER TWO

THE CHURCH IN SOCIETY

The "cultured despisers" of religion see no special reason to read serious explorations of Christian discourse
and prefer to regale themselves with cartoons of its absur-
dity. As for daily newspapers they peddle habitual scorn,
especially about Christianity, since it is difficult to defend
what look like vestiges of previous dominance. In the
"spirituality" sections of bookshops you will find little,
but bizarre, journalistic exposés varied by scholarly promotion of gnostic wisdom or "mystic" junk. There is
not much on the shelves by way of a serious and popular presentation of Christianity, apart from Evangelical
works in specialized shops.

—David Martin,
Christian Language and Its Mutations

The Church lives in society, and sociologists can, and do,
study religion as a phenomenon that can be investigated in
society. In this chapter I want to untangle some of the ideas
being put forward today about how the Church is to function in this world the philosophers and sociologists have
helped to create.

It is often said today that the practice of religion and its
influence in the modern world have declined dramatically

over the last three hundred years; and there is certainly a lot of evidence for this contention.[1] Then, often enough, there are sociologists who go on to produce a kind of law of secularization; for example, we read that any sort of church based on a belief in revelation is doomed to extinction, because the existence of such a church is in fact incompatible with life in a modern liberal democratic society. Religion and modern society are said to be irreconcilable, not because religion is shown to be intellectually incompatible with liberal democracy, but because liberal democracy engenders a complex of attitudes that leave no space for religion.

It is possible to agree with the evidence of decline and at the same time dispute the general law. That is, we might agree that secularization has increased dramatically but deny the claim that a religious viewpoint is an impossibility for modern man. I think it is true that sociology has shown that the place of organized religion in modern society has declined dramatically and, furthermore, that secularization is now best summed up as an attitude rather than as an intellectual position. It is indifference to religion, not the scientific mentality or a conviction that the idea of revelation is not only ridiculous but immoral, that has produced a society that neither believes in God nor fears hell.

There are many different sorts of answers to the question of why this regression of belief in God and decline in religious practice happened. The answers depend to a large extent on the standpoint of the person asking the question. If the questioner does not believe in God and thinks that prayer is useless, then he will be satisfied with a historical account of how the idea of God has in fact been replaced by a picture of the world drawn, he probably believes, in

[1] See above, introduction.

terms of the truths of modern science. The development of secularism, for this type of inquirer, will be understood as going hand in hand with a view of the universe based on reason. You can understand the universe perfectly well without cluttering it up with unnecessary entities like God, and therefore it is obvious that the existence of any sort of church becomes more and more irrelevant.

Another inquirer, however, may be more interested in the human dimension of the matter. In this case he will be likely to concentrate on answers that deal with the development of freedom in society and the liberation of the human personality from the external restraints imposed by religious practices. He may be interested in the overcoming of the tensions and lack of internal harmony, with the alienation, to use the more technical word, that religious belief is said to induce. This person will want answers that emphasize that secularization has been brought about because we want a freer society, a society in which the individual has a better chance of overcoming internal tensions and contradictions.

Most accounts of the process of secularization over the last 350 years are based on these developments in science and on the changes in the perception of our autonomy in relation to the rest of existence. Often enough, the two accounts are viewed as two strands of one explanation. For example, it is often said that the rise of modern science provided the necessary background for the development of human freedom and the overcoming of alienation; or, again, it has sometimes been emphasized that the heightened sense of individuality associated with the Renaissance and the Reformation made people more receptive to the development of a science in which God was no longer at the center of the universe.

We see, then, that the roots of secularization are complex and of long standing, and it is the business of philosophy and the history of ideas to disentangle and describe these roots and then to evaluate them. This is the sort of work that people like Charles Taylor and many others have done in a learned, insightful, and helpful manner. In this book, however, I am not concerned directly with the question of why secularization has come about; rather, my concern is with trying to understand how it affects the day-to-day understanding of the world the Christian now has to live in. Secularization is a fact of life, but what is the proper response of the believer to this secularized world?

The most common answer to this question runs like this: Organized religion, viewed sociologically, is anchored, insofar as it is anchored anywhere, in civil society rather than in the state. After Vatican II, in practice at any rate, the Church has given up on the theory that she is a perfect society that is a counterpart to, and often in competition with, secular governments. Instead, she has effectively disestablished herself (where this had not already been done for her), and now understands that her mission (however she understands this mission) has to be carried out at the same level, or on the same field, as other nongovernmental groups. This anchoring of the Church in civil society, so this answer continues, results in a clearer demarcation of the roles of the state and of the Church; and such a demarcation can only work for the benefit of both. The state and the Church are now in a position to work together in a more effective way because they are in the main concerned with different areas of life; and from this it follows that both state and Church will be mutually enriched, and the Kingdom of God on earth will be an ever more possible reality.

Something like the above is what many people in the Church now seem to believe. Before we clap our hands too loudly, however, let us at least realize that the process of mutual recognition and cross-fertilization is not an easy one and has caused, and will go on causing, endless difficulties. One set of difficulties has arisen because the upholders of secularization, which has brought about the clear demarcation of spheres, often hold that secularization is a law telling us not only what has happened but what is going to happen. Obviously this view will put something of a brake on the "happy families" view of state and Church. Then, secondly, there are those who want to hold that the new arrangements provide ample scope for the Church to get on with her work but who seem to view this work as essentially political in nature. I will discuss both these views below, but we should at least see that neither view leaves much room for a belief that the work of the Church is essentially sacramental and liturgical.

The view that there is some sort of cross-fertilization between religion and the society brought about by the Enlightenment is true, but I do not think it is true in any way that we can program or predict. It is partly for this reason that it is worth continuing to argue for the right of the voice of religion to be heard in the marketplace.

This long-term and unverifiable work of cross-fertilization demands both recognition of the new status of the Church and the fortitude not to be swamped by the allurements of the secular city. David Martin has written about this long-term, problematic, but important dialogue between the Enlightenment and religion:

> It seems to be the case that once religion is eased out of its complete implication in the social totality, it reveals within

itself sources of criticism which can infiltrate the social order just as two hundred years ago the philosophers of the Enlightenment infiltrated the social order of France. Perhaps light in the sense of religious illumination and the light of Enlightenment are destined for continuous dialectic and dialogue, not the supersession of the one by the other.[2]

Once we give up on the existence of God, it is obvious there is no longer any room for the Church, and, certainly, the "hard" Enlightenment gave up on God and wanted to get rid of the Church. But there was also a softer version of the Enlightenment that was prepared to leave us with a rather nebulous, do-nothing God. Believing in this God left the way open for appeals to "higher values", or God could also act as an entity who in some way or other underwrote progress and social reform. But whether it was hard or soft Enlightenment, God had been dethroned, and his plans were seen as being placed firmly in the hands of mankind. I want now to examine two contemporary statements about secularization: one of these illustrates the uncompromising Enlightenment position that God is dead, and "let's get on with things"; the other, a more tentative approach, maintains that God is not very dead, and being convinced of this helps to provide fuel for social criticism and political change.

Steve Bruce, in his book *God Is Dead: Secularization in the West*,[3] makes the point that secularization for most people is not the result of the conscious rejection of Church teaching brought about by the impact of "science and rationalism". He is quite right about this. Most of those who never go near a church have probably never heard of the

---

[2] David Martin, *Christian Language and Its Mutations* (Aldershot: Ashgate, 2002), p. 169.

[3] Oxford: Blackwell Publishers, 2002.

Enlightenment, and their attitude toward religion, wherever it comes from, is certainly not based on an intellectual dialogue with David Hume or Isaac Newton: "To understand the mass of the population it is not self-conscious irreligion that is important. It is indifference. The primary cause of indifference is the lack of religious socialization and the lack of constant background affirmation of belief." [4]

Bruce is a proponent of a hard-line secularization theory; that is, he thinks that secularization is not something that simply happened in modern Western society; rather, he argues that it is something that had to happen. Modernization *necessarily* leads to a decline of religion in society and, as a result, in the individual as well. This had to happen because our urban and democratic society leaves no room for centers of influence, called churches, that teach doctrines that have no obvious relevance to daily life and that appear to run counter to the *ethos* of the prevailing climate of opinion in contemporary society.

> The primary secularizing effects of science came not from its direct refutation of religious ideas but through the general encouragement to a rationalistic orientation to the world that science has given; the embodiment of that rationalistic outlook in bureaucracy as the dominant form of social organization; and the role of technology in increasing our sense of mastery over our own fate. [5]

This may be an accurate account of the convictions that go to make up the basic attitudes of modernity, but, put down in this summary fashion, it is hardly a reassuring one. So far as I can make out, Bruce thinks these facets of modernity

[4] Ibid., p. 7.
[5] Ibid., p. 117.

not only make secularization inevitable, but he also thinks they are desirable. It seems to be generally agreed that something like Bruce's description is in fact true, but that is as far as we can go. No one except sociologists of a certain sort and those who have been mesmerized by their statistics seems to believe that things necessarily had to develop the way they have. That is not to say that the description of the present situation is wrong, but it is, very definitely, to hold that there is no metaphysical or natural law that determined that things had to turn out as they in fact have. Steve Bruce gives us a picture of the modern world in which religion is rapidly declining, and, he seems to be saying, "a good thing, too", and it had to be so.

There are, however, many voices raised to say that this is all too swift. Owen Chadwick in his Gifford Lectures, *The Secularization of the European Mind in the Nineteenth Century*, discusses the position of those who say that secularization does not exist. They say "that secularization only exists in the minds of those who wish it to occur, and are puzzled when it does not occur; in short that it is merely a word of propaganda".[6] Obviously, the work of Steve Bruce, who apparently believes in a law of secularization, gives some substance to this charge. The dogma (that is, that there exists a law of secularization) has been caricatured by David Martin as "God is dead. Therefore secularization must be occurring. Therefore secularization is a coherent notion."[7]

---

[6] Owen Chadwick, *The Secularization of the European Mind in the Nineteenth Century*, Gifford Lectures, 1973–1974 (Cambridge: Cambridge University Press, 1975), p. 2.

[7] "The whole concept appears as a tool of counter-religious ideologies which identify the 'real' element in religion for polemical purposes and then arbitrarily relate it to the notion of unitary and irreversible process" (David Martin, cited in Chadwick, ibid.).

But David Martin is not the only example of those who object to the use of the term. Consider the words of the well-known sociologist of religion Peter L. Berger:

> The assumption that we live in a secularized world is false. The world today, with some exceptions . . . , is as furiously religious as it ever was, and in some places more so than ever. This means that a whole body of literature by historians and social scientists loosely labelled as "secularization theory" is essentially mistaken.[8]

Something seems to have gone wrong: Bruce and Berger cannot both be right. Religion cannot both be declining and not declining at the same time and in the same world. It is obvious that a little conceptual analysis is in order. To help us see the situation a bit more clearly, I want to consider briefly another analysis of secularization that seems a fair and informative piece of work. José Casanova has argued that theories about secularization are actually made up of three different propositions. First of all, there is the view that modernity necessitates the decline of religion. This I have called hard-line secularization. The assumption that religion will tend to disappear with progressive modernization Casanova says is a "notion which has proven patently false as a general empirical proposition".[9] The evidence for his position is drawn from Spain, Poland, Brazil, Evangelical Protestantism, and Catholicism in the United States. His analysis and his arguments bear out Berger's contention that the world is "as furiously religious as ever". Casanova traces the proposition "genealogically" back to the Enlight-

[8] Peter L. Berger, *The Desecularization of the World* (Grand Rapids, Mich.: William B. Eerdmans, 1999), p. 2.
[9] *Public Religions in the Modern World* (Chicago and London: University of Chicago Press, 1994), p. 7.

enment and shows it to be what it is: a belief.[10] And, he thinks, it is a belief that is in trouble.

> It is ... in terms of a crisis of Enlightenment rationalism and of the idea of progress, indeed as a crisis of secularity itself, that one may look for an explanation of the world-wide character of the contemporary religious revival across all civilizations. When secular ideologies appear to have failed or lost much of their force, religion returns to the public sphere as a mobilizing or integrating normative force.[11]

Next, Casanova argues that the second strand in theories of secularization is what he calls *differentiation*. He maintains that the valid part of secularization theory is the differentiation between the religious and the secular spheres. Religion is private in the sense that it is not an aspect of the way the state organizes society, and differentiation has often been brought about because of a conflict between the state and the Church. Poland is one example of this process, which ends by altering, not just the relationship between Church and state, but the nature of the Church as well:

> In Poland, Catholic resistance and church-state conflicts were part of the struggle for the right to a private and social sphere free from totalitarian intervention. But the transformation of Polish Catholicism marks the passage from a

[10] In a footnote (ibid., p. 300, n. 26) Casanova writes: "Robert Wuthnow has offered the intriguing hypothesis that the reason for the widespread irreligion one finds among social scientists may derive from the social science discipline's own insecurity and from their related need to maintain a clear and rigid separation between the two cognitive fields. According to Wuthnow the more precarious the cognitive status of any scientific discipline, the greater the professional need to maintain an irreligious attitude. Robert Wuthnow, 'Science and the Sacred', in Philip E. Hammond, ed., *The Sacred in a Secular Age* (Berkeley: University of California Press, 1985), pp. 187–203."

[11] Casanova, *Public Religions*, p. 227.

struggle centred around the corporatist interests of the church as an institution to a struggle first for human and national rights, and then, after the founding of the KOR and the emergence of Solidarity, for the rights of civil society to autonomy and self-determination.[12]

On the other hand, thirdly, he holds the related proposition, that "modern differentiation *necessarily* entails the marginalization and privatization of religion, or its logical counterpart that public religions *necessarily* endanger the differentiated structure of modernity, to be no longer defensible".[13] We can see what he means here by thinking about the United States:

> It was the 1973 Supreme Court decision legalizing abortion by subsuming it under a woman's right to privacy that galvanized the American Catholic church into the political arena, beginning the process that led the bishops to expand the principle of the moral protection of human life and of the sacred dignity of the human person to the two main subsystems, capitalist markets and sovereign states.[14]

Casanova's careful analysis of what secularization means shows that Bruce's hard-line position, that is, that secularization is a kind of scientific law that prescribes the withering away of religion, is no law at all. Yet we have to be careful, because Casanova's rescue of religion from irrelevance is bought at too high a price. First of all, it is only by displacing the focus of what religion means that it is saved from being relegated to the sidelines and so becoming the occupation of only a diminishing minority. Sec-

[12] Ibid.
[13] Ibid., p. 7.
[14] Ibid., p. 228.

ondly, Casanova's settlement glosses over the aggressive hostility to Christian principles in secular society.

It would be unjust to say that Cananova's theory of secularization does not try to take account of the other-worldly aspects of Catholicism, but as a sociologist he is not directly concerned with these. He writes:

> The Catholic church, while still counting on a large reservoir of traditional cultural allegiance among large sections of the faithful, will have to learn from the American experience, concentrate on its pastoral tasks, and develop some form of voluntary, denominational, revivalist expression to reproduce itself successfully *as a private religion of individual salvation.*[15]

It would be all too easy to conclude, from Cananova's position, that it is the "causes" themselves promoted by the Church that will help her to retain her influence and increase her membership. He may not mean to draw this conclusion, but to speak of Catholicism as "a private religion of individual salvation" tends to obscure this fact.

Catholicism has to do in the first place, and essentially, with the Passion and death, the Resurrection and the Ascension of Jesus Christ. It is this mystery of our redemption that the Church has to try to present and to make real to the modern world. When we forget this, then we are in danger of identifying our temporal agenda, no matter how worthwhile that agenda may in fact be, with the Mystery of Faith. It is not just left-wing people who tend to forget or deny this; it is anyone who begins to mistake his cause or principle of action for the definition of Christianity.

[15] Ibid., p. 223 (my emphasis).

Secondly, Casanova's analysis underestimates the hostility toward Catholicism. Christianity really is despised by the opinion makers in Western Europe and North America.[16] The term "opinion makers" means, of course, the people who work in newspapers, radio, and television. But, for the most part, the ideas these people propagate are not their own. The real opinion makers are in the universities and the legal system. Peter Berger puts it this way:

> There exists an international subculture composed of people with Western-type higher education, especially in the humanities and social sciences, that is indeed secularized. This subculture is the principal "carrier" of progressive, enlightened beliefs and values. While its members are relatively thin on the ground, they are very influential, as they control the institutions that provide the "official" definitions of reality, notably the educational system, the media of mass communication, and the higher reaches of the legal system. They are remarkably similar all over the world today, as they have been for a long time (though . . . there are also defectors from this subculture, especially in the Muslim countries).[17]

The truth of Berger's view seems indisputable. During the last few years the evidence for its truth has become especially striking in the activity of the courts in the area of social policy. Since the 1990s appeals courts in the United

[16] The life and work of the enormously influential philosopher of law H. L. A. Hart, who is an example of "devout atheism", is a case in point. He and his wife ridiculed religious belief in private, even if their views were carefully concealed. The natural law philosopher John Finnis was a pupil of Hart's, and "it was only after Herbert's death that Finnis became aware of the full extent of his antipathy to religion." See Nicola Lacey, *A Life of H. L. A. Hart: The Nightmare and the Noble Dream* (Oxford: University Press, 2004), p. 347.

[17] Berger, *Desecularization*, p. 10.

States and Canada have held that the definition of marriage as the union of a man and a woman violates constitutional equality guarantees:

> Recently, Canadian courts went one step further ordering a change in the legal definition of marriage from the union of a man and a woman to the "union of two persons". Judicial decisions on marriage mark the culmination of a series of cases that have considered the legal implications of homosexual conduct. Those decisions have promoted a view of sexual conduct as a matter of private, personal choice that the state must respect and recognize as a matter of constitutional law.[18]

The Chief Justice of the Province of Quebec has spelled out the view of many judges that they have replaced Christianity as the moral teacher of society:

> We have become an instrument of "governance", in the wide sense of the word. We are becoming the new priests of civil society, in a way, because we are making decisions about same-sex marriage ... about euthanasia and abortion. We are making decisions about many other controversial issues which have a very large moral content and moral connotation.[19]

The favorite philosopher of the Supreme Court of Canada is John Stuart Mill.[20] Mill was a complex and careful thinker, but it is easy to abstract a rather anodyne view of

[18] D. M. Brown, "Sexuality and Constitutional Choice: The Case of Same-Sex Marriage", in R. E. Hauser, ed., *Temperance: Aquinas and the Post-Modern World* (Grand Bend, Ind.: University of Notre Dame Press, forthcoming).

[19] Chief Justice Michel Robert, as reported in the *Ottawa Citizen* of May 4, 2004.

[20] See the appendix to this chapter, which is taken from "Sauvé and Prisoners' Voting Rights: The Death of the Good Citizen?" by David M. Brown, *The Supreme Court Law Review*, second series, vol. 20 (2003): 297.

his thought that sees him as the champion of individual rights against undue pressure from either society or government. It is this reading of Mill that seems to be axiomatic to many judges. There is, however, a great deal more to Mill than this, and it is important to see that this reliance on Mill brings no comfort to anyone interested in the future of institutional Christianity in Western society.

This reliance on Mill owes a great deal to the influence of H. L. A. Hart, who was Professor of Jurisprudence at Oxford and who also taught at Harvard as well as in California and Israel. He was a positivist who thought that law, as law, could have any content whatsoever, but that there was room for a critique of existing laws and for law reform. This critique of existing laws and plans for their reform he elaborated by using Mill's *On Liberty*, and he argued that democratic states were entitled to enforce moral norms as moral norms only if these norms were required to avoid harm and to ensure that individual freedom was respected.[21]

We have already seen that Mill shared Comte's view that a new doctrine of science and society was required for the new age of the nineteenth century.[22] One aspect of this new doctrine was to be a religion that was to replace Chris-

---

[21] "His positivist view asserted that law could have any content whatsoever: hence it could be used to further the welfarist and other goals of the social-democratic government of which Herbert approved and which he saw as to some extent reflected in successive Labour administrations. Yet the moral and practical question of how law *should* be used—its proper limits and its desirable scope—was pressing. Herbert's work, particularly in the field of criminal justice, had become increasingly concerned with these prescriptive questions. He now turned to the elaboration of a liberalism which finds its roots in J. S. Mill's *On Liberty*, which somewhat later found expression, in revised form, in John Rawls' hugely influential *A Theory of Justice*" (Lacey, *Life of H. L. A. Hart*, p. 256).

[22] See above, pt. 1, chap. 6, "Comte: 'Policing the Sublime'".

tianity by taking the best of all existing religions. In Comte's case, this religion was the means for the findings of the sociologists to be made acceptable to the masses as well as for enhancing the status of the sociologist. Mill broke with Comte on how the new religion of humanity was to be made palatable to ordinary people, but he did think that something like a religion of humanity was required to take the place of orthodox Christianity. This strain in Mill's thinking is summed up by Maurice Cowling:

> The careful reader may find himself thinking that Mill's immediate political doctrine is libertarian because a libertarian polity is more likely than any other to facilitate agreement and that the whole of Mill's political writing is impregnated with a desire to destroy existing political orthodoxies because that would be the best way of completing the destruction of the authoritarian church-Christianity he knew and disliked.[23]

It is not necessary to accept everything Cowling has to say about Mill to see that he is pointing to a sinister strain in the Comte-Mill view of society that ends up in a theory of government by experts. Furthermore, the religion of these experts was to be a new religion replacing Christianity.[24]

Berger is right about another point. It is worth noting that the judges in the higher reaches of the law take in each other's washing. The Canadian judgments cite American cases, and the Americans in their turn use the work of their

[23] *Selected Writings of John Stuart Mill*, ed. Maurice Cowling (New York and Toronto: New American Library, 1968), p. 10.

[24] The centrality of religion was an important principle of Victorian thought, and all the enemies of Christianity [in Victorian times] followed Mill in wishing to find a religion to believe in in place of Christianity", Maurice Cowling, *Religion and Public Doctrine in Modern England* (Cambridge: Cambridge University Press, 1985), 2:107.

Canadian colleagues. The international flavor of the sub-culture is all too evident.

The fact that the subculture is hostile to religion does not show that Casanova's view is wrong. After all, it may be that it is in struggling against these élites that Christianity will be brought back to the center of things. However, Berger's words should remind us that the struggle is going to be a good deal more difficult than some of the friends of modern culture in the Church seem to imagine.

I am convinced the presence of the Church, going about her own sacramental and liturgical business, is in itself a powerful suasion both for the argument that she deserves a space in which to operate and that she has a right to raise her voice about social issues. Within this perspective, liturgy is revealed in some of its importance. If liturgy is the source and summit of the Church's life, then it is also one of the most important ways in which the Church is strengthened to fulfill her role and to have an impact on secular society.

Appendix

The Use of Political and Legal Philosophers by the Supreme Court of Canada[1]

Name	Cases referring to philosopher	Cases actually quoting philosopher
Political philosopher		
1. John Stuart Mill	14	13
2. Aristotle	9	7
3. Plato	3	1
4. Alexis de Tocqueville	2	2
5. Jeremy Bentham	2	2
6. G. W. F. Hegel	2	0
7. Immanuel Kant	2	0
8. John Milton	2	1
9. Robert George	1	1
10. Alexander Hamilton	1	1
11. Thomas Jefferson	1	0

12.	John Rawls	I	I
13.	Joseph Rax	2	2
14.	Voltaire	I	I
	Legal theorist		
15.	William Blackstone	16	16
16.	Ronald Dworkin	8	5
17.	Oliver Wendell Holmes	4	4
18.	H. L. A. Hart	3	I

[1] The search was conducted of the Quicklaw database "Supreme Court Judgments" on all decisions involving Charter issues since 1985. This table does not purport to represent an exact compilation of all references, but only serves as an approximation.

CHAPTER THREE

Swimming against the Tide

> Much contemporary moral philosophy, particularly but
> not only in the English-speaking world ... has tended
> to focus on what it is right to do rather than on what it
> is good to be, on defining the content of obligation rather
> than the nature of the good life; and it has no concep-
> tual place left for a notion of the good as the object of
> our love or allegiance or, as Iris Murdoch portrayed it in
> her work, as the privileged focus of attention and will.
>
> —Charles Taylor, *Sources of the Self*

The modern world is a dangerous place for the Church,
and it seems that many Catholics would like to reject it
completely. At the same time they are willing enough to
live with what people usually mean by progress. For example, most people are grateful for and make use of the advances
in medicine when it comes to their own sickness, even when
they may be doubtful about the use to which some of these
advances are put. Most are content to have the benefits of
technology both for practical uses like electricity in the home
and for recreational uses like CDs. There are all sorts of
good things about modern life that most people never had
in earlier times; and there is something distasteful about people who are quite happy to use these gifts of modernity

while at the same time condemning the modern world without qualification.

It is obvious that discrimination is required, and it is also obvious that this is a hazardous business. In this book I have been largely concerned with making the point that a lot of baggage that is at best unnecessary, and at times actively harmful, has been taken on board by the Church. Now I want to emphasize that the ideal of learning about the world from those with no or little connection with the institutional Church is both good and necessary. It is good because truth is a value that does not depend on who teaches it or from whence it comes. Furthermore, it is useful to know about the world in which we are trying to promote the truth.

Newman said that St. Philip Neri "lived in an age as traitorous to the interests of Catholicism as any that preceded it, or can follow it".[1] Yet Philip thought the best way to meet this situation was,

> not with argument, not with science, not with protests and warnings, not by the recluse or the preacher, but by means of the great counter-fascination of purity and truth.... Phillip preferred, as he expressed it, tranquilly to cast in his net to gain [souls]; he preferred to yield to the stream, and direct the current, which he could not stop, of science, literature, art, and fashion, and to sweeten and to sanctify what God had made very good and man had spoilt.[2]

In this spirit I want first of all to consider the work of Iris Murdoch and, then, say something about Charles Taylor.

[1] John Henry Newman, *The Idea of a University* (New York: Image Books, 1959), p. 238.
[2] Ibid., p. 239.

Iris Murdoch saw through a good deal of what was wrong with modernity, and much of what she wrote points in the right direction and has much to teach us. Above all she tried to vindicate the idea of transcendence, that there was "something deep" in experience that was an ineradicable aspect of our experience no matter how much we tried to ignore it. Catholic liturgy needs badly to recapture this dimension of transcendence, and Iris Murdoch can help us to see why. She was a professional philosopher and also a distinguished novelist. Her novels give us a vision of the modern world as it is without the grace of God, and her philosophy shows how the novelist understood this modern world in the light of her interpretation of Plato's philosophy. Plato, for her, "is not only the father of our philosophy, he is our best philosopher".[3]

To call Iris Murdoch either a philosopher who wrote novels or a novelist who worked away at philosophy is to fail to do justice to her extraordinary and twofold achievement. We need another category for her, and perhaps that of prophecy may be called into service. Prophets are people who see things that are hidden from most people and then go on to express these insights in a way that makes sense to those who hear what the prophet says or who read what he writes. When hidden things are described in an intelligible way, then description often includes directives about how people are to behave. A prophet might, for instance, say that the real cause of existential *angst* is overeating and that discontent would disappear if people ate less junk food and visited their local gym more often. The prophet might go on to say that if his prescriptions are not followed, the

---

[3] Iris Murdoch, "Literature and Philosophy: A Conversation with Bryan Magee", *Existentialists and Mystics* (London: Chatto & Windus, 1997), p. 6.

population will only become more unhappy, and society will be in danger of collapse.[4]

Prophets swim against the tide. Just because they see things differently, their message will strike most people as odd and probably as unwelcome. Often enough the prophet himself will find what he sees and has to communicate to be a burden imposed on him by circumstances over which he has no control. Jeremiah in the Old Testament tried to evade God's command to prophesy by saying he was too young and did not know how to speak.[5] Even in the ordinary secular understanding of prophecy the nagging certainty that important things are being ignored or suppressed forces some people into witnessing to what they believe in, even though from many points of view they may want to keep silent and do nothing. This willingness to suffer for the truth, or at least for what is believed to be true, distinguishes the prophet from the man who thinks that criticizing the powers that be is in and by itself a sign of integrity and insightful thinking. Most criticism in politics, the Church, and the arts uses a conventional and predictable rhetoric that is anything but a sign of integrity and insightful thinking.

When I say that Iris Murdoch was a prophet, I mean first of all that she had a compelling vision of what the world was really like and then, secondly, that she had a unique skill in understanding and communicating this vision. She was both an accomplished and a courageous philosopher as well as an outstanding novelist. Her philosophical abilities and her literary talents nourished and helped to per-

---

[4] It should also be pointed out that prophecy, according to St. Thomas, is a gift connected with the imagination and has nothing to do with the moral quality of the prophet.

[5] "Then I said, 'Ah, Lord GOD! Behold, I do not know how to speak, for I am only a youth'" (Jer 1:6).

fect each other. This complex and mysterious process has been studied and ably discussed in much detail, and I have nothing to add about it here.[6] The bottom line for our purposes is that her work in philosophy and literature, taken together, has had, and I suspect will continue to have, an enormous impact on how we understand the world we live in.[7]

This impact will not necessarily be direct, in the sense that more and more people will read Iris Murdoch and that this will influence the way they think and behave. The concerns of professional philosophers can seem very far removed from the ordinary consciousness, and their influence on the way we look at our lives is usually indirect. In the long run what philosophers think helps to create what an eighteenth-century writer called the climate of opinion, that complex of ideas and sets of reactions to those ideas that are often so close to the people of a particular time and place that, when recognized at all, they are viewed as being the expression of common sense or what everybody knows to be true. This is not to say that ill-defined ideas and habitual reactions to those ideas are always comfortable or supportive. They are, though, an aspect of the social environment in which people live. This is true of the concerns expressed by Iris Murdoch the philosopher, but we have also to remember that her vision of what life was really like was also communicated through her novels, and these, too, have helped to form and sharpen our understanding of experience.

[6] See, for example, Murdoch, "Literature and Philosophy", p. 3.

[7] "The philosopher Charles Taylor ... wrote ... that 'summing up her contribution is impossible. Her achievement is much too rich, and we are much too close to it.' What is sure is that she is read in Japanese and Russian and French, and belongs to her worldwide readership as much as she does to the British, who notoriously underestimate their major artists" (Peter J. Conradi, *Iris Murdoch: A Life* [New York and London: W. W. Norton, 2001], p. 595.

208 THE NIGHT BATTLE

One strand in the contemporary climate of opinion is a sense of loss with regard to the ordinary certainties of life. The visible, tangible world of which we all have immediate experience is, so we are told, "really" a restless patter of electrons that bear little obvious relation to what we see and touch. History is no longer a record of past events because we now realize that the past is a construction out of preset experiences based on present needs and interests, not on any sort of objective referent. Novels and poetry, we are assured, are not primarily about telling a story or the recounting of emotions and aspirations; rather, they reveal structures about language and meaning of which the author or poet may be largely unaware. Religion has also been taught to deliver the same ambiguous and hidden message. Only the very naïve, we are assured, would imagine that statements in the Creed, for example, have anything to do with stating the way things are. What religious language shows us is a complicated structure of hidden meanings that are not open to ordinary believers. The hidden meanings are not, however, buried in total obscurity, because they are open to the inspection of experts who are trained to describe what lies behind the worship and religious language in general.

This sustained criticism of our ordinary certainties has created a climate of opinion in which unease and insecurity are the dominant notes. Iris Murdoch wrote that "metaphysical problems now reach the popular consciousness in the form of a sense of loss, or being returned to a confused and pluralistic world from which something 'deep' has been removed".[8]

What is this "something deep"? One answer is that the "something deep" that has been removed is the sense of a real-

[8] In Iris Murdoch, *Metaphysics as a Guide to Morals* (London: Penguin Books, 1993), p. 7.

ity that is more than ourselves and that does not depend on ourselves for its existence. We all really think, when we are away from our study, our conferences, and our books, that ordinary experience is about a reality we do not create but that has to be accepted. We try to understand this reality in many different ways. First of all, through ordinary direct experience; we perceive this otherness; we hear it, we see it, and we feel it. Then, we go on to try to understand this something beyond ourselves through science and religion, through history and art, and through literature and poetry. In other words, there is something that transcends, or goes beyond, human experience. It may be that what transcends human experience is unfriendly, indifferent, or even hostile to us, but whatever its character may be, it is not dependent upon us.

We can accept this apparently obvious claim about the "something deep" without throwing discredit on the real advances made in the twentieth century by the philosophy of language. Because we think there is a reality we have to get to know, this does not imply we are forced to accept a naming theory of language or to deny that language plays a constitutive role in understanding our experience. Our experience means something to us, and we can refine and discriminate this meaning by language. The real question is: Do we find meaning, or do we create it? Iris Murdoch was on the side of those who want to say we find and do not create the meaning, even if it is also true and important to maintain that we cannot do this without language.[9] This is to do no more than state a position, but it is important to see what is at stake. If transcendence, even in the minimal

---

[9] See, for example, Charles Taylor, "Language and Human Nature", *Human Agency and Language* (Cambridge: Cambridge University Press, 1985), pp. 215–47.

way I have sketched out, does not exist, then Christianity could never be anything more than a human construct. It might be important; it might be mysterious; it might be helpful; but it will not be true.

There is, then, something other than we are. Put in this simple way, there is no one who could disagree. There is an element in all experience that transcends or goes beyond ourselves. Sometimes this other is an object of perception, like trees or buildings or lakes, and even Berkeley did not deny that there was an objective perceptual order, although his account of what constituted this order is distinctly odd. Sometimes, though, the other of experience is not the object of perception, although we still have no difficulty in maintaining it has some sort of independent existence. For example, the law of gravity is in some sense a construct of human intelligence, but what it describes in no way depends on us. An airplane whose jet engines have stopped working is going to fall to the ground no matter how the passengers may feel about the matter, and it will do so whether or not the passengers are familiar with the scientific formulation of the law. Plato argued that moral, political, and aesthetic experiences are all characterized by an element that transcends or is beyond our awareness of an ethical constraint or our conviction that the laws of the state should promote justice and protect the innocent or our satisfaction in hearing a Mozart symphony well played. All these experiences involve what Iris Murdoch called "something deep".

They are something deep because they are not on the surface of the experience. The recognition that an airplane is hurtling toward the earth is something that can be reported on by a physicist as a good example of the operation of the law of gravity; a psychologist could discuss what it is like to be aware of an obligation; a sociologist could conduct an opinion poll on the public's attitudes toward a political question; and a physiologist could describe the effects of volumes of sound on the auditory organs of the audience listening to the Mozart symphony. On the other hand, the experience of falling to one's death in a plane about to crash is something more than a good example of the law of gravity; the awareness of the obligation not to put a loved one out of agonizing pain by euthanasia is not adequately described as the result of an overactive superego; nor are questions of how justice is to be realized in our society to be determined only by a poll of what most people imagine they think. Finally, an essay on the physiology of hearing is not the same thing as a discussion on the merits of a symphony or of the way it has been played.

It is possible to deny there are any deep meanings in this sense. You can hold that the so-called deep meanings are all subjective and therefore of little use in understanding the way things really are. You can say, that is, that the terror of the people in the plane, the anguish of the relative of the child dying of cancer, serious and unselfish political activity, and the educated discrimination of those evaluating the performance of the symphony—all this, you can say, is personal and subjective and therefore does not really count in a cool and scientific understanding of the world. But this is clearly wrong. Whatever reality is like, we are not going to find out what it is like by denying the obvious. The experience of terror in the face of violent death, the experience of anguish when faced with hard moral decisions, the experience of principled anger in the face of social evils, and the experience of delight and satisfaction in the encounter of a skilled and thoughtful performance of music are real. How exactly they are real and how they are to be understood are perfectly valid questions. What is not, however, acceptable is to deny they exist and so to say that, even if they exist, they do not matter.

The gateway to something deep is through the personal or the subjective. Personal or subjective here does not mean idiosyncratic or out of kilter; but it does convey the two-fold conviction that reality is more than appears on the surface and that we penetrate beneath the surface with our whole being, not merely with our heads.

If we ask why we try to go beyond the surface of experience, the answer is that by nature we are all looking for something we know not what. "We look before and after, / And pine for what is not; Our sincerest laughter / With some pain is fraught", said Tennyson,[10] and his words well describe that restlessness for something better, or something more complete, that affects us all. We are people who want things, and this is true even when we are confused about what we want and about how to get it. Nonetheless, the drawing of something beyond ourselves characterizes all our experience.

Plato called this something beyond ourselves *the good*. We must not imagine this good is only a moral good in the narrow sense of something that is the source of rules or laws. Plato meant by the good what would satisfy all our intellectual, spiritual, and physical needs in a unified experience. It is the search for this good that lies behind all our personal experience, and only the possession of this good will satisfy us completely. But this is only half the story; we look for the good because it exerts an attraction on us. The good is not an external object that we think we ought to go looking for; it is, on the contrary, a pervasive presence in our lives that draws us to itself. Like a magnet, it pulls us

[10] "In Memoriam".

away from the surface of our everyday experience toward a mysterious world; it is a world of which we are only dimly aware, but it is one in which we obscurely realize we will eventually be satisfied.

Iris Murdoch was passionately committed to this idea of transcendence, and her philosophical position centered on the idea of an objective good that was anchored in reality; or, to put it more strongly and more accurately, this objective good *was* reality. Because it was anchored in the way things really are, it did not depend on what either society or powerful individuals might have decided it should be or, indeed, on any sort of human activity. This objective good is something we all hanker after, although no one is explicitly aware of this at the beginning and most people never understand this basic truth about the human condition.

Some, however, are roused to seek the good in an explicit way. Plato thought that we recognize the good in our experience through coming into contact with what is beautiful. Beauty forces itself on us and awakens in us a desire to possess it, "to get it for ourselves". This desire for what we experience as beautiful, and what we do not actually possess, is an element in what we mean by love. We have, then, three terms: the good, the beautiful, and love. Plato's position is that we become aware of the good through our experience of the beautiful. Our experience of the beautiful is not that of a disinterested observer but of someone who wants it for himself, and so we desire the good (as beautiful). This desire for the good as beautiful is called falling in love. Beauty is something that in various ways we all desire; and so love becomes a central theme for Plato and for Iris Murdoch.

Toward the end of Plato's dialogue on love, *The Symposium*, there is a report of an account by a wise woman called

Diotima on the beginning of love and of its growth toward a vision of a beauty that is flawless and everlasting.[11] This Platonic ladder has been the subject of endless discussion. This discussion has been confused, perhaps distorted, because Plato's discussion of human love focuses exclusively on the love of men for others of their own sex. This has resulted in an overemphasis on the issue of homosexuality by way of either condemnation or enthusiastic approval. But both attitudes obscure the point of Plato's discussion, which is our desire for the good. We desire the good because we recognize it in our everyday experience through the experience of what is beautiful, and we recognize that we need that good of which our experience of beauty has made us aware. John Rist has put the matter quite simply in a way that avoids the homosexual character of Plato's discussion, a characteristic which, so far as the search for the good is concerned, is not essential.

> Perhaps it is easier to come to grips with Plato's proposals if we look not at the Form of the Good but at the Form which he seems to have recognized first—because it is the object of love—and which, because of its physical manifestations, he says (in the *Phaedrus*) is the most obvious: the Form of Beauty. Plato holds that, whereas all objects of physical beauty are comparatively beautiful (Helen is beautiful when compared with the girl next door, but not when compared with Aphrodite), there is nothing that could be more beautiful than the form of Beauty itself. It is not only incomparably beautiful, but it sets a standard against which all other beauties can be measured. Such a standard is not man-made, though all of us can, at least dimly, recognize it.[12]

---

[11] *Symposium* 209E–212C.
[12] John M. Rist, *Real Ethics* (Cambridge: Cambridge University Press, 2002), pp. 33–34.

But love has to be understood as a desire for something or someone particular. We begin to grasp the good through love, not love in general, but through a love of the personal, the immediate. We fall in love, that is, not with something general, but with a particular person, and we become more and more aware of the uniqueness of the person we love as our experience develops and matures. Plato thought that beauty hit us in our ordinary experience and that from that experience we could grow in knowledge of the good. The beginning of this process, though, the bottom rung of the ladder, is anchored into the ordinary world of experience; and it is in this ordinary world of experience that we first begin to learn to perceive and discriminate as accurately as the subject matter allows. Plato, that is, thought that what we can experience in time and space only gave us a low-grade sort of knowledge. He says it is only opinion when compared to the objects of mathematics, for example, which are universal and not mixed up with particularity and sense data.[13] The angles at the base of any isosceles triangle, to take an obvious example, are equal, because this is the real nature of this sort of triangle, and any diagram of this truth will only imperfectly exemplify, or portray, this real nature. However, without sense experience we would never be able to begin to think mathematically. We need to use experience in such a way that it becomes for us the road to a reality greater than itself.[14]

We cannot even find the beginning of the road or put our feet on the bottom rung of the ladder if we think there

[13] Plato discusses this in the *Republic*, bk. 6, "The Four Stages of Cognition: The Line" (509D–511E).

[14] In fact, Plato thought we needed a teacher to help us find the truth suggested by sense experience. See his *Meno*.

is a shortcut to the real world behind appearances, a shortcut that will allow us to ignore what experience can teach us. Ordinary experience, when carefully attended to, sharpens our capacity for making distinctions and, even more generally, for being open to and aware of a reality that is more than we are and different from what we are. The ability to see what is more than we are and different from what we are depends in practice in focusing on what is unique and particular in experience and in paying attention to the way things are. It is only by a patient, open sensitivity to the richness of everyday experience that we will become the sort of people who will transcend what is given to us in everyday life and begin to strive after and finally live in the presence of the good. The novels of Iris Murdoch are full of examples of this careful discrimination brilliantly described.[15]

The reality of the good is discovered through a love that focuses on learning to see and be drawn to what is unique in the object of our desire. If we think there is an objective good, then we have to give some account of how the existence of this good affects us. Plato's answer is clear: The good affects us as an object of desire. That is, we *want* the good in a way that is more than sexual desire but certainly not less. Everyone hankers after the good; it is the way we are, but this usually chaotic and undisciplined desire has to be trained and developed until it can be called love. Desire for the good may show itself as sexual desire, as the love of fame, or as the love of wisdom. Love is the key to finding and keeping the good and is therefore central to Plato and

[15] "She was a particularist in the sense that Gerard Manley Hopkins was a particularist in his poetry; and her attraction to oddities of character and distinctive persons and scenes was linked to her inspiration as a writer" (Stuart Hampshire, in *New York Review of Books*, November 15, 2001, p. 24).

Iris Murdoch's philosophy.[16] "Eros", she says, "is the desire for good and joy which is active at all levels in the soul and through which we are able to turn toward reality. This is the fundamental force which can release the prisoners and draw them toward the higher satisfactions of light and freedom." [17] Yet we do not desire the good directly; rather, we desire it because we find it given to us as something or somebody beautiful:

> The steps by which the lover must proceed, either alone or with guidance, are these: First, begin with the beauty you can see in someone's body and fall in love with that. Then, as if you were climbing the steps of a ladder, continue one rung up and there you will fall in love with physical beauty in general. Take another step up and you will reach the beauty of law and custom and from there it is just one more rung to reach the beauty of the different branches of knowledge. Then, finally, ascend to the very top of the ladder, to the recognition and study of that ultimate knowledge which is the knowledge of Beauty itself.[18]

Beauty awakens in us the love of something beyond itself, and this something we call the good. Murdoch's work is a unique and compelling restatement of a Platonism that shows up the shallow certainties of modernity to be both inadequate as well as dangerous. It is not surprising that her vision was regarded as cranky or wrongheaded. No one denied her skill as a novelist, but the philosophy that underlay her novels was looked on by the English-speaking philosophical

---

[16] "One of the few things which *Socrates*, according to Plato, claimed to know about (and thought enormously important) was 'love matters' (*Symposium* 177D)" (Rist, *Real Ethics*, p. 87).

[17] Murdoch, *Existentialists and Mystics*, p. 415.

[18] *Plato's Symposium* 211C; trans. Avi Sharon (Newburyport, Mass.: Focus Publishing, 1998), p. 62.

establishment as hardly more than competent[19] in the dominant themes of Anglo-American philosophy and wrong-headed in her efforts to reinvigorate a kind of Platonic realism.

Finally, though, in spite of her lucidity and courage, she got important things wrong.[20] First of all, she wanted a theology in which God had been replaced by the good. "We need a theology", she said at the end of her Gifford Lectures, "which can continue without God."[21] In this she was quite consciously trying to go back to Plato and so to reject any sort of Christian Platonism. Christian Platonism was clear that it was easier to love God than the "Idea of the Good"; and this is clearly the case even if *Idea* here was objective and self-maintaining.[22] She was fascinated by Christianity and could not leave it alone, but she did not think it was true.[23]

[19] "I do not think Murdoch ever fully understood analytical philosophy, or that she was ever able to teach it successfully at St. Anne's College, Oxford, where she was for a few years a tutorial fellow" (Hampshire, *New York Review of Books*, p. 24).

[20] See Fergus Kerr, O.P., in chap. 4, "Back to Plato with Iris Murdoch" of his *Immortal Longings* (London: SPCK, 1997), pp. 73–75, for analysis of the element of silliness in Iris Murdoch's work.

[21] Murdoch, *Metaphysics*, p. 561.

[22] "Augustine's God, as the God of his Christian Platonist predecessors, is person and therefore more readily understood as lovable. He represents the Platonic Form of the Good as the standard of goodness, but is less of an ontological curiosity" (Rist, *Real Ethics*, p. 42).

[23] This fascination with Christianity is treated unsympathetically by A. N. Wilson, *Iris Murdoch as I Knew Her* (London: Hutchinson, 2003). "There is a nobility in the 'tragic Christians' like Schweitzer who doubted the objective truth of Christianity, but still chose to deny himself, take up his cross and follow Christ by giving his whole life to running an African hospital. Merely talking about Jesus as another Buddha at dinner parties, and exalting 'The Good' to anyone prepared to listen, is not comparably impressive" (p. 203). Well, perhaps not; on the other hand, she did fight in the very hostile environment of Oxford philosophy in the fifties for some sort of objectivity in morals and for the importance of beauty. Wilson himself describes this period

Next, Eros, as she herself explicitly taught and is also clear from her novels, is a force that can go wrong. It can find expression in the "unbridled appetite of the tyrant",[24] and it also finds expression in "falling in love" with someone else, and love by itself in this sense is no reliable guide to seeking and finding the good.[25]

There is in her work a fundamental ambivalence that extends far beyond the sexual sphere. This can be seen even in her effort to vindicate Plato's affirmation of objective and transcendental value. On the face of it, this vindication is an integral part of her battle to establish morality as an authentic aspect of human experience that cannot be reduced to a scientific, or any other, world view. Yet, at the same time, her concern for human freedom leads her to view even objectivity itself as a curb on freedom, and this is one reason why she insists that the idea of final causality has no place in morality; or, to put it bluntly, that life has no purpose. If life has no purpose, then the watchwords of moral discourse become, as the existentialists quite rightly see, authenticity, integrity, and aspiration. In her efforts to free goodness itself from being dominated by anything external to it, she has effectively neutered its capacity to be a concrete and determinate guide to human actions.

Yet she did point us in the right direction; both her criticism of the contemporary scene and her efforts to vindicate the philosophy of Plato show this. Her discussions of

---

of her life as "Philosopher—A Girl among Chaps" (pt. 2, chap. 2). A much more detailed and authoritative account of this environment is to be found in Nicola Lacey, *A Life of H. L. A. Hart: The Nightmare and the Noble Dream* (Oxford: Oxford University Press, 2004).

[24] Murdoch, *Existentialists and Mystics*, p. 415.

[25] "Love in this form may be a somewhat ambiguous instructor. Plato has admitted that Eros is a bit of a sophist" (ibid., p. 417).

Plato's concern for objective and transcendental values, values that are the true object of desire, bear all the marks of a thinker haunted by the truth. She has much to teach us, even if what she teaches us has to be handled with care.

Charles Taylor, in *The Ethics of Authenticity*, has also subjected the modern scene to a searching analysis, particularly in its technological and bureaucratic elements as well as in its individualism. Taylor's sophisticated appraisal of modernity is based on a well-argued conviction that neither the "boosters" nor the "knockers" of modernity have it right. There are real dangers for humanity in the present situation, but that same situation gives us the chance to go beyond it without losing the positive elements. To use a word we have met with several times already, we have to transcend the present situation without wanting to destroy the real values enshrined in technology, bureaucratic structures, and individualism. The following passage helps to capture Taylor's approach:

> There is a tension between underlying ethical ideals and the ways these come to be reflected in people's lives, and this means that a systematic cultural pessimism is as misguided as a global cultural optimism. Rather, we face a continuing struggle to realize higher and fuller modes of authenticity against the resistance of the flatter and shallower forms.[26]

The struggle, then, to be neither a detractor nor an advocate is going to involve our taking the idea of self-realization seriously. Taylor is perfectly well aware that self-realization can become a code word for selfish and irresponsible behavior; but he wants to hold onto the phrase because he believes it is the best way of describing the ideal of the individual in today's

---

[26] Charles Taylor, *The Ethics of Authenticity* (Cambridge, Mass.: Harvard University Press, 2002), p. 94. (This was originally published in Canada in 1991 under the title *The Malaise of Modernity*.)

world. Subjectivity and freedom are real goods, and they encapsulate modernity. On the other hand, self-realization has to be understood as having a necessary relation to something outside the individual. Self-realization is the realization of the self, but there has to be something toward which the self is working, otherwise it is involved in a "self-immuring" that is stultifying. "To shut out demands emanating from beyond the self is precisely to suppress the conditions of significance, and hence to court trivialization." [27]

> Only if I exist in a world in which history, or the demands of nature, or the needs of my fellow human beings, or the duties of citizenship, or the call of God, or something else of this order *matters* crucially, can I define an identity for myself that is not trivial. Authenticity is not the enemy of demands that emanate from beyond the self; it supposes such demands. [28]

Taylor's analysis of modernity is subtle and accurate, and at first sight it provides a welcome assurance that there is room in the modern world for God and perhaps even the Church. However, the idea that there might just be room in the modern world for God, and perhaps even for the Church, as this idea has in fact been played out, is not a reassuring one. Religion, it would seem, has now become a value, and perhaps even an important one, which must be allowed to play its role under the courts' understanding of the rule of law. But, it appears, at least according to the judges, that this rule of law requires only that the courts find some sort of space in which religion can operate.

In an address entitled "Freedom of Religion and the Rule of Law", the Chief Justice of Canada actually uses Taylor's

[27] Ibid., p. 40.
[28] Ibid.

arguments in *Sources of the Self* to illustrate and support what the Supreme Court is doing in the area of social policy concerning religion; and what the Supreme Court is doing is "trying to create a space within the rule of law in which religious beliefs and practices can manifest [*sic*]".[29]

If Taylor has said that the "call of God" matters "crucially", then we have the required goal that will lift our search for self-realization out of selfishness and narcissism. However, what we have to undertake now is the ungrateful task of showing that escaping from selfishness is not the same activity as vindicating Christianity. I do not suppose for a moment that Taylor thinks otherwise, but it is worth pointing out that a world in which Christianity *could* flourish is not to say either what that Christianity would be or what form that flourishing would take.

Taylor's own view of Christianity is in harmony with his analysis of modernity. That is, the analysis is based on his understanding of the human situation and then, it seems to me, a reinterpretation of Catholicism that uses a Christian vocabulary to explain his own views. The following passage shows what I mean:

> Redemption happens through Incarnation, the weaving of God's life into human lives, but these human lives are different, plural, irreducible to each other. Redemption-Incarnation brings reconciliation, a kind of oneness. This is the oneness

---

[29] The Right Honourable Beverley McLachlin, P.C., Chief Justice of Canada, in *Recognizing Religion in a Secular Society*, ed. Douglas Farrow (Montreal and Kingston: McGill-Queen's University Press, 2004), p. 33. She writes further: "Casting all this back into Charles Taylor's theoretical framework, the Charter has articulated and laid bare, for discussion and application, both the goods of religious freedom and the hypergoods, the core values, it reflects" (p. 33). It is, presumably, the "hypergoods" that determine how much space is to be allowed to religious practice.

of diverse beings who come to see that they cannot attain wholeness alone, that their complementarity is essential, rather than of beings who come to accept that they are ultimately identical. Or perhaps we might put it: complementarity and identity will both be part of our ultimate oneness.[30]

What Taylor writes here is entirely compatible with his general philosophical position. What he calls "Redemption-Incarnation" fits in with and illustrates his view that we are not ourselves without other people (which I think is true), but his use of Christian words here has little to do with what the words mean in the Creeds or the tradition of the Church. I suspect that this observation would not trouble him, but we ought to be clear that he appears to have removed any hint that what he calls *Incarnation* has to do with the second Person of the Trinity taking our flesh through the agency of the Holy Spirit in the womb of the Virgin Mary. Taylor has shown Catholics that they do not have to be like rabbits immobilized by a cobra when they hear the words *modernity* or *secularization*. He has created a space, but his own brand of filling has to be handled with care.

There is a further strand in Taylor's position that goes a good deal farther than merely creating a space for Catholicism. He contends, in addition, that secular society has become the bearer of the values of the gospel. The Church may have carried the message of Christianity in the past, but a necessary condition for doing so in the future will be taking Christian values away from the care of the Church so that they will be able to flourish more effectively in secular society. I think a great many people do

[30] Charles Taylor, *A Catholic Modernity?* (New York and Oxford: Oxford University Press, 1999), p. 14.

believe something like this, and it is therefore worthwhile to see what Taylor is driving at.

We live in a world in which the language of human rights seems to be more important (even to Catholics) than do the affirmations of the Creed. Part of the reason for the success story of rights talk over Church talk is just this failure, as it is judged to be, of the visible ecclesiastical structure to understand, much less live up to, the treasures of the gospel.

> The view I'd like to defend, if I can put it in a nutshell, is that in modern, secularist culture there are mingled together both authentic developments of the gospel, of an incarnational mode of life, and also a closing off to God that negates the gospel. The notion is that modern culture, in breaking with the structure and beliefs of Christendom, also carried certain facets of Christian life further than they ever were taken or could have been taken within Christendom. In relation to the earlier forms of Christian culture, we have to face the humbling realization that the breakout was a necessary condition of the development.[31]

Taylor's position, as one might expect, given his eminence as a philosopher, is subtle and light years away from a good deal of anti-Church rhetoric. He believes that "modern liberal political culture" is characterized by the acknowledgment of universal human rights, such as "to life, freedom, citizenship, self-realization",[32] and furthermore, this realization is unconditional. What he seems to mean by this is that whatever the failures in practice of the liberal democracies to ensure that these rights are recognized, it remains true that in theory no one is excluded from enjoying them.

[31] Ibid., p. 16.
[32] Ibid.

On the other hand, when the Church, or Christendom, was a viable and powerful entity, this universal application of human rights, or the universal right to rights, was in fact impossible. For example, in a confessional state like Elizabethan England or seventeenth-century France there is obviously no room for religious freedom as we understand it. Consequently, the confessional state had to disappear if the right to religious freedom was to be realized. One way or another, Taylor seems to think this is true of all human rights: the seeds are in the gospel, but before they could come to fruition, they had to be rescued from the Church. A good deal of this analysis seems both accurate and humane, at least if we confine it to the triumph of the rhetoric of modern liberal political culture. But are the ideals of modern liberal political culture what Christianity is really about?

I think not. Taylor is involved in a complex operation that involves showing that much of what is admirable in modern society has its roots in the gospel; then he wants to show that these values required a free and open society if they were to come to fruition. On the other hand, he does not seem to think that modern society can quite handle this job by itself, because it looks on itself as self-sufficient and, in principle, capable of meeting all the needs of modern man. That is to say, the criticism that modern liberal political culture seems to leave no room for anything beyond itself is acknowledged by Taylor, and he argues for the necessity and viability of what he calls *transcendence*. He is not completely happy with the term, but he uses it to insist that "human flourishing" as the unique focus of our lives is a truncated, crippled view of our destiny as human beings. Taylor takes human flourishing to be the best way of talking about the humanism of modern culture devoted to the vindication of human rights, but he also thinks this language leaves out something vital about the human condition. If we are going to appreciate our situation properly, then we should recognize our need to transcend the boundaries of everyday existence, where we either flourish or do not flourish as human beings.

> Take any conception of human flourishing that makes no reference to something of intrinsic value beyond human flourishing, and we have something that is dangerously partial and incomplete, particularly because it cannot see that even things that negate this flourishing—solitary death, unremarked suffering, waning powers—can have the deepest human significance, just because they have more than human significance.[33]

Taylor's analysis helps us to understand the way Christian values have enriched modern culture, and at the same time it warns us that, in forgetting transcendence, this culture is defective and potentially hostile to the very values it professes and defends. But, while, to use his expression, we do not have to be "like rabbits and remain mesmerized by a cobra", I would think a very skillful mongoose will be required if Catholics are not going to be fatally poisoned.[34] The Church is more than a preacher of a message; she is also the sacramental means of providing that "deepest human significance" of which Taylor writes so movingly. Taylor's own position owes a good deal to Hegel's view, summarized in Taylor's own words, that "religion cannot see its vocation as in opposition to the truly rational state."[35]

---

[33] Ibid., p. 109.

[34] Taylor's unwillingness to discuss his Catholicism is disconcerting. See Kerr, *Immortal Longings*, p. 155.

[35] Charles Taylor, *Hegel* (Cambridge: Cambridge University Press, 1975), p. 485

The essence of what religion enjoins is given authoritative embodiment in the *Sittlichkeit* of the state. Without the concrete expression of ethical life in the state, the moral precepts of religion remain uncertain in their exact expression, undetermined, and subjective in their application.[36]

This may be what Hegel thought, but it strikes me that to advise Catholics to accept it would be a counsel of desperation. Given what the modern state actually thinks about Catholic principles, it would be foolhardy to think that Christian values would be preserved and developed by present-day political institutions. Taylor probably thinks that the Church is not doing a very good job of this preserving and developing, but that is another question. It is another question because if we believe in the Church, we accept the fact that she is the Mystical Body of Christ and that, in an ultimate if often imperfect way, she teaches in his name and carries on his redeeming work through the sacraments and in the liturgy. It would not be cooperation but capitulation to hand over the gospel to the state.[37]

---

[36] Ibid.

[37] Fergus Kerr, in *Immortal Longings*, shows how Taylor is very clearly his own man and does not fit into any one recognizable school: "He accepts the case against the modern liberal-existentialist self but, although he has been familiar all along with contemporary French thought, in a way that few Anglo-American philosophers are, he refuses to celebrate the decentred subject, in the wake of Lacan, Foucault, Derrida, et al. On the other hand, for all his proximity to communitarianism, he clearly does not want to get back to that in any of its hierarchical or organistic versions" (p. 136). It is evident that Taylor is not enamored of the institutional Church, and it is not clear what role she is supposed to play other than handing over her gospel values to civil society—or perhaps the state—in as tidy and peaceful a way as possible.

PART THREE

THE LAMB'S HIGH FEAST

At the Lamb's high feast we sing
Praise to our victorious King,
Who has washed us in the tide
Flowing from his pierced side;
Praise we him, whose love divine
Gives his sacred blood for wine,
Gives his body for the feast,
Christ the victim, Christ the priest.

—Ambrosian hymn, seventh century

The Church at her deepest, truest level is the living presence of Christ working among us, and in us, through his sacraments. Christ came to share in our humanity so that every one of us could become partakers of his divinity. We are presented with this truth every time we go to Mass and the priest says at the offertory: "By the mystery of this water and wine may we come to share in the divinity of Christ, who humbled himself to share in our humanity." [1] We may not always sense his presence; there will be times of obscurity and darkness; but in a faithful and serious sacramental life, we know that God is gradually remaking us into the image of his beloved Son. And, just as the Father was well pleased with the Son, so he will be well pleased with us—if we remain in the Son.

[1] In 2 Peter 1:3–4 we are told that we have been granted all things "that pertain to life and godliness" so that we may "become partakers of the divine nature". In the *Summa Theologiae* 2, 2, St. Thomas teaches that through God's gift of the theological virtues we are taken into the life of God himself.

In harmony with this understanding of the Church and sacraments, we have already noted[2] that Vatican II taught that the liturgy is the summit of all the Church's activities and the source from which all her power flows and that, in the liturgy, "the work of our redemption is accomplished."[3] The *Catechism of the Catholic Church* takes up this theme and quotes Vatican II's Constitution on the Sacred Liturgy, saying that the liturgy gives to the faithful the power to bring home to themselves and to others "the mystery of Christ and the real nature of the true Church".[4] Liturgy matters, then, because it is vital to the Catholic understanding of what it means to lead a Christian life.[5] Liturgy is related to Christian truth, and Christian truth is required for what Plato called "living well".[6] One of the themes of *The Mass and Modernity* is that to live a good life requires a difficult and ongoing effort to "seek the things that are above" (Col 3:1) and that the worship of the Church is supposed to do just that: to remind us of the things that are above and to help us seek them. But, furthermore, the liturgy is not going to do this unless what actually goes on in church is based on Christian truth and can be seen to be based on Christian truth.

[2] See introduction.

[3] *Sacrosanctum Concilium* 10 (A 142).

[4] "For it is in the liturgy, especially in the divine sacrifice of the Eucharist, that 'the work of our redemption is accomplished,' and it is through the liturgy especially that the faithful are enabled to express in their lives and manifest to others the mystery of Christ and the real nature of the true Church" (CCC 1068, quoting *Sacrosanctum Concilium* 2).

[5] This is an argument from authority, and St. Thomas teaches that in theology such arguments are of the greatest importance. See *Summa Theologiae* I, 1, 8 ad 2. Although such arguments are not very highly regarded today, the teaching of the Council and of the *Catechism* should at least provide a clue as to why liturgy is important.

[6] *Apology* 21 A.

There is an old saying, dating from the *Indiculus*, attributed to Prosper of Aquitaine, written about 435–442,[7] to
the effect that what is believed can be seen from the prayer
of the Church. *Lex orandi, lex credendi*; that is, literally, the
law of prayer is the law of faith. Sometimes this principle
was used to argue that we could base the faith itself on the
liturgy of the Church. This is not, however, what the Council of Ephesus said; in Karl Rahner's words, it taught that
the liturgy is "a witness to the infallible belief of the praying Church".[8] The faith does not come from the liturgy,
but the liturgy is supposed to teach the faith and help the
worshipper to go beyond himself to the source of all truth
and goodness. "Let us be mindful ... of the sacraments of
priestly public prayer, which handed down by the apostles
are uniformly celebrated in the whole world and in every
Catholic church, *in order that the law of supplication may support the law of believing.*"[9]

Rahner, in a hopeful entry in his *Theological Dictionary*,
says that with the document on the liturgy of Vatican II
one of the major tasks of "our generation" must be the
recovery "from within of the sense of the Church as a worshipping community".[10] Well, there may have been a recovery of the idea of the Church as a community, but the
argument of my book is that the worship of the community that has been recovered is no longer manifestly the

[7] Denzinger (1953 ed.), 139.

[8] Karl Rahner, *Theological Dictionary* (New York: Herder and Herder, 1965),
entry "Lex Orandi".

[9] Denzinger (1953 ed.), 139 (my italics). The Latin runs: "ut legem credendi lex statuit supplicandi". *Statuere* means to support but can also have an
even stronger sense, something like "in order that the law of supplication
may *firm up*, or *buttress* up, or *cause to stand*".

[10] Entry "Liturgy".

worship of the transcendent God who took our flesh to redeem us.

Liturgy matters, then, because one of its main purposes is to point the worshipper toward the truth; to remind him that he must go beyond himself and his community to the God who is, who was, and who is to come. The liturgy should teach and help the worshipper to experience in a deep way that is more than verbal that his need for goodness, for truth, for beauty, and for love are grounded in the reality of God.

But the seeds of a genuine renewal "fell upon thorns, and the thorns grew up and choked them" (Mt 13:7). The modern world has been increasingly dominated by the theory and the practice of secularism. And then, too, the flavor of postmodernism is everywhere. Postmodernism may not be the inevitable result of the Enlightenment and of the other movements we have outlined, but it was certainly not a surprising one. The use of reason and the imagination to discover and describe a reality that is more than a social construction of something or other is now looked on as an impossible project; worse than that, it is viewed as unsophisticated. The hard, painstaking work of scholars to describe the real as it is and of artists to evoke hints of a sublime and a mysterious other, an other that is more than a product of the artist's own psyche, is judged to be a relic of a modernist mentality that is still mistakenly looking for a *grand-discours* or metanarrative. But, so they say, there are no metanarratives that tell us the truth about reality, and this is so because there is no reality.

There are different strands that have contributed to this condition. Many of these strands that we have dealt with, such as the Enlightenment with its concern for justice, human rights, and due process, or again, the "rise of modern science", with its applications in health and technology, or the Romantic Movement, with its historical, communitarian, and imaginative concerns, have persuasive and desirable elements, and I have been at pains to underline this side of the matter. Nonetheless, the overall thrust that carries them is hostile to the Christian revelation. The efforts of various sorts of Christians to accommodate the gospel in order to make it acceptable to the world has proved to be, not surprisingly, destructive of the Christian message.

But what are we going to learn from the present liturgical wilderness and from the forces that have created it? Modernity has left little room for a Catholicism that revolves around the transcendence of God the Father, of the particularity of the revelation of God the Son, and the community as, in itself, a sort of eighth sacrament of the abiding presence of God the Holy Spirit working among us. As a result of these attitudes, the liturgy has been badly damaged, but that is not to say it has been destroyed. The Church has taken a wrong turning in her efforts to reach the world we live in, but the effort itself is in line with the Church's mission to bring the mercy of Christ to a fallen, poor, and broken world. The various influences that have helped to distort the liturgy also have within them the themes for a genuine renewal of the sacramental life.

Such a renewal of sacramental life, however, will have to be based on a clearer recognition of the context and implications possessed by the ideas that have so powerfully affected the Church and her liturgy. This recognition cannot result from turning our backs on the forces that have created our world, but it will mean using them with more discrimination and drawing different lessons about what they have to teach us from those that have in fact been drawn in the recent past. The lessons to be learned are very old ones and consist in maintaining that liturgy is the worship of a transcendent God, that worship is through, with, and in the unique, particular life of Jesus Christ, and that it is the Holy Spirit who sweetly and powerfully brings about and fulfills our yearning to be united with each other in the "bond of peace" (Eph 4:3).

In the first chapter of this part, I discuss the meaning of the *Paschal Mystery*, that is, the mystery of Christ's Passion and death, his Resurrection and Ascension. The mystery really is of central importance and in practice has been much invoked by thinkers in today's Church. Unhappily, the expression has come to be used in such an extended way that all too often one or other of its aspects is emphasized to the detriment of the mystery itself; the most egregious example of this is to identify the mystery with the Resurrection in a way that obscures its essential relationship to the Passion and death as well as to the Ascension of our Lord.

In the second chapter I maintain that a renewed awareness of the transcendence of God will go a long way toward reestablishing that awe, beauty, and reverence which should characterize Catholic worship. At the same time, I also show that a heightened awareness of the otherness of God will come about only with a deeper grasp of the particular, historical character of Christ's life and teaching.

In the third chapter I point out that there must be an altogether more serious and lucid penetration of the supernatural aspect of the Christian *community*. There is no word that has been more abused in the years since Vatican II, yet there are few words more important for an understanding of the liturgy. Awe and reverence have to manifest themselves; they have to be put into act; and this is done through the liturgy of the Church, the Church that is, in St. Paul's teaching, the *Body of Christ*.

In the fourth chapter, I discuss the importance of the Old Rite of Mass for a renewed liturgy. The Tridentine Mass, or whatever it should be called, at least pointed toward God even when it was badly celebrated. This is not to say that the solution to our troubles is a wholesale return to this way of celebrating, but we must at least try to see what it possessed and what the *Novus Ordo* (the new rite of the Mass approved by Pope Paul VI) in practice puts in its place. What the Old Rite possessed was a clear lesson in the transcendence of God; while the way the *Novus Ordo* is often celebrated puts the community in the place of this reference to God.

In the fifth chapter I put forward some practical suggestions that, I think, would go a long way toward reestablishing the liturgy as the worship of God, a worship that is offered by the Mystical Body of Christ through the work of the Holy Spirit. These suggestions are probably little more than a "wish list", but they are seriously meant. On the other hand, while I think the liturgy should support or firm up the teaching of the Church,[11] it cannot by itself repair the present situation. Nevertheless, a restored liturgy would be a powerful force in a genuine renewal of the Church.

[11] See introduction.

CHAPTER ONE

THE PASCHAL MYSTERY

He had told His friends to do this henceforward with
the new meaning "*for the anamnesis*" of Him, and they
have done it always since.

Was ever another command so obeyed? For century
after century, spreading slowly to every continent and
among every race on earth, this action has been done,
in every conceivable human circumstance, for every conceivable human need from infancy to extreme old age
and after it, from the pinnacles of earthly greatness to
the refuge of fugitives in the caves and dens of the earth.

—Dom Gregory Dix, *The Shape of the Liturgy*

The phrase "the Paschal Mystery" has been used so often
in recent years that it has ceased to have a precise meaning.
Because of the relative novelty of this term in Catholic theology, it is associated in many minds with reckless change
and the destruction of hallowed customs and practices. For
example, when a devout Catholic is refused Communion
because he is kneeling down and told to stand up because
"the Paschal Mystery has taught us that we are an Easter
people", the would-be communicant remembers at least that
this humiliating experience is somehow bound up with the
term he from now on regards with suspicion and contempt.
Then again, the Society of Saint Pius X has charged that:

The theology of the *"paschal mystery"*, to which the door was left open at the occasion of Vatican II, is the soul of the liturgical reform. Because it minimizes the mystery of the Redemption, because it considers the sacrament only in its relation with the *"mystery"*, and because the conception that it makes of the *"memorial"* alters the sacrificial dimension of the Mass, this *"theology of the paschal mystery"* renders the post-Conciliar Liturgy dangerously distant from Catholic doctrine.[1]

It is not difficult to find examples of what is being objected to: the trouble with the position of the Society is not in its description of the present situation but in its diagnosis of the causes. To see what the Society is reacting against we need only return to a book already mentioned, *Signs of Freedom*, by German Martinez.[2] His understanding of the Paschal Mystery, he says, stems from "a theological approach based on a paschal vision of the communities that experience the risen Lord's continued presence". He contrasts such an approach with what he calls "a pre-Easter historical interpretation".[3] The "pre-Easter historical interpretation", which he finds inadequate, is, quite simply put in the words of the *Catechism*, that "[Jesus Christ] instituted the Eucharist as the memorial of his death and Resurrection, and commanded his apostles to celebrate it until his return".[4] But

---

[1] *Address to the Holy Father*, by the Superior General of the Society of Saint Pius X, Bishop Bernard Fellay, in *The Problem of the Liturgical Reform—A Theological and Liturgical Study* (Kansas City: Angelus Press, 2001), p. i. Cardinal Ratzinger deals with this criticism in "The Theology of the Liturgy", in *Looking Again at the Question of the Liturgy with Cardinal Ratzinger*, ed. Alcuin Reid, O.S.B. (Farnborough: Saint Michael's Abbey Press, 2003), pp. 18–31. Much of what I say in this chapter is based on the Cardinal's arguments.

[2] German Martinez, *Signs of Freedom: Theology of the Christian Sacraments* (Mahwah, N.J.: Paulist Press, 2003); see above, pt. 1, chap. 5, "Hegel: God Becomes the Community".

[3] Martinez, *Signs of Freedom*, p. 139.

[4] CCC 1337.

how does Martinez understand the Paschal Mystery? We can note three key points:

1. The celebration of the Eucharist is based on "the post-resurrection faith experience of the early community".[5]

2. "Current biblical scholarship and eucharistic theology disclaim the strictly historical and literal interpretation of the Last Supper as the foundational event of the Eucharist."[6]

3. His discussion of the Paschal Mystery is from the perspective of the idea of "transformation", which includes the notions of "freedom" and "liberation". "As signs of the freedom of Christ who confronted the reality of evil, sacraments are both the present celebration of that freedom by God's grace in the power of the Spirit and the individual's commitment to the same freedom."[7]

The success of the Enlightenment project is here seen to be complete. What Kierkegaard called the "scandal of particularity", or what Hegel termed the "positivity of the Christian religion", has been effectively set aside; the control that history should have over the development of doctrine is ignored; and the self-building of man in the community is triumphant:

> The Church, born from the Paschal Christ and his Spirit, is then the basic and universal sacrament. As such it is capable of generating the paschal gift as its basis. The Eucharist unceasingly initiates and builds the community as the definitive Church and yet at the same time is also "becoming" the body of Christ.[8]

---

[5] Martinez, *Signs of Freedom*, p. 138.
[6] Ibid., p. 139.
[7] Ibid., p. 305.
[8] Ibid., p. 183.

This might all be true, but it is not. It is merely a very able presentation of the results of the Enlightenment project[9] through Latitudinarianism,[10] Moral Religion,[11] and the triumph of the community, and all this presented within the context of liberation. I am not going to try to argue against the position except to say that it is not the perspective of the *Catechism of the Catholic Church*, and I have already made it clear that this is the standard I am using in writing this book. The point of introducing the troubled layman, the Society of Saint Pius X, and a modern theologian is to remind the reader that I am dealing with real convictions about liturgical life and the Paschal Mystery.

This present situation is deeply troubling, but the spokesmen for the Society of Saint Pius X, in questioning the Paschal Mystery, have put themselves in a false position. This is so because the Paschal Mystery really is central to Christian thought and experience, and the Council in highlighting the centrality of Christ's death and Resurrection was teaching a profoundly traditional doctrine. What the mystery should mean for a practicing Catholic is expressed in a late medieval text designed for the laity:

> After this consecration ... saith the priest in the eighth part of the canon an orison which beginneth thus: *Unde et memores etc.* In the which orison the priest incited us to have mind of the passion of our Lord Jesus Christ, of his resurrection and of his glorious ascension, to the end that by his passion we be incited to charity, by his holy resurrection we be

---

[9] See above, pt. 1, chap. 1.
[10] See above, pt. 1, chap. 2.
[11] See above, pt. 1, chap. 3.

incited to faith, and by his glorious ascension to hope of our health.[12]

This does not exhaust the theological significance of the mystery, but in highlighting the response of the believer at Mass it does help us to see that the notion of the Paschal Mystery is central to Catholic experience.

On the other hand, it is worth noting that the expression is not used with any great frequency in the Council documents themselves, and the phrase is not to be found in the index of the two standard English translations published shortly after the Council.[13] The case is very different with the Latin version of the documents published later, where the index provides abundant references under *paschale mysterium*.[14] The reason for this apparent discrepancy is the increasing postconciliar tendency to use the phrase *Paschal Mystery* as a general heading to cover any discussion of the sacraments; and this practice is especially true when dealing with the Eucharist. There is no conceptual difficulty with this way of using the phrase, but the practical result has been ambiguity of meaning in practice.

Fr. Louis Bouyer, the French Oratorian, whose work before the Council did a great deal to deepen the understanding of the Paschal Mystery in relation to the sacraments of the Church, set out clearly what he meant by the term in his *Dictionary of Theology*:[15] "For Christians the

[12] Anonymous, "The Noble History of the Exposition of the Mass" (ca. 1470), cited in Francis Clark, S.J., *Eucharistic Sacrifice and the Reformation* (London: Darton, Longman and Todd, 1960), p. 553.

[13] Edited by Walter M. Abbott (1966) and Austin Flannery (1975).

[14] *Conciliorum Oecumenicorum Decreta*, 3rd ed. (1973); the liturgical year, the Eucharist, fasting, justification, the sacrament of penance are all listed under the heading *Paschale Mysterium*.

[15] Louis Bouyer, *Dictionary of Theology*, trans. Rev. Charles Underhill Quinn (New York: Desclée, 1965).

paschal celebration becomes the celebration of the death and resurrection of the Saviour; while the Jewish Passover and everything that it had signified for the Jews in the first covenant is the major source for the Christian interpretation of the passion." [16]

Fr. Bouyer then points to another dimension of the mystery that was often overlooked, and this concerns Christ's return to the glory of the Father at the Ascension. In the perspective of the Paschal Mystery, the Ascension is not merely the definitive ending of Christ's earthly life; it is also the return of the eternal Son to the Father, bringing with him all those he redeemed through his Passion and Cross. Through his Cross and Resurrection, Christ carries us with him away "from the dominion of darkness ... to [his] kingdom" (Col 1:13), "which is a sharing in 'the inheritance of the saints in light'". [17]

> Thus the *mystery* of Christ, as explained by St Paul and as celebrated in the liturgy of the ancient Church, is the paschal mystery, i.e., the one that was accomplished on Passover, which the Christian Passover commemorates, and which constitutes the definitive Passover of the new and eternal covenant. The *Parousia* of Christ, finally, is described in turn as the definitive accomplishment of this Passover in eternity (cf. Luke 22:16 and Matt. 26:29). [18]

The ambiguities in the usage of the term stem from the fact that, while it is true that there is one mystery, it is also possible so to stress only one or two of its aspects that the meaning of the whole is seriously deformed. This can happen in any number of different ways. For example, the com-

[16] Ibid., p. 335.
[17] Ibid.
[18] Ibid.

mon practice of describing the mystery as the Passion and
Resurrection, as even the *Catechism* tends to do,[19] can easily obscure the eschatological aspect of the mystery, that is,
that Christ, having passed into glory, will come again. Or
again, sometimes the mystery is presented in such a way
that it signifies only the Resurrection, leaving aside not only
the Ascension but the suffering and death of Christ as well.
No one can talk about everything all the time, but the complexity and richness of the mystery ought to be a warning
that it is not a simple concept to be bandied about as seems
opportune to those for whom change has become the hall-
mark of serious liturgical concern.

We should then examine the three moments of the mystery to understand something about its theological significance from the standpoint of its liturgical representation.
The three moments of the liturgical celebration are summed
up in the familiar refrain: *Christ has died; Christ is risen; Christ
will come again.*

1. *Christ Has Died*

Fr. Bouyer wrote that all Christian worship is but "a continuous celebration of Easter"; and this celebration "pre-
serves us ever in the sentiments of the early Christians, who
exclaimed, looking to the past, 'The Lord is risen indeed',
and, turning towards the future, 'Come, Lord Jesus! Come!
Make no delay'."[20] Everyone seems to be familiar with this
understanding of the mystery, at least at the verbal level,

[19] E.g., "The Paschal mystery of Christ's cross and Resurrection stands at
the center of the Good News" (CCC 571).

[20] Louis Bouyer, *The Paschal Mystery*, trans. Sister Mary Benoit, R.S.M.
(Chicago: Henry Regnery, 1950), p. xv.

but then they conclude that the celebration of Easter, which is the *Paschal Mystery*, consists of only two moments, or aspects: there is the Resurrection and then the coming of our Lord in glory. This cannot be right, because before the Resurrection there was the Passion and death of Christ that took away the sins of the world.

Of course, Fr. Bouyer does not think the Paschal Mystery is only the Resurrection and anticipation of the future coming of Christ; in fact, a good deal of his important book deals with the sacrifice of Christ and its relation to the Eucharist.[21] Fr. Bouyer wrote his book in the 1940s, when no one would have thought of discounting the Passion and death of Christ as central to Christianity and to the celebration of Mass. He thus took for granted what he left out because he was trying to deepen and enlarge the vision of Catholic theologians and liturgists. Unhappily, after the Council, what Fr. Bouyer had taken for granted was quietly dropped; and a good deal of popular Christianity now seems to have left the idea of Christ's suffering, and of his expiation of our sins on the Cross, to one side and concentrated on a preaching of the Paschal Mystery that is incomplete and consists only of Resurrection and anticipation. But such a liturgy without an intimate connection with the Passion and death of Christ is a crippled one and untrue to both the teaching of Vatican II and the tradition of the Church.

Anyone writing today about the Pascal Mystery in a way that includes the Passion and death of Christ is fighting on

---

[21] "The Christian religion is not simply a doctrine: it is a fact, an action, and an action, not of the past, but of the present, where the past is recovered and the future draws near. Thus it embodies a mystery of faith, for it declares to us that each day makes our own the action that Another accomplished long ago, the fruits of which we shall see only later on in ourselves" (ibid., p. xiii).

two fronts.[22] On the one front, he has to explain why the Church teaches that the Eucharist is a sacrifice and to do this in intelligible language. In the course of this explanation, he will have to argue against the Protestant view that the Lord's Supper is *only* a calling to mind of our redemption by Christ; and then he will also have to show, against many modern Catholics, that the idea of sacrifice is an integral aspect of the Christian faith. On the other front, he will also have to argue against some traditionalist Catholics who hold a *post-Reformation* theory of sacrifice that is largely discredited in the Church today.[23]

There is, however, something else that must be made clear. The Paschal Mystery includes the sacrifice of Christ, yet it also possesses the dimensions of the Resurrection and Ascension. The bearing of these different elements on one another is the province of the professional theologian, but at a minimum we can say that any discussion that does not include all three moments of the Paschal Mystery, that is, Christ's Passion and death, his Resurrection, and his Ascension, will be so imperfect as to be misleading.[24] The medieval writer I have cited above got it right: in calling to mind Christ's death, we are reminded of his sacrifice and so are moved to a more profound charity; in recalling his Resurrection, we are called to

[22] Cardinal Ratzinger gives an admirable example of this in his "Theology of the Liturgy", in *Looking Again at the Question of the Liturgy*, pp. 18–32.

[23] These post-Tridentine "destruction theories" of the Eucharist are discussed in an eminently fair-minded way by Clark, *Eucharistic Sacrifice*, chap. 20. The author shows that De Lugo and Bellarmine faithfully adhered to the teachings of the Council of Trent that Christ's sacrifice is *not* repeated in a bloody manner.

[24] F. X. Durrwell, *The Resurrection*, trans. Rosemary Sheed (London: Sheed and Ward, 1964), discusses these questions in a way faithful to the Council of Trent and to Scripture; see especially chap. 2, no. 3, "The Death and Resurrection in the Framework of Sacrifice", pp. 59–74.

a deeper faith; and in treasuring the memory of the Ascension, we are led to a more vivid exercise of the virtue of hope.

There are three matters we have to discuss concerning Christ's death in relation to the Paschal Mystery. In the first place, Christ redeemed us by his Passion and death and was a sacrifice for our sins: "For Christ our Paschal Lamb, has been sacrificed" (1 Cor 5:7), "Christ ... offered for all time a single sacrifice for sins" (Heb 10:12). Secondly, the Church teaches that this sacrifice is perpetuated in the Eucharist: "At the Last Supper, on the night He was betrayed, our Savior instituted the Eucharistic Sacrifice of His Body and Blood. He did this in order to perpetuate the sacrifice of the Cross throughout the centuries." [25] Thirdly, this sacrificial aspect of the Mass has to be understood in relation to the teaching of St. Augustine that Fr. Bouyer sums up as "true sacrifice is every work done to establish us in a holy fellowship with God." [26]

a. *Christ Redeemed Us through His Suffering and Death*. St. Thomas Aquinas says that Christ endured every human suffering; not in the sense that he endured all suffering specifically; that would be impossible, as Thomas says with his usual massive common sense: the same man cannot suffer the pain of both being burned to death and being drowned. But, he says, speaking generically, Christ did experience every human suffering,[27] and this suffering can be considered from several different standpoints. First of all, there is the physical suffering:

> In His head He suffered from the crown of piercing thorns;
> in His hands and feet, from the fastening of the nails; on

---

[25] *Sacrosanctum Concilium* 47 (A 154); cf. CCC 1323.

[26] Bouyer, *Paschal Mystery*, p. 331.

[27] *Summa Theologiae* 3, 46, 5.

His face from the blows and spittle; and from the lashes over His entire body. Moreover He suffered in all His bodily senses: in touch, by being scourged and nailed; in taste, by being given vinegar and gall to drink; in smell, by being fastened to the gibbet in a place reeking with the stench of corpses, *which is called Calvary;* in hearing, by being tormented with the cries of blasphemers and scorners; in sight, by beholding the tears of His Mother and of the disciple whom He loved.[28]

In addition to all this, we should recall the moral and spiritual factors of the Passion and death of Christ. There was desolation in the garden; our Lord was betrayed by one of those closest to him; and Judas sold him, apparently, because Jesus refused to play the political role for which Judas and the Zealots hoped. The three apostles went to sleep when he needed them most; the leaders of his nation and of his church mocked him, mistreated him, and forced the Roman governor to condemn him to death. Finally, there were the crowds that followed his progress into Jerusalem with shouts of "Hosanna to the Son of David" and then turned on him—as is the way with crowds—and five days later screamed for his death.

But, when all is said and done, why do we commemorate this particular death? Why is this one, isolated tragedy so important that we are still remembering it two thousand years after it happened? History and the world today are full of the most hideous cruelty and appalling wrongdoing. Why are we not remembering all these victims of mankind's infinite capacity for cruelty? "Homo homini lupus", said St. Augustine, man is a wolf to his fellowman, and nothing in the distant past or in the twentieth century or today in

[28] Ibid. (STD).

the twenty-first has shown him to be wrong. The reason, bluntly put, that we recall this one particular death is that on the first Good Friday they crucified Jesus Christ, who was God made into our flesh. It is because the man on the Cross was also the Son of God that we recall his cruel scourging and unjust condemnation. It is because Jesus Christ was from all eternity with the Father that we remember his betrayal by his friends and retrace his painful way to Golgotha. It is because he took flesh, for our sake, of the Virgin Mary and then, as he was dying, gave her to St. John to be the Mother of the Church that we commemorate his agony and bitter death. It is because from the dead body, pierced with a lance, flowed the waters of baptism and the blood of the Eucharist that we remember his being taken down from the Cross and all the sad human business of preparing the dead for burial.[29]

The way to our reconciliation with God, with each other, and within ourselves is through this mysterious life-giving death of Christ. *Why* this should be so, we do not know; but we know it to be so. There is no natural or metaphysical necessity that Christ should have redeemed us by suffering; but hidden in the mysterious design of God's will it was so.[30] Christ suffered, Christ died, and since then suf-

---

[29] "There was a virtue in His death, which there could be in no other, for He was God. *We*, indeed, could not have told beforehand what would follow from so high an event as God becoming incarnate and dying on the Cross; but that something extraordinary and high would issue from it, we might have been quite sure, though nothing had been told us. He would not have humbled himself for nought; He could not so humble Himself (if I may use the expression) without momentous consequences" (J. H. Newman, "The Incarnate Son, a Sufferer and Sacrifice", *Parochial and Plain Sermons* [San Francisco: Ignatius Press, 1997], p. 1231).

[30] "It was not necessary ... for Christ to suffer from necessity of compulsion, either on God's part, who ruled that Christ should suffer, or on Christ's own part, who suffered voluntarily" (STD 3, 46, 1).

fering has been part of our way back to the Father when it is identified with the pain of Christ.

> We believe ... that when Christ suffered on the cross, our nature suffered in Him. Human nature, fallen and corrupt, was under the wrath of God, and it was impossible that it should be restored to His favour till it had expiated its sin by suffering. Why this was necessary, we know not; but we are told expressly, that we are "all by nature children of wrath", ... [and] the Son of God then took our nature on Him, that in Him it might do and suffer what in itself was impossible to it. What it could not effect of itself, it could effect in Him.[31]

It was, then, through Christ's bitter suffering and death that we were saved from our sins; and we call this death a sacrifice because Christ out of his obedience and love offered himself to the Father for those sins. It is this offering in love and obedience that constitutes the essence of sacrifice for a Christian:

> True sacrifice is every work done to establish us in a holy fellowship with God, every work tending to the attainment of that good in which alone we can be truly blessed. It stands to reason then that even the mercy upon which we draw to help our neighbour is not a sacrifice if it is not exercised for God.[32]

On the other hand, Christ's obedience and love were shown in his acceptance of the suffering of his Passion and death. "He was wounded for our transgressions, he was bruised for our iniquities; upon him was the chastisement that made us whole, and with his stripes we are healed" (Is 53:5). It

---

[31] Newman, "Incarnate Son", p. 1236.
[32] Augustine, cited in Bouyer, *Paschal Mystery*, p. 330.

was through Christ's wounded, tortured body that we see the sacrifice of Christ's love and obedience; it was through Christ's Passion and death that the Son made satisfaction for our sins.

This book is a book about liturgy, not directly about theology, but it would help us to understand the sacrifice of Christ if we remembered that our redemption from sin and death is also the work of God.[33] The initiative, to put it simply, was on the part of God, who out of love for his fallen creation willed Christ's death. It was for us, not for himself, that the Son in union with the Father's will gave himself up to suffering and death.[34]

The central conceptual problem in the Christian view of redemption is the existence of sin and death in a world we believe was created by an all-powerful and loving God. But, since this is the way things are, we have to think about the Passion and death of Christ as the way God chose to heal us. St. Thomas says: "From the beginning of His conception Christ merited our eternal salvation; but on our side there were some obstacles, whereby we were hindered from securing the effect of His preceding merits: consequently, in order to remove such hindrances, *it was necessary for Christ to suffer*."[35] In the liturgy God puts us into contact with

[33] This perspective on the liturgy is firmly established in *Sacrosanctum Concilium* itself, in section 5, where the document cites various texts from the New Testament, including 1 Timothy 2:4, to the effect that because God wished all men to be saved, he, the Father, sent the Son into the world to redeem the world.

[34] "Aquinas prefers to locate the effect of the passion in the changeable creature instead of the transcendent God" (Romanus Cessario, O.P., *The Godly Image: Christ and Salvation in Catholic Thought from St. Anselm to Aquinas* (Petersham, Mass.: St. Bede's Publications, 1990), p. 164. This excellent book should be required reading for anyone writing about the redemption today.

[35] STD 3, 48, 1 ad 2.

this work of Christ, who gave himself up for our sins so that we could begin to live a new life in him.

> Christ's passion removes both the obstacle of original sin and those sins which stem from them. The priesthood of Christ, however, figures in this satisfaction, since he offers God a renewed humanity. Authentic worship of the Father transforms the human person, making him or her a sharer in the fruits of Christ's passion by faith, love and the sacraments.[36]

It seems to be the case that today people find this sort of language foreign and are not at all ready to think much about Christ in terms of a sacrifice for sin. In a Toronto Catholic paper,[37] for example, in an unsigned editorial review of Mel Gibson's *The Passion of the Christ*, the reviewer wrote: "Atonement as one bloody death on the cross has little to say to modern people about how one man's death two thousand years ago affects us today. This is the right question." The review ends with an attack on "the Church's failure to educate" and an entirely predictable assertion that modern man has moved beyond the view "popularized" by St. Anselm in the twelfth century, which identifies Jesus as the sacrificial lamb:

> This metaphor, probably borrowed from the sacrifice on the Jewish Day of Atonement, has had a long grip on our imagination. It must be stressed, however, that it has outlived its usefulness, as have most of the metaphors used over the course in time in the Church—the necessary justification, the holy ransom, etc.

I do not think this review represents progress in theology; what it does represent (much as the writer of the editorial

---

[36] Cessario, *Godly Images*, p. 162.
[37] *Catholic New Times*, March 21, 2004.

might resent its being said) is a capitulation to the spirit of modernity—not even postmodernity. Such language is not a refinement or more intellectually respectable presentation of Catholicism; it is a repudiation of the Paschal Mystery itself. There is no arguing with this mentality, so let us go to the words of a poet, St. Paulinus of Nola (353–431), who lived long before the Scholasticism of the Middle Ages and seems to have been prompted to write neither by controversy nor even didactic motives, but only out of love. In the first six lines he expresses both Christ's sacrifice for sin as well as mankind's share, through its humanity, in that sacrifice:

> Look on thy God, Christ hidden in our flesh.
> A bitter word, the cross, and bitter sight:
> Hard rind without, to hold the heart of heaven.
> Yet sweet it is; for God upon that tree
> Did offer up his life: upon that rood
> My life hung, that my life might stand in God.

He then goes on to ask what he can do to repay what Christ has done for him; and he answers there is nothing he can give to God except Christ's sacrifice:

> Christ, what am I to give Thee for my life?
> Unless take from Thy hands the cup they hold,
> To cleanse me with the precious draught of death.
> What shall I do? My body to be burned?
> Make myself vile? The debt's not paid out yet.
> What'er I do, it is but I and Thou,
> And still do I come short, still must Thou pay
> My debts, O Christ; for debts Thyself hadst none.

But, finally, united to Christ's sacrifice, Paulinus offers everything he has out of love for the crucified:

What love may balance Thine? My Lord was found
In fashion like a slave, that so His slave
Might find himself in fashion like his Lord.
Think you the bargain's hard, to have exchanged
The transient for the eternal, to have sold
Earth to buy Heaven? More dearly God bought me.[38]

b. *The Sacrifice of Christ Is Perpetuated in the Mass.* There
was one sacrifice for sin on the Cross, and there are many
Masses. Is the Mass a sacrifice only in the sense that we
join our sufferings and sacrifices to the one true sacrifice of
Christ on the Cross, or is there something more to it than
this? The traditional Catholic view is that there is a great
deal more to it than this. In a doctrine taught again by
Vatican II and reaffirmed in the *Catechism*,[39] the Church
holds that there is one sacrifice for sin offered by Christ on
the Cross but that this sacrifice is made present daily on the
altars of the Church. Mass is not merely a service for making Holy Communion available to the faithful; it is the per-
petuation through time of Christ's saving work. Christ is
not crucified again and again, but his sacrifice is made present
and offered over and over again. St. Thomas More summed
the matter up in a relatively untechnical way:

> Who saith that Christ is daily new crucified? Truth is that
> the Church saith that Christ is at the altar every day offered,
> his own blessed body in the sacrament. This is of truth, the
> Church saith that Christ is our daily sacrifice. But no man
> saith that he is daily crucified of new, and daily put to new
> pain. But as he was once crucified and killed and offered

---

[38] Paulinus of Nola (353–431), "The Word of the Cross", in *Mediaeval Latin Lyrics*, trans. Helen Waddell (London: Penguin, 1952), p. 51.

[39] "The Sacrament of the Eucharist", 1322–1419; and on the sacrifice, especially 1362–72.

on the cross, so is that one death-oblation and sacrifice daily represented, by the self same body: that only quick [living] sacrifice and oblation that God has left unto us his new Christian Church, instead of all the manifold sacrifices and oblations of his old synagogue, the Jews.[40]

There is a passage from the *Sentences* of Peter Lombard (d. ca. 1160) that sums up the doctrine of the Fathers of the Church and of the early Scholastics on the Eucharistic Sacrifice. Peter asks "Whether what the priest does is properly called a sacrifice or immolation; and whether Christ is daily immolated or was only once immolated". He then goes on:

> To this we may briefly reply that what is offered and consecrated by the priest is called a sacrifice and immolation because it is a memorial and a representation of the true sacrifice and holy immolation made upon the altar of the cross. Christ died once, upon the cross, and there he was immolated in his own self; and yet every day he is immolated sacramentally, because in the sacrament there is a recalling of what was done once.[41]

The language is technical and is not in much favor today. On the other hand, it does make clear and precise the teaching of the *Catechism* and sums up the teaching of the Fathers of the Church on the sacrificial character of the Eucharist.

c. *Christ's Sacrifice and Ours.* There is a familiar theme in the prophets that can be summed up in the words of the words of Psalm 51:16–17:

---

[40] Cited in Clark, *Eucharistic Sacrifice*, p. 558.
[41] Ibid., p. 75.

For you take no delight in sacrifice;
    were I to give a burnt offering, you would not be pleased.
The sacrifice acceptable to God is a broken spirit;
    a broken and a contrite heart, O God, you will not despise.[42]

This text and ones similar to it are often taken as showing, as Kant thought, that moral and spiritual religion must
get rid of the idea of sacrifice. But the prophets were not
trying to rid religion of the idea of sacrifice as such; what
they were trying to do was to shift it from the external
destruction of beasts, and even human beings, to an internal offering of the mind and heart to God. St. Augustine
puts this in a marvelously concise way:

> Let us see how, even where God says that He does not
> wish sacrifice, He shows that He does wish it. God does
> not desire the sacrifice of immolated beasts but he does
> desire the sacrifice of a contrite heart. Thus, in what the
> Psalmist says God does not wish, is implied what God does
> wish.[43]

God still wishes sacrifice; and what he wants from us is "a
broken and a contrite heart". There is another famous text,
this time from the New Testament, that teaches the same
lesson:

> I appeal to you therefore, brethren, by the mercies of God,
> to present your bodies as a living sacrifice, holy and accept-
> able to God, which is your spiritual worship.

---

[42] Or again: "I will accept no bull from your house, nor he-goat from
your folds.... If I were hungry, I would not tell you; for the world and all
that is in it is mine" (Ps 50:9). Another famous text is from Micah 6:6–8,
ending with the lines: "What does the LORD require of you but to do justice,
and to love kindness, and to walk humbly with your God?"

[43] Cited in Bouyer, *Paschal Mystery*, p. 330.

Do not be conformed to this world but be transformed by
the renewal of your mind, that you may prove what is the
will of God, what is good and acceptable and perfect. (Rom
12:1–2)

St. Peter Chrysologus (ca. 406–450) gives a moving interpretation of this text in the following words:

"I exhort you to present your bodies." By requesting this,
the Apostle has raised all men to a priestly rank. "To present
your bodies as a living sacrifice." O unheard of function of
the Christian priesthood, inasmuch as man is both the victim and the priest for himself! Because man need not go
beyond himself in seeking what he is to immolate to God!
Because man, ready to offer sacrifice to God, brings with
himself, and in himself, what is for himself! Because the
same being who remains as the victim, remains also as a
priest! Because the victim is immolated and still lives! Because
the priest who will make atonement is unable to kill! Wonderful indeed is this sacrifice, where the body is offered
with [the slaying of] a body, and blood without bloodshed.[44]

So, it is not sacrifice as such that is inimical to Christianity,
but the wrong idea of sacrifice, and it is important to see
that the offering of "our selves, our souls and bodies to be
a reasonable, holy, and lively sacrifice unto thee" as the old
Book of Common Prayer expressed it,[45] is not an invention of
Vatican II but is in accord with the most authentic Christian tradition. On the other hand, we still have to understand that these sacrifices have value only because they are

[44] Fathers of the Church, Sermon 108, *Saint Peter Chrysologus: Selected Sermons, and Saint Valerian: Homilies*, trans. George E. Gauss, vol. 17 (New York:
Fathers of the Church, 1953), p. 169.

[45] *Book of Common Prayer* (Cambridge: Cambridge University Press, 1969),
p. 164.

united to Christ's sacrifice. It is Christ's atoning sacrifice that is offered at Mass, and it is this sacrifice that takes our own poor offering to the Father. The point is put very strongly and very clearly by Fr. Bouyer. After saying that the "oblation of himself which Christ made upon the Cross and renews at Mass" does not dispense us from offering ourselves but rather makes us "capable of offering ourselves", he goes on to say:

> We do not offer to Christ what we call figuratively our "sacrifices", but we do offer to God *His own sacrifice*, the oblation of the Crucified, which alone saves and reconciles us, and which alone can communicate some value to the sacrifice that we ourselves shall make later. There is in this confusion a reversal of value which would logically end in pure Pelagianism. In any case, its immediate result is a grossly naturalistic conception of the Mass.[46]

Here Fr. Bouyer gives expression to the traditional faith of the Church that it is only through being joined to the sacrifice of Christ that our own efforts at self-denial, even when done out of compassion for the Savior's suffering, have any value; it is only "through him, and with him, and in him"[47] that our sacrifices are accepted by the Father as part of the redeeming death and Resurrection of Christ.

2. *Christ Is Risen*

In the letter to the Romans, St. Paul says, "We know that Christ being raised from the dead will never die again; death no longer has dominion over him. The death he died he

---

[46] Bouyer, *Paschal Mystery*, p. 328.

[47] "Per ipsum, et cum ipso, et in ipso"; the phrase is found as the ending of all four Eucharistic Prayers.

died to sin, once for all, but the life he lives he lives to God" (Rom 6:9–10). The Resurrection of Christ is the central motif of the Paschal Mystery; but it does not replace either his suffering and death or his "glorious Ascension into heaven". If we concentrate on the Resurrection to the exclusion of the other two elements, then the Paschal Mystery will lose its cutting edge as a celebration of Christ's saving death and will be robbed of the dynamic introduced into the liturgy by the longing desire for Christ's coming.[48]

It remains true, though, that the Resurrection is central to Christianity. In the face of ridicule and indifference, the Church has asserted to an unbelieving world that Jesus Christ arose in his human body.[49] The Resurrection showed that life in Christ was stronger than death and that, deep at the center of things, a door had closed, a chapter had ended. "Death, you shall die in me; hell, you shall be destroyed by me", cries the Church in the name of Christ.[50] For the friends of Christ, the grave is no longer the end but the

---

[48] See below, the discussion on the Ascension.

[49] See above, "Hume and Atheism", pp. 103–10. The impression that no intelligent and modern person could possibly believe in the Resurrection is so firmly rooted that it is worth saying that this is not the case. Wittgenstein, whose philosophy provides little support for traditional Catholicism, nevertheless wrote: "What inclines even me to believe in Christ's Resurrection? It is as though I play with the thought.—If he did not rise from the dead, then he decomposed in the grave like any other man. *He is dead and decomposed.* In that case he is a teacher like any other and can no longer *help*; and once more we are orphaned and alone. And must content ourselves with wisdom and speculation. We are as it were in a hell, where we can only dream, and are as it were cut off from heaven by a roof." Quoted in Norman Malcom, *Wittgenstein: A Religious Point of View?* (Ithaca, N.Y.: Cornell University Press, 1994), p. 17 (emphasis in original). One can think what one likes about Wittgenstein's argument as an argument; my point here, though, is that Wittgenstein, who was surely an "intelligent and modern person", did not find the notion of Christ's Resurrection to be inherently absurd or unthinkable.

[50] *The Liturgy of the Hours*, first antiphon at Evening Prayer for Holy Saturday.

beginning of a life that will never end. Behind everything done at Mass is the strange, stubborn fact of the Resurrection in his human body of our Savior Jesus Christ. It is a fact that defies explanation; it is a fact that is often openly derided; and it is a fact that seems to have been almost too big to handle even by those closest to him. Nonetheless, it is the Resurrection that gives meaning and truth to all the symbols of our faith and the practice of our religion. To see and understand that the Eucharist is a celebration of Christ's victory over sin and death is an exercise of faith, and it is also the way in which God strengthens and vivifies that faith.

For the Easter Octave there is an addition to the First Eucharistic Prayer that states that our Lord *rose in his human body*. Now unless this is true, then all we are doing at Mass is giving expression to what we would like to be the case; or perhaps making a statement of community solidarity; or perhaps trying to tell ourselves, in a quaint, old-fashioned way, that the universe is unfolding as the planners think it should. But what we are celebrating, or should be celebrating, is the Lord's victory of life over death, and unless Christ rose in his human body, then, in St. Paul's words, "our preaching is in vain and your faith is in vain" (1 Cor 15:14).

The Resurrection is not the wisdom of the world; and the Resurrection certainly does not voice the hopes of the chattering classes. But the wisdom of the world and the noise of the opinion makers often make it difficult to make a convincing case, even to ourselves, of what we believe. We do need some sort of basis for what we believe, a basis that will be strong enough to support us when we are tempted by sin, by despair, by doubt, or by difficult questions, sometimes from those in our own family. The worship of the Church satisfies this very real need for support for our Christian convictions by providing the imagination with an experience that presents the reality of the truths of faith in a powerful and convincing way. It is a great foolishness to ignore the imagination, because the world, the flesh, and the devil go after us through our imagination. "The world", says Newman, "sweeps by us in long procession":

> its principalities and powers, its Babel of languages, the astrologers of Chaldaea, the horse and its rider and the chariots of Egypt, Bal and Ashtoreth and their false worship; and those who witness, feel its fascination; they flock after it; with a strange fancy, they ape its gestures, and dote upon its mummeries.[51]

In this dramatic passage Newman is warning us of the victory of the power of sight over the power of faith. In comparison to the glamor and the glitter, the power and the glory of this world, how utterly unreal the message of the gospel often seems to be.

In the liturgy we are given a living contact with what we cannot understand clearly enough always to argue for convincingly. The worship of the Church is the gracious gift of the mercy of God to an insecure, distraught, and confused humanity. It is not as though the material and visible aspect of our worship becomes somehow unspiritual and second-rate when we begin to reflect on the hidden mysteries of our faith. The outward and visible signs bring us the reality and the power of the risen Christ, but that reality and that power are displayed, shown forth, made manifest, found, experienced in and through what we see, hear,

---

[51] John Henry Newman, "Faith and Sight", *Fifteen Sermons Preached before the University of Oxford between A.D. 1826 and 1843* (London: Longmans, Green, 1900), p. 132.

smell, touch, and see. The sacramental and liturgical worship of his Church is God's gift to human beings with bodies and souls. It is God's gift; and our way back to him is through this worship.[52]

3. Christ Will Come Again

The third moment of the Paschal Mystery is the Ascension of Christ, and the unknown medieval writer I cited earlier in the chapter connects the Ascension with the virtue of hope. This is a profound and important connection and one that is utterly traditional, but it needs reaffirming, and it is important to see why this is so.

The Ascension is not very close to the heart of the practice of most people's Catholicism; and it is not difficult to see why. The Ascension is often thought of and presented as a kind of coda to the end of the earthly life of Christ, or as little more than a sort of signing off of a mission successfully accomplished. But Christ's Ascension, as the *Catechism* puts it, "signifies his participation, in his humanity, in God's power and authority".[53]

> The heavenly liturgy celebrates the ongoing event of the return of the Son—and of all others in him—to the Father's house. It is the feast, the banquet, even the marriage, of the beloved and his bride. All is not yet completed, but the great event of history is now present at the heart of the Trinity; there, one with the Father, it becomes a wellspring.[54]

[52] See below, chap. 2, "With Desire I Have Desired".

[53] CCC 668.

[54] Jean Corbon, *The Wellspring of Worship*, trans. Matthew J. O'Connell (San Francisco: Ignatius Press, 2005), p. 41.

When we recall the Ascension, we should realize that Christ, the Head of the Church, reigns in glory and that through the sacraments of the earthly liturgy he shares his risen and ascended life with us. When we think about eternal life and the promises of the risen Christ we are led to practice the theological virtue of hope.

> The hope of which we speak now, attains God by leaning on His help in order to obtain the hoped for good. Now an effect must be proportionate to its cause. Wherefore the good which we ought to hope for from God properly and chiefly, is the infinite good, which is proportionate to the power of our divine helper, since it belongs to an infinite power to lead anyone to an infinite good.[55]

It is the power of the Holy Spirit that fuels our hope and that makes us persevere in hope; it is the bridge from *believing* there is a God to actually *wanting* him above everything else. With God's help we can hope for the reality of Christ's coming at the end of time, when he shall have destroyed "every rule and every authority and power. For he must reign until he has put all his enemies under his feet. The last enemy to be destroyed is death" (1 Cor 15:24–25). In hope we realize that we can really desire the promise of eternal life with Christ because we have some taste of what is to come through our sacramental life; in our sacramental life we already have a hint, a foreknowledge, of the glory that is to come. In one of the finest passages of the Constitution on the Sacred Liturgy of Vatican II we find the words:

> In the earthly liturgy, by way of foretaste, we share in that heavenly liturgy which is celebrated in the holy city of Jeru-

[55] STD 2, 2, 17, 2.

salem toward which we journey as pilgrims.... *We eagerly await the Saviour*, our Lord Jesus Christ, until He, our life, shall appear and we too will appear with Him in glory.[56]

We eagerly await: we eagerly await our Savior because, like the disciples on the road to Emmaus, we have already begun to recognize him in the breaking of the bread. We recognize him, not just as the God who shared our humanity and has now returned to the Father: we also recognize him as the Lord of all time and history who shares his triumphant love and life here, now, with each one of us. If we recognize that new life he gives us in the sacraments, then we will hunger and thirst for more; and, hungering and thirsting for more, we will say from the depth of our hearts, and not as a trite formula: Lord Jesus, come in glory. In emphasizing this dimension of the liturgy, it is clear that *Sacrosanctum Concilium* pointed the way to the restoration of an aspect of the worship of the Church that had not been sufficiently emphasized in the years before the Council.[57]

In the Paschal Mystery, the Church celebrates the Passion and death, the Resurrection and the Ascension of the Lord. If we emphasize the Resurrection, we must not do so in a way that overlooks the intrinsic connection of the death and Passion to Christ's triumph over sin and death; nor must we so concentrate on the death and Resurrection as real events in history (which, of course, they were) that we diminish the dimension of the ever-present activity of the triumphant Christ, who continues his work through his Body, the Church.

[56] *Sacrosanctum Concilium* 8 (A 141–42).

[57] "The reference to the *Parousia* is not highly developed in SC but, given the concision of the theological summaries in the Liturgy Constitution, it cannot be overlooked" (Aidan Nichols, O.P., *A Pope and a Council on the Sacred Liturgy* [Farnborough: Saint Michael's Abbey Press, 2002], p. 24).

CHAPTER TWO

"WITH DESIRE I HAVE DESIRED"

(LUKE 22:15, AV)

> So they call him the beloved and the yearned-for since
> he is beautiful and good, and, again, they call him yearn-
> ing and love because he is the power moving and lifting
> all things up to himself, for in the end what is he if not
> Beauty and Goodness, the One who of himself reveals
> himself, the good procession of his own transcendent
> Unity? He is yearning on the move, simple, self-moved,
> self-acting, pre-existent in the Good, flowing out from
> the Good unto all that is and returning once again to
> the Good.
>
> —Dionysius the Areopagite, *The Divine Names*

As we saw in the previous chapter, in the liturgy we celebrate, not only the Passion and death as well as the Resurrection of Christ, but also "his glorious Ascension". The
Ascension of the Lord is the element in the Paschal Mystery that turns our attention away from an exclusive concern with the past and introduces a note of longing
expectation into our worship. The letter to the Hebrews
says that Jesus "is able for all time to save those who draw
near to God through him, since he always lives to make
intercession for them" (Heb 7:25), and through our cel-

ebration of the Paschal Mystery we enter into this unend-
ing intercession of Christ on our behalf. In the Eucharistic
Sacrifice we are made aware that Christ's victory over sin
and death has become a reality that is shared with us in the
here and now, and this awareness awakens in us the response
"Come, Lord Jesus!" [1]

At the Last Supper when our Lord first offered the bread
and wine as his body and blood, he began to speak to his
disciples and said: "With desire I have desired to eat this
passover with you before I suffer" (Lk 22:15, AV). This mysterious phrase, which seems deep with hidden meaning,
shows us that Christ's attitude toward eating this last meal
was one of intense feeling that went far beyond a cool statement about what he intended to do. It was as though he
were saying that his whole being—spirit, mind, and body—
was united in an overwhelming desire to give himself and
all he was, not only to those in the upper room, but to all
who would follow him in the ages to come.

The phrase translated "with desire I have desired" is one
of Hebrew origin[2] and was used by the translators of the
Old Testament to indicate intense longing; for example, in
Genesis, Laban says to Jacob, "You longed greatly for your

[1] "Jesus died and rose 'once and for all,' and that event now lives on
through all of history and sustains it. But when in his humanity he takes his
place beside the Father and from there pours out the life-giving gift of the
Spirit, he does not cease to manifest and carry out the liturgy. There is but
a single Passover or Passage but its mighty energy is displayed in a continual
ascension and Pentecost (Jean Corbon, *The Wellspring of Worship*, trans. Matthew J. O'Connell [San Francisco: Ignatius Press, 2005], p. 59).

[2] "This is a Septuagintism (found verbatim in Gen 31:30).... It could also
translate a construction now attested in Palestinian Aramaic ... 'and I Abram
wept with grievous weeping'" (*The Gospel according to Luke*, introduction,
trans., and notes by Joseph A. Fitzmyer, The Anchor Bible, vols. 28–28A
(Garden City, N.Y.: Doubleday, 1981–1985), 2:1395.

father's house" (Gen 31:30). The Greek word for desire (ἐπιθυμία) can be a morally neutral word, as when the prodigal son is hungry and desires food; it more often has a negative ring about it; but it can also indicate something good. It all depends on the object desired: if the desire is for something reprehensible, then it is an evil desire, and most often in the New Testament the Greek words for desire indicate a yearning for something evil.[3] Sometimes, though, the object of desire may be something good, and then the desire is a good one: for example, in St. Matthew we read that "many prophets and righteous men have desired to see those things which ye see" (Mt 13:17, AV), and St. Paul said "I desire to be dissolved and to be with Christ" (Phil 1:23, DR). In the liturgy we are supposed to be given a sense that we are entering into the eternal intercession of Christ and to desire what has been only half revealed to us. The object of our desire, that is, what we desire, is God himself.

In the tradition of the Church, the presentation of Christ's saving work to the Father is called the *heavenly* liturgy; and our desire for God should be kindled and sustained by the Eucharist. The earthly liturgy through the Paschal Mystery is an activity in which there are both divine and human elements[4] that together draw us to the Father.

The renewed interest in the place of the Ascension and of the heavenly liturgy is a return to very ancient Christian themes, and they are still of greatest importance. I believe

---

[3] See William F. Arndt and F. Wilbur Gingrich, *A Greek-English Lexicon of the New Testament and Other Early Christian Literature*, 5th ed. (Chicago and London: University of Chicago Press, 1958), entry ἐπιθυμία.

[4] CCC 1077–1112, "The Liturgy—Work of the Holy Trinity". At the same time it is the work "of the whole Christ, head *and body*" (1187, emphasis mine).

that much of the excitement and sense of liberation that accompanied the first heady days after the closure of Vatican II was the sense of returning to a world that was not confined to the past but was a recapturing of the sense of expectancy and of urgency that seems to have characterized the early Christians. The fact that these post-conciliar expectations were pitched too high and were sidetracked does not alter the fact they were elicited by a response to genuine Christian principles. In discussing some of these principles I want to turn to an ancient writer known as Dionysius the Areopagite.[5] Whoever this unknown author really was, he has had an enormous influence on the Christian Church over the centuries. It is true that this influence has waned as well as waxed, but it has never entirely disappeared, and today he is enjoying something of a renaissance even outside of strictly theological circles through the work of French thinkers such as Jean-Luc Marion.[6]

---

[5] The writer is sometimes called "Pseudo-Dionysius" to distinguish him from the Dionysius of Acts 17:34, who was said to be among those "who joined [Paul] and believed". The writer used the same name and identified himself with the disciple of St. Paul, a literary device designed to preserve the author's anonymity. However, to call him "pseudo" implies a sort of falsity or double dealing. Hans Urs von Balthasar sets the record straight in some remarkably fine pages on Dionysius in *The Glory of the Lord: A Theological Aesthetics*, vol. 2, *Studies in Theological Style: Clerical Styles* (San Francisco: Ignatius Press, 1984), especially pp. 144–54. Some translators, notably Andrew Louth, follow the French and use "Denys" rather than "Dionysius". Here I have followed the more common usage.

[6] Jean-Luc Marion, *God without Being*, trans. Thomas A. Carlson (Chicago: University of Chicago Press, 1995). I should make it very clear that I am not interested here in the use Marion makes of Dionysius. I think this use is profound and potentially very important, but this is not my concern in this book. I mention him only to show the abiding influence (and interest) of Dionysius.

It is, I think, a mistake to confine the influence of the Areopagite exclusively to the mystical tradition of the Church. Certainly, he has had an enormous impact on how we think about the individual soul's approach to God,[7] but there is more to it than that. Hans Urs von Balthasar claims that "virtually all medieval philosophy up to the Aristotelian renaissance and the whole of theology up to Thomas [is] derived from the fecundity of these two [Augustine and Dionysius]." [8] It is clear that Dionysius still has important things to say.

One of the themes that Eastern Christianity took over from Greek philosophy was the conviction that reality was essentially one. What it could not find in Greek philosophy, however, was the biblical teaching that this reality was the free creation of Almighty God. We sometimes hear that God needed to create in order to have an object for his love. To this the Church has said that the Blessed Trinity is a unity of love that is already perfect and complete in itself. God created, not because he had to or needed to, but because out of his freedom he chose to do so. Again, there was no preexisting "matter" or "stuff" that he used as though he were a sculptor molding a statue out of clay. There was, to emphasize the point, no clay, or anything answering to it, before God brought everything into existence:

[7] "Interest in Denys could not lapse for long, for, whoever he was, his writing exercised an enormous influence on the so-called mystical tradition of the mediaeval West. As interest in that tradition increases as the twentieth century wears on, so curiosity, at least, about Denys and his writings has grown" (Andrew Louth, Denys the Areopagite [London and New York: Continuum, 1989], p. 2).

[8] "And even with Thomas himself: if Aristotle supplies the exact categories, Denys supplies not just the great frame for the plan of the Summa, with procession and return and many essential adagios" (Von Balthasar, Glory of the Lord, 2:148).

For you did create all things,
and by your will they existed and were created.[9] (Rev 4:11)

If God created everything there is, he is beyond or other than what was created. Dionysius put this *otherness* of God in a striking way:

> the inscrutable One is out of the reach of every rational process. Nor can any words come up to the inexpressible Good, this One, this Source of all unity, this supra-existent Being. Mind beyond mind, word beyond speech, it is gathered up by no discourse, by no intuition, by no name. It is and it is as no other being is.[10]

The only reason we can talk about this unknown and hidden God is because he has revealed something about himself in the Bible, and this gives us a vocabulary in which to speak about and pray to God. "Cause of all existence, and therefore itself transcending existence, it alone could give an authoritative account of what it really is."[11]

This cause of all existence that is beyond everything there is has revealed itself, through Jesus Christ, as a Trinity of Persons, Father, Son, and Holy Spirit, and Dionysius prays that this Trinity will guide us to a point where we will be united with his ultimate reality. We have to start our reflections with our belief in the blessed Trinity and not add what we believe about God as a hurried afterthought that gives a respectable veneer to our ruminations

---

[9] "We believe that God needs no pre-existent thing or any help in order to create, nor is creation any sort of necessary emanation from the divine substance [cf. *Dei Filius*, can. 2–4: DS 3022–3024]" (CCC 296).

[10] Pseudo-Dionysius, *The Divine Names* 588B, in *The Complete Works*, trans. Colm Luibhéid (New York: Paulist Press, 1987), pp. 49–50.

[11] Ibid.

about the modern world and the place of faith—any sort
of faith—in the modern world.[12]

> Trinity!! Higher than any being,
>   any divinity, any goodness!
>   Guide of Christians
>   in the wisdom of heaven!
> Lead us up beyond unknowing and light,
>   up to the farthest, highest peak
>   of mystic scripture,
>   where the mysteries of God's Word
>   lie simple, absolute and unchangeable
>   in the brilliant darkness of a hidden silence.
>   Amid the deepest shadow
>   they pour overwhelming light
>   on what is most manifest.
>   Amid the wholly unsensed and unseen
>   they completely fill our sightless minds
>   with treasure beyond all beauty.[13]

If we look at these quotations together, we get the following picture. God is beyond any thought or concept that
we can have of him. He has, however, revealed himself as a
Trinity of Persons and given us a language in which we can
talk about him. This Trinity, furthermore, has created all
there is, including the world of our everyday existence. This
revelation by God about his nature, the fact that existence
is his creation, and his providing us with a language to talk
about these mysteries can be looked on as going out from

---

[12] See "Introduction: Suspending the Material: The Turn of Radical Orthodoxy", in *Radical Orthodoxy*, ed. John Milbank, Catherine Pickstock, and
Graham Ward (London and New York: Routledge, 1999).

[13] Pseudo-Dionysius, "The Mystical Theology", in *Complete Works*, p. 135.

God to us. God's relation to his creation from this point of view is that of a loving and sustaining cause. But, in his praise of the Trinity, Dionysius asks to be led up from where he is now to the hidden mystery of the being of God. He does not say he can get there by himself, but he asks for help to be "uplifted to the ray of the divine shadow which is above everything that is";[14] and here we have God functioning as a great magnet drawing all there is to himself.[15]

There are, then, two different movements. In the first of these, God gives existence, revelation, and language. And in the second, he draws what he has created back to himself. These two movements are often said to provide the structure for the *Summa Theologiae* of St. Thomas Aquinas, and a consideration of what he has to say may help us to see the intrinsic importance of the plan.

> We may consider a twofold order between creatures and God:—the first is by reason of creatures being caused by God and depending on Him as on the principle of their being; and thus on account of the infinitude of His power God touches each thing immediately, by causing and preserving it, and so it is that God is in all things by essence, presence and power. But the second order is by reason of things being directed to God as to their end.[16]

St. Thomas, in the same place, then goes on to emphasize that this return by creatures to God is made possible through the Incarnation and says that lower creatures are directed to God by higher ones, "and to this order pertains the assumption of human nature by the Word of God, Who

[14] Ibid.
[15] Cf. John 12:32: "... and I, when I am lifted up from the earth, will draw all men to myself."
[16] STD 3, 6, 1 ad 1.

is the term of the assumption; and hence it is united to flesh through the soul." [17]

It has been argued by Fr. M.-D. Chenu, O.P., that St. Thomas' plan for the *Summa* is taken from Neoplatonic sources.[18] I think the question is intrinsically important and interesting, but whatever is to be decided about sources and influences, it must be said that there is a way of considering God's relationship to his creation that is common to both the East and West, and any discussion about liturgy that ignores this, or replaces it by some other sort of theory, is going to go badly awry from the very beginning.

There is, then, a going out of God in creation, and there is also our response to this loving initiative. Our response, though, is only possible through the love of the Father for the Son who shared our human nature.

> What comes into view, contrary to hope, from previous obscurity, is described as "sudden". As for the love of Christ for humanity, the Word of God, I believe, uses this term to hint that the transcendent has put aside its own hiddenness and has revealed itself to us by becoming a human being.

---

[17] Ibid.

[18] M.-D. Chenu, O.P., *Toward Understanding Saint Thomas*, trans. A. M. Landry and D. Hughes (Chicago: Henry Regnery, 1964). "Beyond the scientific world of Aristotle, Saint Thomas appeals to the Platonic theme of emanation and return. Since theology is the science of God, all things will be studied in their relation to God, whether in their production or in the final end, in their *exitus et reditus* [going-out from and coming-back to]" (p. 304). There is an extended treatment of Fr. Chenu's views, as well as of those who disagree with him, in Ghislain Lafont, O.S.B., *Structures et méthode dans la "Somme théologique" de Saint Thomas d'Aquin* (Paris: Desclée de Brouwer, 1961). A contemporary argument against Chenu's interpretation is to be found in: Christopher T. Baglow, "Sacred Scripture and Sacred Doctrine in Saint Thomas Aquinas", in Thomas G. Weinandy, Daniel A. Keating, and John P. Yocum, eds., *Aquinas on Doctrine: A Critical Introduction* (London and New York: T & T Clark International, 2004), p. 11.

But he is hidden even after this revelation, or, if I may speak in a more divine fashion, is hidden even amid the revelation. For this mystery of Jesus remains hidden and can be drawn out by no word or mind. What is to be said of it remains unsayable; what is to be understood of it remains unknowable.[19]

Furthermore, our response to the Father in Christ is only possible because God himself draws us to himself through our prayers and efforts to draw closer to him.

Let us stretch ourselves prayerfully upward to the more lofty elevation of the kindly Rays of God. Imagine a great shining chain hanging downward from the heights of heaven to the world below. We grab hold of it with one hand and then another, and we seem to be pulling it down toward us. Actually, it is already there on the heights and down below and instead of pulling it to us we are being lifted upward to that brilliance above, to the dazzling light of those beams.[20]

The response to love is to love in return, and Dionysius makes it clear in several places that at the heart of the liturgy is the love of Christ for his people. The response to this divine initiative is not merely to think about it but to experience it through the liturgical action.[21] The attitude

---

[19] Pseudo-Dionysius, *Third Letter*, "To the Same Monk Gaius", 1069B, in *Complete Works*, p. 264.

[20] Pseudo-Dionysius, *Divine Names* 680C, p. 68.

[21] "The liturgical action is an invitation to allow the whole of one's life to be transformed, to be deified, to become a vehicle for God's love in the world. The liturgical invitation is addressed to human beings of body and soul: it is expressed in symbols and concepts, in liturgical actions and gestures, and hymns and prayers. To understand and respond is to enter into the meaning of these ceremonies, which is God's *philanthropia*, his love for all humanity. And that response is required of all who take part in the liturgy" (Louth, *Denys the Areopagite*, p. 108).

of the worshipper should share some of the desire Christ showed when he instituted the Eucharist.

Dionysius uses *eros* for this yearning after the God who himself longs to share himself with us:

> Indeed some of our writers on sacred matters have thought the title "yearning" (ἔρωτος ὄνομα) to be more divine than "love" (τῆς ἀγάπης). The divine Ignatius writes: "He for whom I yearn has been crucified." In the introductory scriptures you will note the following said about the divine wisdom: I yearned for her beauty (ἐραστὴς ἐγενόμην τοῦ κάλλους ἀυτης). So let us not fear this title of "yearning" (τὸ τοῦ ἔρωτος ὄνομα) . . . What is signified is a capacity to effect a unity, an alliance, and a particular commingling in the Beautiful and the Good.[22]

The liturgy of the Church shares in this pattern as a response, or an answer, to the hidden unknown God who has revealed himself in Jesus Christ, the Christ who desires we should desire him. We have to anchor our thinking firmly in these two principles. First of all, if our liturgy is to be in "spirit and truth" (Jn 4:23), it must point toward the Trinity that has been revealed in Jesus Christ. The focus of our worship is on a God who out of his goodness has shared himself with us. Secondly, it is also vital to hold in mind that God not only goes out to us but also draws us to himself. Christ said, "I am the way, and the truth, and the life; no one comes to the Father, but by me" (Jn 14:6). Christ, we might say, points us in the right direction through the shadows and obscurity to the hidden God. But this is not all, because through his love and with his love and in his love, we are drawn back to "the

---

[22] Pseudo-Dionysius, *Divine Names* 709B, p. 81.

Father of lights with whom there is no variation or shadow due to change" (Jas 1:17).

Our earthly liturgy has to do with what we can see, hear, touch, and taste, and acts of liturgical worship can be perceived by anyone who has the use of his senses. What is experienced, however, has a meaning and a dimension far beyond the walls of the Church. In ordinary life we say a red traffic light shows we should stop our car and wait; in other words, the traffic light is more than merely a red light; it contains a meaning that is a command to stop and wait. It does not matter here whether you think there is some sort of natural connection between something red and stopping or whether you want to say that stopping for a red light has to be understood within a complex of words and things that enable us to move efficiently and safely through traffic in a city. What does matter here, though, is to see that the things we perceive are important to us only because we are aware of them as meaning something. Whether they possess the meaning "in themselves" or whether we endow things with meaning in an arbitrary way has nothing much to do with the things themselves. Finally, whether both what we perceive and what we mean are mutually dependent on each other through a continual process of refinement of both our perception and our meanings is irrelevant for the moment. It is the end result that interests us, and this is that in experience we cannot separate awareness and meaning.

Very often the reaction to some of the various deformations of the liturgy of which Bishop Garriga spoke[23] is to call for a liturgy that is more spiritual and points beyond itself. At first sight it is hard to quarrel with this demand, but it is worthwhile seeing what it involves. First of all,

[23] See above, pp. 142–43.

what does a more "spiritual" liturgy mean? All too often the phrase seems to be based on an attitude that plays down, or even denies, the importance of the visible and tangible. It is as though we are being told that "really" or "in the final analysis" our bodies are not important, because the heart of the matter is the meanings conveyed by the liturgical actions. Secondly, we have to ask to what it is that these meanings direct our attention. Here, again, caution is in order. Once we get rid of political or social candidates who were providing the ultimate focus for liturgy and replace these by God, there still remains the question of who we believe this God to be and how we are to understand his role in liturgical action.

There is a very natural temptation at this point to look on liturgy as a stage or step in a purer and even a more Christian worship of God, but, as a step or stage, it could in principle be dispensed with as we grow in religious and spiritual maturity. The visible and the tangible aspects of the liturgy serve their purpose as a useful means, perhaps even a necessary means, by pointing us in the direction of God and in some way taking us to a deeper realization of God. Once, however, they have done their work, we should strive after contact with God that will not be encumbered or even contaminated by images and ideas drawn from our ordinary experience. While such a position is understandable, it is wrong, because to strive after what we imagine to be a purer worship is to misunderstand liturgy in a basic and dangerous way. It is also, I believe, to misconceive the nature of Christian mysticism.

We can see what is wrong with this in two stages. In the first place, there is the fact that human beings have bodies and are not even "essentially" pure (or impure!) spirits. The second stage on this wrong road begins when we start to think that our contact with the mysterious being of God, who is Father, Son, and Holy Spirit, is through an experience that is separated off from ordinary liturgical life. The body, we are tempted to say, provides the soul or spirit with the means to grasp symbols as well as to understand meaning, and this is correct. But then we go on to say that to reach the Holy of Holies we must pass to a more privileged and more private as well as essentially nonliturgical way of praying. This is the second great mistake.

The body is a partner in the spiritual life and not something to be disregarded and with luck or a strange experience left behind. Any sane spiritual life has to be based on the facts of the case, and the fact is that human beings have bodies, and the body requires to be nourished and developed in the ways of God. The tendency to regard ourselves as essentially spiritual and the body as being an unfortunate and unprepossessing drag on the flight of the spirit is wrong. In the thought of St. Thomas, human beings are not made up of two distinct entities called body and soul; rather, they are what Aristotle called "ensouled bodies". This same teaching is to be found in the Second Vatican Council and in the *Catechism*.[24]

I do not think we should regard these statements about human nature as so many conclusions, based on natural reason, that have now closed the door on any further philosophical discussion. The position taken by the Church about human nature has been motivated by the conviction that

[24] For example, CCC 365: "The unity of soul and body is so profound that one has to consider the soul to be the 'form' of the body [cf. Council of Vienne (1312): DS 902]: i.e., it is because of its spiritual soul that the body made of matter becomes a living, human body; spirit and matter, in man, are not two natures united, but rather their union forms a single nature." The *Catechism* also cites *Gaudium et Spes* of Vatican II.

there is a truth concerning this nature in Christian revelation and that the philosophy of St. Thomas is the best way of expressing this truth. This is quite a different thing from saying that the Church's view of human nature draws its authority from Aristotle or even St. Thomas. This becomes important when we think about liturgy. One of the criticisms of a traditional approach to liturgy is that such a liturgy is based on what is called a classical view of human nature. Those who talk this way seem to mean by *classical* a view of things based on Aristotle and Plato. Now that we have been removed, or have removed ourselves, from this foreign and meaningless view of man, it becomes obvious, so it is argued, that a radically new approach to liturgy must be adopted.

We can think what we like about the internal incoherence of this sort of argument, not to say the startling premises on which it is based, but there is no doubt that it has had a powerful influence; and the motive power behind much of this approach to worship is found in the Enlightenment view that there is one true moral religion (or faith) that is essentially interior. Rather than trying to deal with all the sources and consequences of this powerful dynamic, I only want to show that the view of human nature required for a sane liturgy can stand on a fairly simple, but accurate, understanding of the demands of the gospel. In the example I shall use, these demands were understood in a particularly exacting way. Still, the life was actually lived by the hermits and men living in small communities in Egypt between about 250 and 500. These men, usually called the *Fathers of the Desert*, through their way of life and their teachings developed the institution of monasticism. Their view of human nature was based on their understanding of the Bible, and this understanding was used, not in the interests of philosophical speculation, but in trying to lead a Christian life; and this is true even if their practice might seem outrageous to many latter-day Christians.

The Fathers of the Egyptian Desert are often looked on as men who despised the body in an un-Christian way. No doubt many of them did get things wrong, but the greatest were acutely conscious that the body had to be looked on as a partner and not as an enemy in their striving to fulfill the will of God. In a remarkable chapter in a remarkable book, Peter Brown has argued that "the mood prevalent among the Desert Fathers" contradicts the view that they were motivated by "contempt of the human condition and hatred of the body".[25]

> In reducing the intake to which he had become accustomed, the ascetic slowly remade his body. He turned it into an exactly calibrated instrument. Its drastic physical changes, after years of ascetic discipline, registered with satisfying precision the essential, preliminary stages of the long return of the human person, body and soul together, to an original, natural and uncorrupted state.[26]

Christians, then, did not need Aristotle and St. Thomas to see that, in order to be human, human beings require a body. The Fathers of the Desert might so easily have come up with the view that the body was in the final analysis nothing but a nuisance. It is this sort of idea that is usually attributed to them. But they went into the desert, not to get rid of the body, but to bring the whole person, body and soul, back to something like the state of Adam and Eve in Paradise. In the writing of these ascetics, "we can sense",

---

[25] Peter Brown, *The Body and Society: Men, Women, and Sexual Renunciation in Early Christianity* (London and Boston: Faber and Faber, 1990), p. 222.
[26] Ibid., p. 223.

says Peter Brown, "the huge weight that the myth of Paradise regained placed on the frail bodies of the ascetics".[27]

> The ascetics imposed severe restraints on their bodies because they were convinced that they could sweep the body into a desperate venture. For the average ascetics . . . the imagined transfiguration of the few great ascetics, on earth, spoke to them of the eventual transformation of their own bodies on the day of the Resurrection.[28]

However we might want to judge the Fathers of the Desert, it should be clear that they thought the body had an indispensable role in their efforts to know "Jesus Christ and him crucified" (1 Cor 2:2).

Earlier in this chapter I said that the liturgy must be modeled on the pattern found in Dionysius' *Divine Names*. God's revelation in Christ gives us a language to enable us to say something meaningful about God, and this language, we might say, points us in the right direction through the shadows and the obscurity back to the hidden God. But this is not all, because "through him, and with him, and in him", we are brought back to "the Father of lights with whom there is no variation or shadow due to change" (Jas 1:17). Even if this is true, however, why is it that the liturgy must be a continuing aspect of our life of prayer? Cannot we look on it as a necessary stage in the development of divine intimacy, but only as a stage?

We can try to deal with this very real difficulty in two stages. The first is to return to the principle of the going out and coming in of all things and to look at it from a slightly different point of view. Liturgy is a representation

[27] Ibid., p. 222.
[28] Ibid.

of this procession and return, and it is only in the here and now of liturgical experience, which takes place in the everyday world, that we encounter this fundamental movement. Secondly, if this is true, then a prayer that seeks to pass beyond images and meaning still requires the movement of going out and coming in, a movement that liturgy embodies and teaches.[29]

The Church is the Kingdom of God "now present in mystery".[30] She is "a kind of sacrament [or sign] of intimate union with God, and of the unity of all mankind";[31] and she is at the same time "an instrument [for the achievement] of such union and unity".[32] And so the Church is truly, in von Balthasar's striking words, "the heart of the world and the earthly representation of the heavenly court".[33] The liturgy of the Eucharist is the source and goal of the heart of the world, and so whatever nonliturgical prayer may be, it must be related to liturgical prayer and not be looked on as an escape from our ordinary humanity.

To say that mystical prayer must be related to liturgical prayer is not to say enough. This is so because there is no Christian prayer outside the Mystical Body of Jesus Christ, and the prayer of Christ's Body represents the gradual return of those being redeemed to the glory of God in our homeland. The most personal, inward prayer or an apparently wordless prayer of the heart does not falsify this principle;

---

[29] Von Balthasar puts this conviction of Dionysius like this: "Everything lies in the circular movement between procession and return, the cataphatic and the apophatic, nothing can find fulfilment except by entering into this movement" (*Glory of the Lord* 2:166).

[30] *Lumen Gentium* 3 (A16).

[31] Ibid., 1 (A15).

[32] Ibid.

[33] Von Balthasar, *Glory of the Lord,* 2:166.

that is, such prayer is still the prayer of the Mystical Body and presupposes and requires praying that is more obviously connected with symbols and meanings. This is the last point to be made in this chapter.

If we go back to our red traffic light, we will remember that it is a symbol that is visible but that it also has a meaning. The Church uses objects such as water, wine, oil, and incense that point beyond themselves to meanings. Unless we see the water, the wine, and the incense within this system of meanings, we may be interested in or even entranced by them, but they will not have a Christian significance. To say, however, that the burning incense symbolizes our prayer rising up to God[34] does not entail our forgetting the visible and olfactory sense impressions, because these are aspects of the human grasp of the symbol.

Suppose, though, we do admit that symbol and meaning should not be separated, what is to prevent our holding that there is a mystical, wordless prayer, a prayer without sensible images of any sort? And, furthermore, why cannot we believe that this prayer ought to be removed from what we may even (mistakenly) call the contamination of sense experience and symbolic meanings? In other words, symbols and meaning are for liturgical prayer, but deep, non-formal prayer of the heart requires only a wordless communion with God.

This is obviously a complex subject, but I do not think there are levels of prayer in quite the way the upholders of isolated, nonliturgical prayer want to maintain. It is always the human being who prays, and without denying, and indeed affirming, the importance of mystical prayer, such

---

[34] Cf. Psalm 141:2: "Let my prayer be counted as incense before you, and the lifting up of my hands as an evening sacrifice!"

prayer is possible only because the particular individual is a Christian who has been nourished, and I would maintain sustained even during his prayer, by biblical symbols and meanings.

Symbols and meaning are required to preserve and direct the consciousness that is drawn into a wordless and image-less prayer. This is not merely a psychological imperative; it is a religious one. "The inexpressible", as Dionysius puts it, is bound up with what can be articulated.[35] Even the most mystical, wordless prayer is only possible with the revelation God himself has given to us, because there is no way for the believer, at any rate, to extricate himself from the great *exitus* and *reditus* that constitute the very nature of reality.

The liturgy, with its splendid symbols of light, of incense, and of bread and wine, points to and expresses the power of Christ's Resurrection. But these symbols do not suddenly become unimportant when we realize they express and point to something more than themselves. It is not as though the material and visible aspect of our worship becomes somehow unspiritual and second-rate when we begin to reflect on the hidden mysteries of our faith. The outward and visible signs bring us the reality and the power of the risen Christ, but that reality and that power are displayed, shown forth, made manifest, found, experienced, in and through what we see, hear, smell, touch, and see. The sacramental and liturgical worship of the Church is God's gift to human beings with bodies and souls. It is God's gift; and our way back to him is through this worship.

---

[35] Pseudo-Dionysius, *Letter Nine*, "To Titus the Hierarch", 1105D, in *Complete Works*, p. 282.

We should not imagine that we are going to become more spiritual by trying to ignore that we are a body with a soul. We should not make the mistake of believing that our prayer will become deeper and more contemplative by trying to pretend we are "really" some sort of ghost, called the soul, in a machine, called the body. We are ensouled bodies, or a soul made into who we are by having this particular body and not another one. We are in the here and now. God is with us in the here and now, and we do not leave our bodies to one side as we find our way back to him. What we perceive and hear are not so many veils or disguises behind which God is hiding. It is, rather, the case that our worship, heavy with the sacred freight of the centuries of Catholic worship, is a necessary, if inadequate, glimpse of what God is. And, the worship of Christ's Church is the only covenanted, or promised, gateway to a deeper and more tenacious grip on the God in whom we live and move and have our being.

The Second Vatican Council taught, as we have seen,[36] that the Church is a sort of eighth sacrament. That is, she is a sign that brings about what it shows or displays. And the worship of the Church is one aspect of this showing forth of God, so that God himself make take us back to himself—not just in Palestine in the first century, not just when we die—but here, now, at this moment in and out of time now and forever.[37]

---

[36] See above, pt. 1, chap. 3.

[37] Cf. T. S. Eliot, *Four Quartets* (London: Faber and Faber, 1979), p. 4: "Burnt Norton":

> "Time past and time future
> What might have been and what has been
> Point to one end, which is always present."

CHAPTER THREE

From Communal Divinity
to the Holy Community

> Although it may be misunderstood, man seems to have
> access to something good, to find the possibility of union,
> in the tender love of a comrade in mortality; and even if
> this love is itself open to corruption, still it is a distant,
> weak echo of the love of God and embraces a phantom
> only because of the Good.... Through the very form
> of unity and love, man already possesses a shadowy share
> in the Good.
>
> —Maximus the Confessor, *In De Divinis Nominibus*

Hegel's development of the idea of community in the *Phenomenology* and elsewhere has been the basis of a welcome development of theories that focus on humanity and its needs and aspirations. Hegel made a profound and lasting contribution with his arguments that community is an integral and necessary aspect of being a human being. A community is not a more or less desirable extra for those with a gregarious nature. It is, on the contrary, an essential element in what it means to be human. It is obvious that Hegel's sort of thinking has had an enormous influence on Catholic thought, because, in this case anyway, it is such a powerful restatement of the traditional view that man is a social animal and that only a god or an animal can live in isolation.

> The proof that the state is a creation of nature and prior to
> the individual is that the individual, when isolated, is not
> self-sufficing; and therefore he is like a part in relation to a
> whole. But he who is unable to live in society, or who has
> no need because he is sufficient for himself, must be either
> a beast or a god.[1]

The desire for solitude has always been treated with reserve
in the Church, because all too often it has its source in a
desire to abstract oneself from the everyday checks and bal-
ances that living with other people imposes. The traditional spirituality of the Church taught that there must be
an extended training in the virtues before attempting a sol-
itary life, and developing the virtues requires a community
of some sort.

> For a man appears to himself to be patient and humble, just
> as long as he comes across nobody in intercourse; but he
> will presently revert to his former nature, whenever the
> chance of any sort of passion occurs.... For when the oppor-
> tunity for practising [the virtues] among men is removed,
> our faults will more and more increase in us, unless we
> have been purified from them.[2]

On the other hand, Hegel's emphasis on community was
bought, as we have seen,[3] at too high a price. It was bought
at too high a price because Hegel taught explicitly that community is not only essential for human living; it is also

[1] Aristotle, *Politics*, bk. 1, chap. 2, 1253a 24.

[2] John Cassian, *Institutes of the Coenobia*, bk. 8, chap. 18, in *Nicene and
Post-Nicene Fathers*, 2nd series, ed. Philip Schaff and Henry Wace (Grand
Rapids, Mich.: Eerdmans, 1979–1983), 11:262. See my *Spiritual Combat Revisited* (San Francisco: Ignatius Press, 2003), pp. 261 ff., for a reference to this
text and a discussion of this point.

[3] See above, pt. 1, chap. 5, "Hegel: God Becomes the Community".

required for God to be himself. The community Hegel was really interested in was the state in its ethical dimension; and it was only a matter of time before people began to wonder, quite explicitly, whether God was anything more than a human construct or human projection.

Faced with this development, there are some Catholics who back away from the emphasis on community and try to reassert the transcendence of God and of the worship due to him in a way that seems to undermine the incarnational and social dimensions of the Church. That is, faced time and time again with what Bishop Garriga called auto-celebrations,[4] they come to the conclusion that something has gone seriously wrong, and in this they are right. But then, unhappily, this sometimes leads to the creation of an attitude that in practice seems to want to create a liturgical life that is hermetically sealed off from the world around them with its needs and aspirations.

This will not do, because the attitude itself is fundamentally un-Catholic.

The first and great commandment is to love God with all our heart and mind and soul, and the final purpose of the Christian community is to teach this lesson and to practice it in the worship of God. But there is a second commandment that has to do with loving our neighbor. St. John insists that if we do not love the brother whom we have seen, then we are not going to be able to love God, whom we have not seen (1 Jn 4:20). Yet without a supernatural motivation, the effort to live a community life in any Christian sense is doomed to failure; without the effort to obey the Commandments, there is no Christian community.

[4] See above, introduction: "Wingless Chickens", p. 34.

Newman put this clearly to his fellow Oratorians in Birmingham: "Our only life as a *body*, consists in our sanctification, as individuals." [5] Community costs something; and what it costs is the effort to respond to God's call to live as he wants us to live. However we are going to understand *community* in a natural or secular setting, it should be clear that more than this natural or secular understanding is required for the community to merit being called Christian. The characters of the members of a secular association or group may be admirable; the natural society they constitute may serve many useful purposes; and their intellectual aims be impeccable. Their association may even deserve to be called, in some sense, a community, but it is not a Christian one. In fact, it would probably be better if Catholics avoided using the word *community* about these groups.

If the community is to be Christian, then its foundations and its purposes must be Christian. It is true that community living involves reaching out to other people for whom, often enough, we may have no temperamental, sociological, or intellectual affinity; but this reaching out to others is a consequence of our belief that Christianity necessitates the effort to love other people. Successful community living requires a supernatural or a transcendental reference. The only way a community can be Christian, at least in the sense of displaying the seeds of inclusiveness, is to base itself on Jesus Christ and the demands of Christian living. That is to say, the Christian community must find its source in the celebration of the Paschal Mystery, and the celebration of this mystery demands that the individuals who make up the community make some effort to live the new life

[5] John Henry Newman, chapter address, 1853, in Placid Murray, O.S.B., *Newman the Oratorian* (Dublin: Gill and Macmillan, 1969), p. 239.

that Christ's victory over sin and death has brought to mankind. The worthy celebration of the Paschal Mystery, that is, requires some form of ethical realism. "For Christ, our Paschal Lamb, has been sacrificed. Let us, therefore, celebrate the festival, not with the old leaven, the leaven of malice and evil, but with the unleavened bread of sincerity and truth" (1 Cor 5:7–8). A community without this transcendental reference is not a Christian community.

Once again Newman puts the matter in the right way:

> An Oratory is an individuality. It has one will and one action, and in that sense it is one community. But it is obvious that such a union of wills and minds and opinions and conduct cannot be attained without considerable concessions of private judgment on the part of every individual so united. *It is a conformity, then, not of accident or nature, but of supernatural purpose and self-mastery.*[6]

We can see Newman's thoroughly traditional and valid ideas about community, and about the proper ordering of the love of God and the love of neighbor, by considering the Carthusian martyrs under Henry VIII. The London Charterhouse was a group of men who tried to put God first and, as a result, were welded into a community that was so strong that the only way it could be broken was by killing off its members. My discussion is, if you will, an ostensive definition. I have no formal or essential definition to offer of *community*. One viable sense of the word is a religious community such as I describe in this chapter. Another acceptable usage would be small groupings of people in the country that we still call rural communities. However, I have no idea what the word is supposed to signify in

---

[6] "Remarks on the Oratorian Vocation", in ibid., p. 334 (my italics).

a large modern industrial city. Certainly, I think the practice of tacking on community to such words as *parish* or
even *diocese* does nothing for clarity and does not seem to
me to describe anything more than the wish of some Catholics to find a group of like-minded people. There is nothing wrong with the wish in itself, but I cannot see that it
has anything necessarily to do with a cell in the Mystical
Body of Jesus Christ. Furthermore, creating a community
with sinews, be it religious or secular, is a much more difficult business than many who use the word seem to imagine.

In February 1535 the English Parliament had passed the
Treason Act, under the terms of which a charge of high
treason could be brought against anyone who denied, or
who even refused to acknowledge, that the king was supreme
head on earth of the Church in England. Commissioners
were sent to all the religious houses, including the London
Charterhouse, to require acknowledgment of the king's
supremacy. The prior, St. John Houghton, had set aside
three days of preparation to decide how they were to respond
to the commissioners; on the first, all made a general con-
fession; on the second, all, led by Houghton himself, asked
pardon of each of his brethren in turn for all offenses; on
the third, the prior sang a Mass of the Holy Spirit for
guidance.

> When he did so, and the moment came for the elevation of
> the consecrated Host, all felt in their hearts, and to some it
> seemed that they heard, either as a gust of wind or as an
> echo of harmony, a breath of the Spirit Whose counsel they
> had implored. The celebrant was for some minutes unable
> to continue the Mass, and at the subsequent chapter he spoke
> of his experience thankfully indeed, but with an exhorta-
> tion that all should abide in God's grace with prayer, hum-
> ble and fearful. His own constant prayer was that of Christ

for His disciples: "Holy Father, keep them whom thou hast given me in thy name."[7]

The Carthusians determined not to take the oath. They were tried at the end of April, condemned for treason, and sentenced to death. They died, eighteen in all, either the appalling death of being partially hanged, then disemboweled while still conscious, and finally dismembered,[8] or else they were chained to a stake and left to starve to death in the Tower of London.[9]

In the first place, the monks put the love of God before everything else. They had led an austere, observant community life centered on the Eucharist, the Divine Office, and an intense life of personal prayer. They understood the oath that was being required of them as a denial of the faith they had lived for, and they were prepared to die for it.

It seems clear that in taking this decision they were influenced solely by their conviction that a matter of divine faith was at stake. The Carthusian Order, as such, was in no direct dependence on the papacy, as were the orders of Friars. Nor had Houghton and his companions any concern with

[7] David Knowles, *The Religious Orders in England*, vol. 3, *The Tudor Age* (Cambridge: Cambridge University Press, 1959), p. 230.

[8] "Houghton, the first to die, ... bore the agony of the butchery, aggravated by the tough hair shirt, with what seemed a more than human patience; conscious to the end he died invoking the Lord he had loved and followed to the Cross. He was forty-eight years of age" (ibid., p. 232).

[9] "The first martyrs had been executed as a public spectacle. The publicity had not told against them, and the second group had been dispatched without advertisement. The third and most numerous band was denied even the dignity of a formal trial and execution. They had asked to live as hidden servants of Christ; they died, silent witnesses to His words, hidden from the eyes of all. Chained without possibility of movement in a foul atmosphere, and systematically starved, they were left, as Bedyll put it, to 'be dispeched by thand (sic) of God'" (ibid., p. 235).

the unity of Christian nations, whatever may have been the case with More.... All that can be extracted from Houghton's notes and record sources goes to show that the Carthusian priors and their followers, many of them men of education and wide reading, stood purely and simply by the traditional faith of the Church in the divine commission to Peter. They were thus in the most literal sense martyrs of the faith.[10]

If the monks died for the love of God, it was because they had kept the Second Commandment. "The prior was regarded as a saint by those who knew him in the years when a martyr's death for one in the London Charterhouse would have seemed an impossibility",[11] and "the monks whom Houghton guided were as a body worthy of their prior."

He himself looked upon them as angels of God, and visitors who sought of them counsel and help involuntarily echoed the words of the patriarch: "verily God is in this place." It was commonly said that if a man wished to hear the divine service carried out with due reverence he should visit the London Charterhouse. The rules of fasting and silence were kept in their strictness, and such alleviations as the fire in the cell were often forgone save in extreme cold. The night choirs in winter, where the lessons were long, began after ten and lasted till three in the morning.[12]

The example I have chosen is an example about exceptional men in exceptional circumstances. Yet the example does illustrate very clearly that the love of God must be the object of a Christian's life, while at the same time showing

[10] Ibid., p. 231.
[11] Ibid., p. 226.
[12] Ibid.

that love of neighbor is required if the first love is to be anything more than a formula. The Carthusians' love for their common life, for each other, and for the people who relied on them[13] was the means through which they learned the love of God.

Most of us are not even remotely like the Carthusian martyrs, but they provide us an example of the love of God, trained by a religious rule, it is true, but lived out in the love of those around them and joined together in their common aim that "in everything God may be glorified through Jesus Christ" (1 Pet 4:11).

The words of *Sacrosanctum Concilium* sum up much of what I have been saying and remind us that the mystery of Christ's sacrifice must be at the center of our worship and at the center of our lives, both personal and communal:

> For it is through the liturgy, especially in the divine Eucharistic Sacrifice, that "the work of our redemption is exercised." The liturgy is thus the outstanding means by which the faithful can express in their lives, and manifest to others, the mystery of Christ and the real nature of the true Church.[14]

Awe and reverence in the liturgy are not produced to order; they must be the consequence of people trying to

---

[13] "Lying as it did at the edge of the city, with its orchards and gardens running up among the town houses of the great, the Charterhouse could scarcely fail to be a centre of religious influence. The solemn devotion of the liturgy, the contrast between the silence and austerity there and the noisy, restless, ambitious and sordid whirl of the city streets, the presence within its walls of a number of men of gentle birth and high abilities, attracted to its gatehouse many of the *âmes d'élite* of the time, and facilities seem to have been given for those in need of spiritual direction to visit and confess themselves to the priests, and even to make a prolonged stay in the guest quarters" (ibid., p. 224).

[14] *Sacrosanctum Concilium* 2 (A137).

lead serious Christian lives. I say "trying to lead" because sin and moral failure generally are so bound up with the human condition that it is idle chatter to say that we must be perfect before we begin to take God, and the worship of God, seriously. If some hint of the attitudes that animated the Carthusians could direct modern worship, then most of our problems would be over. However, there are some practical suggestions I have to make that would go a long way to restoring a worship of God that is worthy of him.

CHAPTER FOUR

MR. RYDER COMES TO TOWN

The great historian of the Council of Trent, Hubert Jedin, pointed ... out in 1975, in the preface to the last volume of his history of the Council of Trent: "The attentive reader ... in reading this will not be less dismayed than the author, when he realises that many of the things—in fact almost everything—that disturbed the men of the past is being put forward anew today." It is only against this background of the effective denial of the authority of Trent, that the bitterness of the struggle against allowing the celebration of Mass according to the 1962 Missal, after the liturgical reform, can be understood. The possibility of so celebrating constitutes the strongest, and thus (for them) the most intolerable contradiction of the opinion of those who believe that the faith in the Eucharist formulated by Trent has lost its value.

—Joseph Cardinal Ratzinger, *Looking Again at the Question of the Liturgy with Cardinal Ratzinger*

In *Brideshead Revisited*, Charles Ryder recounts how he earned a good living by painting pictures of country houses just before the wreckers moved in. Harassed by death duties, higher taxes, the Depression of the thirties, and reduced incomes, the owners decided to give up and demolish their homes. Naturally enough, they wanted a keepsake of their home, which to them was more than bricks and mortar; rather, it embodied a way of life and was a treasury of the experiences and memories of their families. Once the house was gone, there remained nothing but Ryder's pictures and the fading memories of the last generation to have lived in the house.[1]

If someone today were to visit the actual site of the vanished building, he might find that some of the materials had been used to construct a no-nonsense edifice designed to serve the needs of the local community. The satisfaction of these needs, of course, would necessitate a certain degree of planning and direction to ensure that these aims were in fact secured. Suppose, for example, the materials of the house had been used to produce a center to accommodate a food bank for the poor of the neighborhood, classrooms for English as a second language, a day-care center, and a shelter for battered women, perhaps even a "quiet room" for "personal reflection". The harmonious satisfaction of the different purposes would have required rules to coordinate the bringing about of these diverse ends. It would be clear, however, that it was the community and its perceived needs that dictated how the remains of the house had been used.

Most people will agree that a home and a community center are not the same thing. Furthermore, it is quite possible to admit they are different and to hold that the new building is of much greater value than a house devoted to the needs of one family. No doubt, there are many aspects of the house reflected and incorporated architectural and aesthetic

---

[1] "After my first exhibition I was called to all parts of the country to make portraits of houses that were soon to be deserted or debased; indeed, my arrival seemed often to be only a few paces ahead of the auctioneer's, a presage of doom" (Evelyn Waugh, *Brideshead Revisited* [Boston: Little, Brown, 1999], p. 216).

values that it is sad to lose. Nonetheless, nostalgia for a past that has disappeared is no reason to halt the development of progress and a more rational use of resources, nor should it blind us to the fact that an image of genteel living had obscured from our eyes the harsh outlines of ordinary existence.

Writing about the liturgy today is like discussing the community center, which is real and in place, and one of Ryder's pictures, which is a fixed reproduction of something that no longer exists. The community center provides a locale where people can actively participate in the life of their community, whereas the picture is only a reminder, so it will be said, of the élitist interests of a leisured and moneyed class.[2] If we criticize the community center in terms of comfort, beauty, or architecture, we will be told that we are making a category mistake. That is, we are applying criteria to the building that are irrelevant. If, for example, I order a ton of gravel to repair a country road, the seller will not be impressed if I refuse the load because all the stones are a dull gray. It is the quantity of the stone that matters, not their color. In a similar way most criticisms of the new liturgy are dismissed because they are said to be irrelevant and show the critic to be unaware of the pastoral and communitarian aspects of the new liturgical arrangements.

Suppose, though, it could be shown that the country house in fact embodied important values and had a function that the community center had not managed to incorporate. If this were the case then, without denying the real values of the new center, it would still be defective if it were looked

---

[2] Perhaps, although it is unlikely, a liturgist might quote the haunting line of T. S. Eliot: "These things have served their purpose: let them be" ("Little Gidding", *Four Quartets* [London: Faber and Faber, 1979], p. 38).

on as an adequate replacement for what had gone before. It can be argued that the lives of some at least of the families who owned such houses embodied moral and intellectual values that were important for the life of society. Community centers are not a home where children are loved and brought up in the tradition of the family who has lived in the house over the years. A family rears its children to live in a certain way, and that way of living also affects the community around it. It is not a question of liking or wanting to copy this tradition; it is merely to point out that the new center does not fulfill this function.

The Old Rite of Mass is like the country house. That is, in many ways it needed refurbishing and even some reconstruction, but it did fulfill its stated function, which was the worship of God the Father, in which Christ himself makes present the mystery of his own Passion and death, his Resurrection and Ascension into glory, and in which the Holy Spirit cooperates with the Church to manifest Christ and his work of salvation.[3]

The intent of the liturgical reform undertaken by the Second Vatican Council was to enhance the celebration of the Paschal Mystery, not to diminish it. The dogmatic constitution *Sacrosanctum Concilium* represented a response to a widely held conviction that the liturgy was in need of a reform that would bring out the community aspect of the Mass and the other sacraments as well as make them more effective in teaching the truths of the Catholic faith. On the other hand, judging at least from the document itself, it is clear that the bishops did not intend that the entire house should be pulled down and a new edifice constructed.

[3] CCC 1099.

There were legitimate reasons for the changes envisaged in *Sacrosanctum Concilium*. All too often what the Sunday Mass in many parishes was like is forgotten by traditionally minded people. No doubt there were exceptional parishes, but the following description by a somewhat disapproving critic of what he calls "Triumphal-era American Catholicism"[4] eloquently exemplifies why it was thought change was necessary:

> To outsiders, the Latin Mass was Kabuki Theater—static and incomprehensible. That millions knelt unprotestingly through the Mass Sunday after Sunday confirmed secularists in their conviction that Catholics were inert hordes. But the details of the Latin hardly mattered to a lifelong Catholic. The stately cadences of the Mass were carved deep in neural pathways and had a clear dramatic structure . . . the total experience—the dim lights, the glint of the vestments, the glow of the stained glass windows, the mantralike murmur of the Latin—was mind-washing. It calmed the soul, opened the spirit to large, barely grasped Presences and Purposes. For a trembling moment every week, or every day if they chose, ordinary people reached out and touched the Divine.[5]

It was this sort of celebration that the liturgists set out to improve, and there was no doubt it needed improving. Instead of improvement, though, there has been loss: a diminishment of that ability "to reach out and touch the Divine" that was once the central thrust of the liturgy. It seems to me to be a waste of time wondering whether or not it was inevitable that liturgical reform should alter this numinous character of Catholic worship, or whether the *Novus Ordo* was drawn up specifically to diminish or destroy this

---

[4] Charles R. Morris, *American Catholic* (Toronto: Random House, 1997), p. 174.
[5] Ibid., p. 175.

transcendental reference; the fact is that this is what has happened. It has been said that *Sacrosanctum Concilium* was a largely conservative document but "carried within it, encased in the innocuous language of pastoral welfare, some seeds of its own destruction".[6] The "seeds of its own destruction" were its emphasis on community, which has so quickly been debased into just one more social grouping, and, closely allied with this, the conviction that liturgy was essentially about instruction. The Mass, it was thought, is a particularly effective way of promoting different sorts of causes by educating people in various sorts of ways.

The imposition of the reforms according to norms that went far beyond anything even suggested by the Council, and in a high-handed and insensitive manner, has certainly verified the truth of Fr. Nichols' observation. The new versions of the liturgy have been accompanied, on the one hand, by indifference to the claims of the Church and a widespread apostasy; and, on the other, by cries for the return of what many call "the Mass of All Time".

It should be noted with regard to the question of indifference and apostasy that I have not argued for a direct causal connection between the implementation of the reforms and the widespread abandonment of the practice of Catholicism. I believe that the way the liturgical reforms were implemented has undoubtedly been a factor in bringing about the present condition of the Church, but I do not think the entire blame for this situation of the Church can be laid directly at the door of the liturgy. The situation is more complex than this, because the principles behind the changes were the result of absorption by many in the Church of ways of thinking that are incompatible with Catholicism.

---

[6] Aidan Nichols, O.P., *A Pope and a Council on the Sacred Liturgy* (Farnborough: Saint Michael's Abbey Press, 2002), p. 12.

In the previous chapters of this book, I have tried to untangle some of the factors that have created the mind-set leading to the liturgical chaos and banality that is all around us, at least in the English-speaking world. I have also argued that the most important factor in creating the present unhappy situation was a misreading of the modern world by those responsible for creating and implementing the norms for the implementation of the liturgical reform. The cultural and intellectual climate of opinion was not understood or, if understood, then misused, both by those who first imposed the reforms and, then, by the various liturgical committees who continued this work. I have shown how diverse this cultural and intellectual climate was and just how many elements that were indifferent, when not hostile, to Christianity it in fact contained. It is these elements that have infected the approach of those in control of the liturgy. Cardinal Ratzinger minced no words when he said:

> The thesis according to which it is the community itself which is the subject of the Liturgy, serves as an authorization to manipulate the Liturgy according to each individual's understanding of it. So-called new discoveries and the forms which follow from them, are diffused with an astonishing rapidity and with a degree of conformity which has long ceased to exist where the norms of ecclesiastical authority are concerned. Theories, in the area of Liturgy, are transformed very rapidly into practice, and practice, in turn, creates or destroys ways of behaving and thinking.[7]

It is hardly surprising in the face of all this that there is cry for a return to "the way things used to be". The expression "the way things used to be" usually means a wish for

[7] Joseph Ratzinger, in *Looking Again at the Question of the Liturgy with Cardinal Ratzinger*, ed. Alcuin Reid, O.S.B. (Farnborough: St. Michael's Abbey Press, 2003), p. 21.

the return of the Old Rite of Mass. It may be true that sometimes this wish is little more than the expression of a rather precious antiquarianism, but all too often it is an anguished plea for a liturgy that draws the worshipper into the hidden mysteries of God made visible in Christ.

I have two things to say in regard to the demand for the wholesale return to the Old Rite. In the first place, I understand and sympathize with the causes for the demand. Faced with bizarre celebrations of Mass and the other sacraments that are sometimes hardly Christian, much less Catholic, it is not surprising that a significant minority of Catholics have fought for a return to the Old Rite. It can seem today to be a choice between either the Old Rite or an intolerable situation. Yet, as understandable as it may be, I do not think a return to the Old Rite would be either practical or sound. Even if the use of the rite of 1962 became much more common than it is, this would only represent a return to the situation that brought about the need for the reforms initiated by Vatican II. It was not infidelity, stupidity, and lack of historical sense that prompted the reforms; which is not to say I think they were entirely successful. Nonetheless, the reforms actually called for by the Council were the work of people who cared about the worship of God, and there were many aspects of the old liturgy that even conservatively minded people hoped would change. A full-scale return to the rite of 1962, even if such a move were within the bounds of possibility (and I do not think it is), would fail because such a return would only re-create the situation that many found so inadequate in the middle decades of the last century. Indeed, the fact that the texts and rubrics of the Old Rite have been immobilized at 1962 means that even developments that are clearly necessary would be difficult to make. A reform of the old calendar,

for example, is certainly called for even if only to provide
for the saying of the Mass of saints canonized since 1962.[8]
It is difficult to see how even more substantial changes could
be made in the Old Rite without causing suspicion and
more dissension.

There is, however, a second reason for thinking that such
a return would not work. The Old Rite is no longer central to the mentality of most practicing Catholics today; and
in fact, when most contemporary Catholics actually attend
an Old Rite Mass for the first time, it appears strange and
foreign to them. That is not to deny that some of them
may like it; that is not the point. The crucial fact is that the
Old Rite is no longer the central point of spiritual reference for most Catholics; they have to be *brought to* the Old
Rite. It is not the point from which they start when they
think about the worship of God. So, while it is true that
the Old Rite taught or reflected a Catholic perspective on
human life and society and contains a great many elements
that modern Catholic worship lacks, nonetheless it is also
true that the Church has to live in the particular historical
epoch in which she finds herself, and at the present time in
North America, at least, there seems to be no widespread
desire for the return of the Old Rite.

There are those who will say that the question of what
people want is not the point and that priests ought to
have the courage to provide the people with "real Catholic
worship". People who talk this way have no sense of the
realities of parish life. The London Oratorian Fr. Frederick
Faber used to say: "All change is for the worse, even when

---

[8] It was said to me, in all seriousness, that the Mass of Padre Pio (who was
canonized in 2003), for example, could be said as a votive Mass on a ferial
day—if one felt so inclined. That is hardly a happy solution and points to a
real need for development.

it is change for the better", and, odd as the proposition may sound, it has to be remembered by anyone actually trying to build up parish life and to not destroy it. There must be liturgical change, but it must be done slowly and must be carefully thought about. More violent change is the last thing we need in the Church today.

If this general recommendation is to have any chance of success, then it must be applied with some knowledge of the realities of parish life. Anyone faced with actually leading a parish, not writing about how it should be done or dictating to others how it must be done, is faced with at least four fundamental ways of looking at things among his people. There are those who want a steady diet of change, and for these people even the slender structure of the rubrics in the *Novus Ordo* is looked on as an intolerable restraint on the development of "meaningful celebrations". Then there are some who want the Old Rite back, and for these even an impeccable celebration of the *Novus Ordo* in Latin is an unsatisfactory substitute for "the real thing". Then there is a large group of those who still go to Mass and for whom "fellowship" or community events seems to be most important. Finally, there are those who want a liturgy that has at least elements of worship in it and that does not change all the time. It does not show courage deliberately to alienate three of these groups in the interests of the Old Rite. It manifests irresponsibility, not to use a stronger word. Things have to change, but on the ground at the parish level, if one may put it that way, this is not as easy a thing to do as those who sit on liturgical committees or who only write books about liturgy seem to imagine.

Things can change, and things must change, but the renewal of the liturgy cannot be addressed merely at the level of the liturgy itself. Angry arguments about fidelity or the lack of it, openness or its absence, conservatism or liberalism, produce much heat and little light. The deformation of the liturgy has to be understood as the result of cultural and intellectual forces that will have to be recognized before anything very serious can be accomplished in the way of serious liturgical reform.

I am not arguing that the present liturgical situation is nothing but an innocent end product of a misreading of the modern world; nor is it even essentially a pardonable capitulation to forces in modernity that could no longer be withstood. On the contrary, present liturgical practice has in fact reinforced a good deal of the anti-God initiatives and false teaching about community. In this way the liturgy itself has exemplified and deepened modern trends that in my view are destructive, not merely of liturgy, but of the Catholic world view itself.

The perennial attraction of the Old Rite is that it provided a transcendental reference, and it did this even when it was misused in various ways. Take the Mass at Versailles in the presence of the king in the eighteenth century. The king sat in a tribune that was more prominent than the altar; "at each end there was a sort of pagoda of gilded wood set in a semi-circular projection—the king knelt in the left hand one, the queen in the right." [9] On occasion

the great nobles formed a vast circle at the foot of the altar and stood, backs towards the priest and the holy mysteries, their faces turned towards their King, who is seen kneeling in a tribune, and to whom they seem to be directing all their mind and all their heart. This usage, you can hardly avoid realizing, implies a sort of subordination, for the people

[9] John McManners, *Church and Society in Eighteenth-Century France* (Oxford: Clarendon Press, 1998), 1:42.

seem to be worshipping the prince, and the prince worshipping God.[10]

Yet even in this center of absolute political power and
in a setting designed to teach a message of royal absolut-
ism, the Mass itself held its own. When I say the Mass
held its own, I mean that it was not merely a celebration
of the community awareness of itself; it was a living testimony that there was another power that even the absolute monarch was forced to acknowledge. It may have been
true that rendering to Caesar the things that were Caesar's
was the thought uppermost in the minds of many who
attended the celebration; nonetheless, the Mass itself was a
reminder of the things that are not Caesar's. The saying of
Mass even at the center of one of the most splendid centers of earthly power and civilization was a testimony to
the transcendence of God, to the reality of the Incarnation, and to the work of Holy Spirit in creating a community that was more glorious than even the court of
Versailles. The Old Rite, even when badly said, did fulfill
its basic function, which was the worship of God the Father
through making present the reality of Christ's saving death,
Resurrection, and Ascension into glory. It may not always
have gotten its message across very effectively, and the Mass
at Versailles is a case in point, but the message was always
there, no matter how carelessly, stupidly, or perhaps, sometimes, wickedly the Mass was used.

The fact of the matter is, though, that just as the country house was pulled down, so the backbone of the Old
Rite has been broken. It follows from this that an effort to
reform the liturgy at the pastoral level has to begin from

[10] Ibid. McManners is citing La Bruyère.

where things are now; and where things are now is best described as involving some version of the *Novus Ordo*. Once again, this has nothing to do with the way one might wish things to be; it has to do with the way things are.

The New Rite can still be seen to enshrine the Paschal Mystery when it is said in a traditional manner. Tradition is not the same thing as development, although it does develop. Newman taught in *An Essay on the Development of Christian Doctrine* that tradition has two aspects; there is a something handed on (in Latin, the *traditum*); and there is the process or activity of handing on this *traditum* (in Latin, *tradere*). Newman's theory requires careful handling, but we can say that today many of those working in liturgy seem to have forgotten there is anything more to tradition than an activity of development with no fixed points of reference in the past, or at least any fixed references that should affect liturgical practice today.[11]

It must be said in fairness to those who want the Old Rite back that there is one element of the reform that seems intent on breaking with any sort of tradition and that this seems to leave the way open to endless experiment and change. *Notitiae* is the publication of the Congregation for Divine Worship, and over the years it has given authoritative interpretations of the Missal of Paul VI. Some of its work is often cited as a case in point. For example, in dealing with the question of the proper way to incense the altar at Mass, we find:

---

[11] I have tried to work out some of the implications of Newman's theory in relation to the development of the spiritual life in *On the Lord's Appearing* (Washington, D.C.: Catholic University of America Press, 1997), pp. 9–34. There I stress the importance of what has been called "the control of the object" for any theory of development.

It must never be forgotten that the Missal of Pope Paul VI has, since 1970, supplanted[12] the one called improperly "the Missal of St. Pius V", and completely so, in both texts and rubrics. When the rubrics of the Missal of Paul VI say nothing or say little on particulars in some places, it is not to be inferred that the former rite should be observed. Therefore, the multiple and complex gestures for incensation as prescribed in the former Missal are not to be resumed. [The text then goes on to legislate how the incensation is to be done.][13]

It is not the legality of the changes in the rules themselves that gives cause for concern so much as the philosophy behind the changes, which seems determined to emphasize novelty over continuity. This is puzzling because, often at the same time, we are told that "nothing has really changed."

When I claim that Mass should be said in a traditional manner, I am not referring directly to particular rubrics, but I do mean that it should be said in a way that reflects the transcendence of God, the supernatural character of the worshipping community (that is, the fact that it is called into being by God), as well as the Catholic view of the reality of sin and of the mercy of God and of the sacrifice of Christ. I also believe that the unfortunate truth of the matter is, more often than not, that the reforms have produced a liturgy that does none of these things: there is no message either in word or action about the transcendent God; the community at prayer is envisaged merely as the local community; and the great Christian mystery of the redemption of mankind through the sacrifice of Christ seems

---

[12] *Supplanted*: I do not know who translated the Latin, but *supplant* in English has the sense of "to trip up or cause to stumble" or, more usually, "to dispossess and take the place of (another), especially by dishonorable means".

[13] Notitiae—Notices on the General Instruction of the Roman Missal (1969–1981), no. 51, Not. 14 (1978), 301–2, no. 2.

to be regarded as an embarrassing relic of an unenlightened age.[14]

The New Rite leaves a great deal too much to the initiative of the celebrant or to his local liturgical committee. The result of this, not surprisingly, is that the way the Eucharist is celebrated from one parish to another differs enormously. The *Catechism* lists several different names for the Mass, each of which "evokes certain aspects" of its "inexhaustible richness".[15] These include: the Eucharist, the Lord's Supper, the Breaking of Bread, the Eucharistic assembly (synaxis), the memorial of the Lord's Passion and Resurrection, Holy Communion, and Mass. It is clear that the *Catechism* means to teach that these terms are in no way contradictory; rather, they mutually support and enrich one another. So they do against a background, or within the context, of a theology of the Paschal Mystery that unites the meaning of the different terms and should thus give a recognizable cohesion to the celebration. When, however, one of the various descriptions becomes dominant, often to the exclusion of the others, then the result is not only liturgical anarchy, but the virtual denial of a Catholic understanding of the Mass. The essential point here is to see that such diversity is compatible with the *Novus Ordo* as it is in fact mandated. There is nothing in the rules governing the way the *Novus Ordo* is to be said that ensures this centrality of the celebration of the Paschal Mystery; and what should be the

---

[14] There is an interesting and helpful discussion about *traditio* and *tradere* in Geoffrey Hull, *The Banished Heart: Origins of Heteropraxis in the Catholic Church* (Sefton, Australia: Robert Burton, 1996), pp. 193–212. There is much to be learned from this book, but apart from the author's conclusions (which are pessimistic, to put it mildly), I think he overestimates what the *traditio* of tradition actually teaches us about liturgy.

[15] CCC 1328.

fundamental thrust of the liturgy is often overlooked or in practice denied. However undesirable this may be from the theological point of view, and for the health of the Church, the fact is there is nothing in the rubrics of the *Novus Ordo* to prevent this from happening.[16]

It seems to me irrelevant to speculate on whether this situation is the result of deliberate planning, indifference to theological principles, or a de facto if hidden conviction that liturgy does not really matter very much except as a way to manipulate people. The fact of the matter is that it is difficult to criticize what goes on in church solely on the grounds of the new Sacramentary; that is to say, the Sacramentary is so porous that it leaves the way open for celebrations that in practice deny the purported aims of the liturgy constitution that called forth the *Novus Ordo*.

The difficulty of achieving a proper balance between the immediate needs of a community and a recognition and celebration of what gives meaning to the very existence of the community is an old and a difficult one. Yet the community that celebrates the liturgy has been called together by God; and the liturgy celebrated by the people of God must be more than a celebration of the particular community. It is clear that a great deal hangs on what we understand by the idea of *community* and how we see it as exemplified, or practiced, in the liturgy.

The notion of the people of God, as we saw in the chapter "From Communal Divinity to the Holy Community", is

[16] "There is a weakness militating against the perception of continuity in the revised rite. This weakness is in a word rubrical. Rubrics, of course, are not an end in themselves: they presuppose the existence and the role of actions in the Mass. If some of the requirements of the previous Mass could do with simplifying, what the revised Mass needs is more rubrics or at any rate more detailed ones" (Derek Hanshell, in *Sacred Music*, vol. 3, no. 1, p. 13).

a religious concept, not a naturalistic one. One of the names for the celebration of the Eucharist is *synaxis*, or gathering; and Dionysius singles this out as the key aspect of the Eucharist:

> Let us reverently behold what is above all characteristic of this (that is, the Eucharist), though also of the other hierarchic sacraments, namely, that which is especially referred to as "communion" and "gathering" (*synaxis*). Every sacredly initiating operation draws our fragmented lives together in a one-like divinization. It forges a divine unity out of the divisions within us.[17]

We seem to be faced with the following situation. On the one hand, for a variety of reasons, a full-scale return to the Old Rite is neither possible nor desirable; yet, on the other hand, the New Rite has failed to win hearts in the way the Old Rite used to do, nor is it succeeding in its aim of presenting through its actions and words the sacrifice of Christ that takes away the sins of the world. I think the only way out of this morass is to move the *Novus Ordo* to what the Old Rite in fact was: the worship of the transcendent God, through participating in the sacrifice of his Son. The role of the Old Rite in this will be to provide a standard of worship, of mystery, and of catechesis toward which the celebrations of the *Novus Ordo* must be moved.[18]

---

[17] *Ecclesiastical Hierarchy* 424C, in Pseudo-Dionysius, *The Complete Works*, trans. Colm Luibhéid (New York: Paulist Press, 1987), p. 209.

[18] "The regaining of the 'inwardness of mystery' is not to be accomplished for the whole Church—and we can be concerned with nothing less—by the retention merely of the old, 'Tridentine' Mass in what could easily become a backwater of Catholicism. It is because it is vital for the fostering of the whole sacral tradition of the Church that the Latin Mass must be a mainstream activity" (Derek Hanshell, "Resacralisation", in *A Voice for All Time*, ed. Christopher Francis and Martin Lynch [Bristol: Association for Latin Liturgy, 1994], p. 203).

CHAPTER FIVE

"Know What You Are Doing"

"Know what you are doing, and imitate the mystery you celebrate: Model your life on the mystery of the Lord's cross."

— From the Rite of Ordination of a Priest

I will now spell out some of the consequences of my contention that the celebration of the *Novus Ordo* must be developed to include characteristics of the Old Rite. The most important of these characteristics is the capacity of the Old Rite to teach the transcendence of God and at the same time to inculcate a sense of Christ's salvific work in the Mass through the operation of the Holy Spirit. The Old Rite does this in a variety of ways that lead the worshipper beyond the immediate ceremonies of the Rite itself to a contemplative encounter with "the nameless God of many names".[1]

By contemplative here I mean an experience that is a largely wordless, serene, and attentive prayer to the presence of God. There is nothing extraordinary about this, and it is common to most people who pray and participate

---

[1] The expression is Andrew Louth's, in *Denys the Areopagite* (London and New York: Continuum, 1989), chap. 5.

in the sacraments; the development of their prayer follows the traditional map of progress in prayer that is to move from the complex to the more simple.[2] At the beginning, prayer consists in petition, meditation, and thanksgiving; but as it develops, it becomes less and less a matter of words, acts of the imagination, and motions of the will and develops into a loving attention to God. St. Francis de Sales says: "At the beginning we consider the goodness of God to excite our will to love him. But love being formed in our hearts, we consider the same goodness to content our love."[3] Sometimes this simple, loving attentiveness to God is called "acquired contemplation"; that is, through our participation in the liturgy, and by our own more private prayer, we gradually learn to remain quiet and content in the presence of God, and so we can be said to be contemplating him rather than meditating *about* him.

> [The soul] no longer needs to meditate in order to learn to know and love God. The way has been left far behind, the soul is resting at its goal. As soon as it begins to pray it is with God and remains in his presence in loving surrender. Its silence is dearer to him than many words. This is what today is called "acquired contemplation". It is the fruit of man's own activity.[4]

This sort of prayer is not a substitute for liturgical prayer, but liturgical prayer should lead to it, and there ought to be

[2] I have discussed this development in *On the Lord's Appearing* (Washington, D.C.: Catholic University of America Press, 1997). The section on "Contemplation", pp. 177–87 deals with the movement from discursive prayer to a quieter, less-structured approach to God.

[3] *Treatise on the Love of God*, trans. Henry Benedict Mackey, O.S.B. (Westminster, Md.: Newman Press, 1951), p. 240.

[4] Edith Stein, *The Science of the Cross*, trans. Hilda Graef (Chicago: Regnery, 1960), p. 86.

enough silence and serenity in liturgical celebrations to allow it to develop. The liturgy is not supposed to lead to a mindless submersion of the individual in a communal experience; it should, on the contrary, leave the individual with a heightened sense of his own self and lead him deeper into the mystery of the God who revealed himself in Jesus Christ and who shares himself with us in the sacraments.

It is not solely the verbal aspects of the Mass that should help to develop this contemplative attitude. In the Eucharist the reality of the presence of the Paschal Mystery is impressed on the worshipper by the structure of the rite itself, by the position of the priest for the Eucharistic Prayer, by the choice of the readings from Scripture, by the use of a formal archaic language (Latin), as well as by the controlled movements and gestures of the officiants; and all these characteristics of the Eucharist help to develop the contemplative attitude. It is from this perspective on liturgy that von Balthasar speaks of the liturgical attitude as one "silent, recollected adoration".[5]

A supporter of a more community-oriented liturgy might be quite willing to admit that the Old Rite did in fact encourage a liturgical attitude of "silent, recollected adoration" and that this is precisely what was wrong with it. Since von Balthasar wrote, there has been the Second Vatican Council with its request for *participatio actuosa*.[6] The

---

[5] "The heroic sense of sharing in a divine adventure, which dominates Gregory of Nyssa's conception of eternity, has given way to a liturgical attitude of silent, recollected adoration" (Hans Urs von Balthasar, *Cosmic Liturgy* [San Francisco: Ignatius Press, 2003], p. 142).

[6] The Latin runs: "cupit mater ecclesia ut fideles universi ad plenam illam, consciam atque actuosam liturgicarum celebrationum participationem ducantur [Mother Church earnestly desires that all the faithful be led to that full, conscious, and active participation in liturgical celebrations which is demanded by the very nature of the liturgy]" (*Sacrosanctum Concilium* 14 [A 144]).

phrase *participatio actuosa* is usually translated by "active participation", and the Council expressly enjoined it upon all those attending Mass. This active participation is the worship of the people of God, and because this participation must be "full, conscious, and active", it is therefore often said to exclude an "old-fashioned" view of liturgy that values elements of silence and recollected adoration. This argument is the source of much that is wrong with contemporary liturgy because it is based on a misconception of what active participation meant for those who first developed the idea; and, after all, it matters how they used it because their usage provided the context for the conciliar request for *actuosa participatio*. The question has been treated in detail and authority in many different places, but it is vital to see that without a correct understanding of how the phrase was used, and should be used, then there will never be even a beginning of a reform of the reform.

If we are going to understand how the phrase was used by those who developed its usage, we should understand that it was not something new introduced by the Council; in fact, it was used by Pope Pius X in a *motu proprio* entitled *Tra le Sollicitudine*.[7] The document is about sacred music, and in it the saint asked for an "active participation in the mysteries and in the public and solemn prayer of the Church".[8] Pius X himself, however, was drawing on an earlier tradition.[9] Dom Alcuin cites Dom Lambert Beauduin,

[7] Cited in Michael Kunzler, "La Liturgia all'inizio del Terzo Millennio", in Rino Fisichella, ed., *Il Concilio Vaticano II: Recezione e attualità alla luce del Guibileo* (Cinisello Balsamo [Milan]: San Paolo, 2000), p. 217.

[8] "Participazione attiva ai misteri e all preghiera pubblica e solenne della Chiesa".

[9] "It must be said that St Pius X did not invent the principle of active participation *ex nihilo*" (Dom Alcuin Reid, O.S.B., "Active Participation and

one of the pioneers of the Liturgical Movement, who stated in the early years of the twentieth century that one of the principal aims of the movement was "The active participation of the Christian people in the holy Sacrifice of the Mass *by means of understanding and following the liturgical rites and texts*".[10]

> We could have no clearer statement of the meaning of active participation at the outset of the Liturgical Movement. Active participation is essentially contemplative, and in no sense is it *primarily* concerned with our doing things in or to the Liturgy. Active participation is a state of being contemplatively connected to the profound actions of the Sacred Liturgy, and from that privileged encounter we receive grace.[11]

Since the Council the phrase has been used by many as though it were the most important reform the Council introduced, and it has been used to judge every liturgical practice.[12] It would seem that this use of active participation as the ultimate standard for liturgical life is wrong; but if the Council was not teaching that everyone at Mass should be, at least ideally, saying and doing everything that everyone

---

Pastoral Adaptation", in *Liturgy, Participation and Music*, Ninth International Colloquium on the Liturgy [Paris: CIEL, November 2003]). Dom Alcuin cites Dom Guéranger and Cardinal Wiseman in the nineteenth century, and St. Giuseppe Tommasi and others in the eighteenth and seventeenth centuries, as having argued for a more liturgical piety that included active participation.

[10] Ibid., p. 4.

[11] Ibid.

[12] "If we can no longer sing a Mass by Mozart or Palestrina because not everyone is capable of singing Mozart or Palestrina, if we can no longer hold solemn processions in Church because those who view them must remain spectators on the periphery, then many expressly liturgical forms will lose, from this point of view, not only their meaning, but in the end their existence as well" (Michael Kunzler, *Liturgia*, p. 220).

else says, sings, or does, then what was it asking for? It
would seem to be the case that in insisting that there should
be active participation, the Council was making the theological point that the liturgy is essentially an action done by
the whole community and that it involves both God and
man. By actively participating in the worship of the Church,
the laity is working out the consequences of its baptism
and confirmation, and the test of liturgy ought to be the
full, conscious, and active participation in the mystery of
the Eucharist; and so *Sacrosanctum Concilium* taught that the
liturgical rites and texts must be followed by those who
share in divine worship. The sort of thing the Council did
want to put an end to, for example, was the practice, still
very much alive before the Council, of the laity saying the
rosary together out loud during the celebration of Mass in
October. The mysteries of the rosary thus became the object
of devotion put in front of the laity and really were a bar-
rier to any full, conscious, and active participation in the
mysteries of the Eucharist. Participating in the Mass, that
is, was almost impossible, even with a Latin-English missal.
We tend today to take it so much for granted that the focus
of the worshipper's attention must be the Mass itself, and
that other devotions and interests must play a subsidiary role,
that it is easy to forget that this was not always the case.
The Council's insistence on active participation must be
understood as a much-needed reform.

Yet while the theological principle of participation is admirable, its application is an altogether different matter; and
the use of the principle has gone hand in hand with what
a German author describes as:

an allergy to both solemnity and Latin together with a misunderstanding about ecumenism which at times has led to

people being ashamed of their Catholicism. This had been coupled with libertarianism in the face of any tradition that should be binding and that has led to a mentality of do-it-yourself liturgy, and also to the practice of incessant commentaries on all and everything during the celebration; and this has put the emphasis on human speech that is not always particularly inspired.[13]

In conclusion, then, we can say that active participation ought first of all to reflect the theological truth that the Mass is a "saving work", and it must be celebrated in a way that does not obstruct participation in this work. On the other hand, this participation should not be the only criterion for judging the authenticity of liturgical celebrations. Then, secondly, it must be remembered that the liturgical attitude ought at least to lead to "silent, recollected adoration", as von Balthasar put it. The liturgy must leave space for the development of interior prayer by those participating in the Mass. Fr. Aidan Nichols has pointed out that silence is one of the themes in a section of *Sacrosanctum Concilium* in which the phrase *actuosa participatio* is found: "'Active participation' means primarily contemplatively engaged participation, not jumping up and down, which is why section 30 of the Liturgy Constitution can include silence under this heading."[14]

Since active participation means primarily this "contemplatively engaged participation" in the saving work of our redemption, I want to return to the work of Dionysius. The view of the Areopagite on the liturgy is profoundly contemplative, and yet, at the same time, he believes

[13] B. Fischer, in Fisichella, *Concilio Vaticano II*, p. 19.

[14] Aidan Nichols, O.P., *A Pope and a Council on the Sacred Liturgy* (Farnborough: Saint Michael's Abbey Press, 2002), p. 19.

that it is in the liturgy that the worshipper both encounters Christ and is made a partaker in the mysteries of our redemption.

In the chapter on Dionysius, I outlined his view, common enough in the intellectual environment in which he lived, that the best way of thinking about God and his relation to creation was the *exitus-reditus* model; that is, God goes out to his creation in order to draw it back to himself. The whole of creation reveals the beauty of its hidden Creator, and the creation itself in its turn glorifies its Creator; "the heavens are telling the glory of God; and the firmament proclaims his handiwork" (Ps 15). The liturgy reveals this twofold procession and is (or should be) characterized by the same fundamental movement of going out and returning, that is, God's relation to his world and the world's relation to its God. This *exitus-reditus* is accomplished through what Dionysius calls *hierarchy*.[15] He uses the word, in the first place, to portray the way the whole of reality, both heavenly and natural, has been created by God; and then, secondly, to describe the transmission of revelation. In fact, Dionysius invented the word *hierarchy* to stand for "a structure or system for 'sourcing' or channelling the sacred, and linked it all inextricably to the single leader."[16] I have structured my discussion for suggestions of a reform of the reform on the three characteristics that Dionysius says are found in both the celestial and ecclesiastical hierarchies. We would miss the point of most of what he says if we were to imagine

---

[15] "In my opinion a hierarchy is a sacred order, a state of understanding and an activity approximating as closely as possible to the divine" (Pseudo-Dionysius, *The Celestial Hierarchy* 164D, in *The Complete Works*, trans. Colm Luibhéid (New York: Paulist Press, 1987), p. 153.

[16] Paul Rorem, *Pseudo-Dionysius* (New York: Oxford University Press, 1993), p. 21.

he is using the word as it is usually employed today to mean the order of bishops. For Dionysius, bishops belong to the earthly hierarchy;[17] they are part of the ordering of the Church, but they are only one aspect of what he means by the word. Hierarchy for Dionysius was the order established by God, but this order extends far beyond the visible Church to include the whole of creation.

The reason God established a hierarchical universe "is to enable beings to be as like as possible to God and to be one with him".[18] "To be as like as possible to God and to be one with him" is the goal of the contemplative life. St. Augustine says over and over again that God became man so that man could become God. If we are going to take these words seriously, then the traditional scheme of development in the spiritual life has to be borne in mind. The focus of our attention in the life of prayer shifts and changes; we begin by concentrating on fighting sin and practicing the virtues (the purgative way); then we begin to penetrate the mysteries of faith in periods of light and darkness (the illuminative way); and then finally we are united to God through a loving but dark awareness of his presence (the unitive way). This movement is not primarily the result of our own efforts but is the consequence of God's grace; it is, as the writer of *The Cloud of Unknowing* put it, *the drawing of this love.*[19] The earthly liturgy is one of the ways this activity of God is made manifest, and the liturgy must reflect the truth both that it is God who is the source of worship and that he works through the agency of other people and other things to draw all men unto himself.

[17] The human hierarchy for Dionysius consists of sacraments, clergy, and laity. See ibid., p. 58.

[18] Pseudo-Dionysius, *Celestial Hierarchy* 165A, p. 154.

[19] See my "The Drawing of This Love", *On the Lord's Appearing*, pp. 76–84.

The characteristics of hierarchy are sacred order (τάξις), knowledge (ἐπιστήμη), and "being-at-work" (ἐνέργεια); and Dionysius links these characteristics to the three stages of the spiritual life. In linking liturgy to the development of our relationship with God, he firmly points us in the right direction—to the hidden God revealed in Christ. His analysis of hierarchy also provides us with a useful principle of organization for drawing together a number of different strands concerning the liturgy.

I. *A Sacred Order* (τάξις)

The Greek word for order here (τάξις) has to do with the ideas of arranging and an arrangement; for example, the drawing up of soldiers in order and a way things are in fact positioned are both an ordering. Dionysius uses the word to express his profound conviction that at the center of reality there is order and not chaos and that this order is, or should be, reflected in our worship of God. With this general principle in mind, we can say, first, that in the celebration of Mass there must be a determined effort to reduce what is personal and local in the celebration and, second, that we should go back to the practice of facing the liturgical East when the Eucharistic Prayer is said.

Whatever is personal and local should be eliminated. One of my contentions in this book is that the liturgical morass in which the Church is sunk is a reflection of the retreat from objectivity in the moral life. The teaching of St. Thomas that human beings are created with a built-in direction, or bent (*inclinatio*), toward what is good and beautiful and that choice does not enter into either the reality of these built-in tendencies or their object is being seriously questioned even in the Church. The atmosphere of "creative liturgy" is a sign of this retreat from an objective moral stance, and it furthers the advance of a subjectivism that will destroy the possibility of any real Christian community. And, along with the disappearance of a Christian community, understood as part of the Mystical Body of Jesus Christ, disappears any hope for the restoration of a liturgy oriented toward the worship of God.[20]

It is often said that the Old Rite of Mass was so exclusively focused on the priest that any consideration of the needs of the community was in fact ignored. Father was a lonely figure at the altar, where he did mysterious things, and the people were passive spectators (as they tend to be called nowadays) at the complicated and largely meaningless rituals performed in a foreign language. Now, things have changed, so it is maintained, and the priest is free to present the prayer and praise of the people in a way that meets the needs of his particular community and in a manner that seems best to him. A great deal of this may be questionable, but it is what a great many priests think. I want to observe at this point that the more individualistic, not to say idiosyncratic, a priest's celebration of the liturgy becomes, the less it is capable of fulfilling its function of representing the prayers and needs even of the particular community he represents. Furthermore, the liturgy is sup-

---

[20] Derek Hanshell, "Resacralisation", in *A Voice for All Time*, ed. Christopher Francis and Martin Lynch (Bristol: Association for Latin Liturgy, 1994): "The priest in the sanctuary and about the things of the liturgy must not only preserve an inner but an outer attitude of prayer. He is not acting just as a private individual but as a *persona* and a public one. We have to rid ourselves of the illusion that the informal can be mixed with the formal in the liturgy, and the more so the better, as if informal were good and formal bad.... The old rubrics of the Mass were designed to make every movement of the priest look natural: natural and right and proper in the circumstances, which were those of the liturgy and sacral and duly ceremonial" (p. 209).

posed to be the Church's participation in the sacrifice of Christ, and the more "personal and local" the celebration becomes, the more it fails to portray this primary object of the Eucharist. One way of keeping the goddess Choice in her place would be to restore a respect for the fixed theological truths embedded in the Mass, for which the interests and needs of the priest and his people are no substitute. I think it is true, as I have been saying, that it is possible to celebrate Mass licitly with little or no reference to these truths; that, after all, is part of the trouble. The recognition of this objectivity of truth, a recognition rooted in a firm belief in God's revelation in Jesus Christ, is an aspect of the tradition of Catholic worship. It is this tradition to which the traditional Mass is an abiding witness and a reproach to much that passes for worship in the Church today. The Old Rite may not by itself be the way forward, but until the New Rite manages to recapture the sense of dealing with the ultimate mysteries of faith and existence, characteristics the Old Rite did possess, then the New Rite will continue its descent into triviality and irrelevance. Of course, liturgical fidelity to the truths of the faith is not necessarily going to mark the beginning of a return to ethical objectivity; on the other hand, though, free-for-all liturgy is most certainly only going to confirm the impression that the Church at the local level no longer seriously believes in the reality of any sort of law whatsoever. In the interest of this greater respect for objectivity, I would drastically reduce the options open to the priest and if possible suppress them altogether, so as to produce a rite that is recognizably the same wherever it is said; and the same holds for the ad-libbed contributions of the priest.

The celebrant at Mass ought to face the liturgical East for the Eucharistic Prayer, or the Canon of the Mass. That is, he should

not be facing the people. There are three considerations here
to be taken into account. First of all, there was nothing in
the Council documents that required the radical reordering
of the sanctuaries that in fact has taken place. Secondly, the
present arrangement teaches all the wrong lessons about God
and the community. Finally, and at a practical level, saying
Mass "facing the people", as it usually described, has turned
priests from being servants at the altar of God into social
animators of varying degrees of competence.

The historical arguments for the present practice are very
shaky indeed, and there is no theological imperative for turning the altars around.[21] Nor was there anything in the documents of Vatican II that necessitated the radical changes in
the reordering of the sanctuaries that in fact took place. As
Cardinal Ratzinger has written:

> To the ordinary churchgoer, the two most obvious effects
> of the liturgical reform of the Second Vatican Council seem
> to be the disappearance of Latin and the turning of the
> altars toward the people. Those who read the relevant texts
> will be astonished to learn that neither is in fact found in
> the decrees of the Council.[22]

Secondly, saying the Eucharistic Prayer facing the people
has taught the wrong lessons both about the community
and about the priest's role in relation to the community.
The function of the priest cannot be completely identified
with being a spokesman for the community. From the perspective of this chapter, we can say that the function of the
priest (in addition to being a representative and spokesman
for the community) is to represent and maintain the God-

---

[21] In the foreword to U. M. Lang, *Turning Towards the Lord: Orientation in
Liturgical Prayer* (San Francisco: Ignatius Press, 2004), p. 9.

[22] Joseph Cardinal Ratzinger, preface, ibid., p. 7.

directed focus of the liturgy. He represents this focus by acting in the place of Jesus Christ. And it was, and is, Jesus Christ
who has made the community a Christian one. I would argue
that the priest cannot perform this function unless he is prepared to submerge his own particular personality into what
he is doing; and this requires a sense that he is doing more
than "presiding" over the celebration. He does "preside", or
at least he is supposed to, but he is also supposed to lead his
people toward the mystery of our redemption; and he does
this not only with words but with actions.

Finally, the practice of saying the Eucharistic Prayer facing the people has imposed a burden on priests saying the
Mass that most of them are unable to fulfill. Czesław Miłosz
has described how the changes in the liturgy affected him:

> The Latin, the shimmering chasubles, the priest's position
> with his face towards the altar and his back to the faithful,
> made him an actor in a sacral theatre. After Vatican II the
> clergy shed not only their robes and their Latin but also, at
> least from where I write this, the language of centuries-old
> formulas which they had used in their sermons.[23]

Whether we think this was a good development or a bad
one, it is what happened. What is not sufficiently taken into
account, however, is that the priest now has the burden of
being at the center of the celebration in a new way: he not
only has to preside over the celebration, but he also has to
maintain the interest of the congregation by being involved
in a process of making the Eucharist more relevant and meaningful. The most important factor in creating this situation
has been the changing of the position of the celebrant at Mass.
No one is up to being interesting and creative on demand and

---

[23] *To Begin Where I Am* (New York: Farrar, Straus and Giroux, 2001), p. 324.

on a regular basis; and it is no criticism of priests as individuals that most of them in fact do not manage to fulfill a task that I think is impossible for anyone to fulfill adequately.

Turning toward the altar after the readings from the Scripture, "conversio ad Dominum", as St. Augustine put it, is an action that would turn both priest and people from instruction to worship.

2. *Knowledge* (ἐπιστήμη)

The Greek word used here for knowledge usually means a knowledge based on principles and reasoning, and this distinguishes it both from a casual knowledge of things and from the practical wisdom about what actually to do in particular cases. Dionysius used knowledge in connection with the idea of being enlightened by the truths of the gospel, that is, of seeing things in a new light. In the illumination afforded by liturgical experience we become aware of the connections and the consequences that flow from our knowledge of the Christian faith. In the final analysis, it is God who illumines the human intellect so that it can see clearly, but he does this in various ways, and one of these ways is the liturgy. There is, or there should be, an illuminative aspect to the prayer of the Church. The expression *lex orandi, lex credendi* means, as we have seen, that "the law of supplication" should support "the law of faith";[24] the liturgy, that is, ought to reflect and teach the Catholic faith on which it is based. This teaching is accomplished by the reading from Scripture and the homily; but it is also the liturgical action itself, taken as a whole, that should support "the law of faith".

[24] See above, introduction to pt. 3.

Preaching ought to be based on the Scriptures as the Church understands them, and it should follow the cycle of the Church's liturgical year; it should be concerned with Christian truth in a way the hearers can understand. In other words, preaching should be dogmatic; not dogmatic in the sense of a hectoring, unthinking rant, but dogmatic as being rooted and grounded, at least implicitly, in the Catholic faith. I have suggested above that the priest's personality ought not to be the center of attention at Mass. This is necessary even when it comes to the homily. It is the truth of the Gospel, not the personal musings of the priest on life in general, that ought to provide the content of the priest's discourse. This is not always clearly understood, and the basis for the misunderstanding can be traced to a misuse of a very old distinction between *kerygma* and *dogma*.

The distinction between kerygma and dogma is found in the work of St. Basil the Great. Kerygma is from the Greek word *herald*, and it was used by Basil to mean the Church's preaching of the gospel to those who do not believe in order to persuade or convert. More recently, especially since the Council, it seems to mean preaching the Christian faith in an effective way:

> [Kerygma is a New Testament] term which in modern use means the word that is preached ... to the Christian community or individual ("unto destruction" or "unto edification") in the name of God, by lawful commission of God and the Church, as the very word of God and Christ, and which efficaciously makes present its utterance in the situation of the hearer whom it summons.[25]

[25] Karl Rahner and Herbert Vorgrimler, *Theological Dictionary* (New York: Herder and Herder, 1965), p. 249.

Kerygma is often contrasted with dogma to the detriment of the latter, but I do not find the theological reason for this in any way compelling. Preaching is important, but the rhetoric used to support this unexceptionable proposition, especially when it seems de facto to diminish the importance of dogma, is misguided. I am not trying to determine in this book how theology ought to be done or to decide about the best way to use *kerygma* or how it should be distinguished from dogma; what I do want to do with the distinction, though, is to remind the reader that liturgy is a great deal more than a kind of preaching. It does not matter for my purposes here whether or not the reader accepts Basil's and Dionysius' view that theology "celebrates the inscrutable mystery liturgically".[26] But what is central to everything I have tried to argue for is the truth that *what the liturgy celebrates is the inscrutable Paschal Mystery*; and it does this in a way that is not merely verbal. Andrew Louth, in writing about the distinction in Basil's work, says:

> *Dogma* . . . is the experience of the mystery of Christ within the bosom of the Church, which is to be kept secret from those outside, from those who do not have faith—it is growing understanding of the faith mediated through the experience of the liturgy of the Church and a deeper grasp of the hidden significance of the Scriptures.[27]

The practical consequence of this should be a determined effort on the part of the clergy to allow the liturgy to do its work without the constant intrusion of their own personality and concerns. At the end of the Letter to the Romans, St. Paul prays that the Romans be strengthened

---

[26] The phrase is from von Balthasar, *Cosmic Liturgy*, p. 98.
[27] Louth, *Denys the Areopagite*, p. 27.

according the gospel he is preaching; and the gospel he is
preaching is "according to the revelation of the mystery ...
known to all nations, according to the command of the
eternal God, to bring about the obedience of faith" (Rom
16:25–26). To bring about the obedience of faith ought to
be the motto for priests, both in their preaching and in
their celebration of the Mass and the other sacraments. The
failure to do this for many different sorts of reasons, not all
of which are by any means the fault of priests themselves,
has helped to bring about the situation described in the
following lines:

> By democratizing and anarchizing, up to and including the
> realm of what, it would seem, were the unassailable truths
> of faith, *aggiornamento* ... struck a blow at the "knowing
> function of the clergy". An entirely new and unusual situ-
> ation arose in which, at least in those places where I was
> able to observe this, the flock at best tolerates its shepherds,
> who have very little idea of what to do. Because man is
> *Homo Ritualis*, a search takes place for collectively created
> Form, but it is obvious that any liturgy (reaching deep into
> one or another interpretation of dogma) which is elabo-
> rated communally, experimentally, cannot help but take shape
> as a relative, interhuman Form.[28]

A liturgy so communal and experimental that it inevitably takes
"shape as a relative, interhuman Form" will be corrected only
when both priests and people begin to realize they are dealing with the "mystery of faith". This is what Cardinal Ratzinger urged in a recent conference at Fontgombault:

> The Liturgy derives its greatness from what it is, not
> from what we make of it. Our participation is, of course,

[28] Miłosz, *To Begin Where I Am*, pp. 324–25.

necessary, but as a means of inserting ourselves humbly into the spirit of the Liturgy, and of serving Him Who is the true subject of the Liturgy: Jesus Christ. The Liturgy is not an expression of the consciousness of a community which, in any case, is diffuse and changing. It is revelation received in faith and prayer, and its measure is consequently the faith of the Church, in which revelation is received.[29]

I think the present three-year cycle is not effective in providing a structure of readings that teach and reinforce the Church's beliefs as they are found in the liturgical year. It is quite true that the new Lectionary provides a richer fare of readings than was available in the Old Rite, and this is certainly a desirable development in itself. Yet, it has been my experience that the complexity of the three-year cycle for Sunday Mass, and even the two-year cycle for weekdays, does not work all that well in everyday parish life. I think the diversity, rather than enriching people, tends to confuse them, and it is therefore counterproductive, as they tend to "tune out" the Liturgy of the Word. This may be because the selections, as has been noted by others, were drawn up more to satisfy the sensibilities of modern Scripture scholars than on traditional liturgical principles. This is ironical because it was the rediscovery of the greater scope of the historical lectionaries that first suggested the reform. Nonetheless, reading long passages from Genesis or from the historical books of the Old Testament, especially on a cold winter's morning or a humid summer day, often seems to be met with little more than stoical resignation on the part of the average parishioner.

---

[29] *Looking Again at the Question of the Liturgy with Cardinal Ratzinger*, ed. Alcuin Reid, O.S.B. (Farnborough: Saint Michael's Abbey Press, 2003), p. 30.

I think there has been a confusion of *lectio divina*, which is a profitable and indeed necessary component of a serious Christian life in modern times, with the proclamation of the Christian mysteries at Mass. By *lectio divina*, I mean the practice of the daily reading of the Scriptures in a quiet meditative way, but this practice is something quite different from trying to instruct people in the truths of Christianity in a way that will enable them to enter more deeply into the Eucharistic Sacrifice as well as strengthen and encourage them to lead their lives in conformity with the demands of that sacrifice.

There is also the question of what version of the Scriptures ought to be read. This is not up to the priest, but the versions foisted on the laity seem to have little to do with the need to make them effective instruments in conveying the truth of Christianity. It has been pointed out, for example, by Alan Jacobs, that most modern translations of the Bible suffer from a divorce between literary people and biblical scholars.[30] Jacobs contends that this happened largely as a result of the Protestant theologians' responses to Catholic charges that they, lacking guidance and correction from a Magisterium, were able to say whatever they liked about the Bible.

> The charge stung: What *was* to prevent this or that Protestant leader from offering a bizarre interpretation of some passage from Scripture and claiming as warrant for it the inspiration of the Holy Spirit? From the need to answer this charge arose *the* characteristic trait of Protestant biblical scholarship: an obsession with method. Method would be the Protestant scholar's Magisterium.[31]

[30] See, for example, Alan Jacobs, "A Bible for Everyone", *First Things*, December 2003, pp. 10–13.
[31] Ibid.

Jacobs goes on to show how this has led to a focusing on such skills as grammar, textual philology, and so on. None of these skills is a training in rhetorical nuances; and the Bible is full of such nuances. If the reading of the Scriptures at Mass is to be more effective, then we must be allowed to use translations that do not sound as though they were written by machines and that, therefore, are incapable of moving the heart. They fail to move the heart because the living images, images that reach us through the conscious mind to the mysterious center of our being, have been torn out of much modern biblical work.[32]

When it comes to the translations of the Sacramentary, and especially the prayers of the Mass, the situation is parlous. Enough has been written about the International Committee on English in the Liturgy (ICEL) to render it superfluous to add very much in the way of argument for the urgent need for revisions. The members of ICEL seem to have had the same cavalier attitude toward metaphor and hidden meanings as do many translators of the Bible, but unlike the translators of the Bible, they displayed less fidelity to the texts with which they were working. The matter has been documented over and over again: there has been infidelity to the texts in the interest of an ideology that is often alien to the traditions of Catholicism. There is no

---

[32] Jacobs sings the praises of the English Standard Version of the Bible and says that: "The key principle that the ESV's translation team employed is simple yet profound: deference to existing excellence. It is a principle that was employed by James' translators themselves, who graciously acknowledged their debt to their predecessors.... What is at work here is the humble recognition that our ancestors in the faith may have had certain skills now neglected or forgotten—may have had their palates trained to detect certain flavours that we today cannot distinguish." I would think there is very little *may* about it, and, furthermore, the principle of deference to the past extends far beyond translations.

more obvious example of drinking from the wells of the modern world than in the translations of the prayers in the Sacramentary. Eamon Duffy has said that just when the Church was being buffeted on every side by the modern world, the various committees of ICEL either caved in to the world or, worse still, actively cooperated in a Pelagianism that runs counter to twenty centuries of Catholicism.

> The verdict must be essentially one of sustained failure to rise to the challenge of the Latin, not merely in its great moments but also in the humdrum bread-and-butter ordinariness of the routine prayers of the Latin propers.... This failure involves more than a simple artistic or literary insensitivity. In almost all cases the distinctive theology of the prayers has been evacuated, and in many cases it has actually been subverted, and replaced by a slacker, often semi-Pelagian theology, far removed from the spirit of the Roman Rite, but redolent of some of the more shallowly optimistic theological currents of the late 1960's.[33]

Again, in the effort to restore order and objectivity, there should be an increased use of Latin. The Vatican Council never intended the virtual abolition of the language of the Latin Rite[34] and foresaw that the Eucharistic Prayer would be in that language, although other parts of the Mass could be in the vernacular. The Dominican Cardinal Browne warned during the debate on the documents that if the vernacular were allowed into the celebration of Mass, then Latin would disappear within ten years. "He was laughed at

---

[33] Eamon Duffy, "Rewriting the Liturgy", *Beyond the Prosaic—Renewing the Liturgical Movement*, ed. Stratford Caldecott (Edinburgh: T & T Clark, 1998), p. 121.

[34] "Particular law remaining in force, the use of the Latin language is to be preserved in the Latin rites" (*Sacrosanctum Concilium* 36 [A 150]).

by the assembly, but as so often, the pessimistic reactionary proved to be more in touch with the flow of events than the optimistic progressives." [35] I think Cardinal Browne was wrong in his assessment that Latin and the vernacular could not be combined, but he was certainly right in his analysis that the dynamic behind much of the changes would in fact destroy the use of Latin. Latin did disappear for all practical purposes and, with it, much of the Church's musical heritage. [36]

I believe that the use of Latin as a universal and hierarchic language in at least one or two Masses at regular intervals in all parishes would serve as a flagship pointing toward God and would help to inform Masses in the vernacular with this spirit. I should be clear, though, that I do think the readings ought to be in the vernacular and that they ought to be read facing the people.

Last, but certainly not least, the question of the part music plays in the liturgy has to be seriously addressed. Once again, as with so many other questions, the right things are being said but seem to have little practical effect. For example, to mark the hundredth anniversary of Pius X's letter *Tra le Sollicitudini*, [37] Pope John Paul II issued a document that says

---

[35] John Parsons, "Reform of the Reform?", *Sacred Music*, vol. 129, no. 2 (2002): 19.

[36] Karol Pope, "About the Use of Latin", *Sacred Music*, vol. 116, no. 3 (Fall 1989): 8: "Latin has practically vanished from our Churches. This is not only a great loss for universal Catholicism, but it is also one of the causes for the chaotic state of Catholic liturgical music. For it made the best of Catholic liturgical music obsolete overnight. Attempts to force vernacular texts under music composed in Latin will produce only the dismal results known from 'adaptations' of Palestrina or Lassus by Protestant choirs. Even chant loses part of its character when divorced from the tongue that took wings by becoming chant."

[37] "The Fitting Role of Sacred Music in the Holy Liturgy", *L'Osservatore Romano*, no. 4, January 28, 2004, pp. 6–7.

that "among the musical expressions that correspond best with the qualities demanded by the notion of sacred music", Gregorian chant was recognized by the Second Vatican Council as "being specially suited to the Roman liturgy"; and since it continues to be "an element of unity" in the latter, it "should be given ... pride of place in liturgical services sung in Latin".[38] There are also some pointed remarks about how the Church has always recognized and promoted progress in the arts, and so "she admits into celebrations even the most modern music, as long as it respects both the liturgical spirit and the true values of this art form."[39]

It will be an interesting exercise to see what effect this document will in fact have, but at least it shows that the arguments and recommendations of this book are not totally out of line with the instructions of the ordinary Magisterium.

3. Being-at-Work (ἐνέργεια)

We saw at the beginning of this chapter that the purpose or end of liturgical worship ought to be the formation of a contemplative attitude. This attitude of "silent, recollected adoration" leads the worshipper to union with Christ and a living participation in the Paschal Mystery. This attitude is not, as is often said, a passive and heedless state of vacancy; on the contrary, it is a vital awareness of the great *exitus-reditus* that is the fundamental reality of the liturgy. This awareness itself takes on the character of what it contemplates; that is, the worshipper begins to sense the reality of God himself, not as a static entity of a theological principle, but as *being-at-work*.

[38] Ibid., p. 6.
[39] Ibid., p. 7.

Being-at-work is a way of expressing Aristotle's notion of ἐνέργεια and is often translated into English as *activity*.[40] For Aristotle this is an ultimate idea, not definable by anything deeper or clearer, but grasped directly from examples, at a glance or by analogy. We begin to formulate the idea of activity when we encounter things in motion: people walk, stones roll down hills, and water flows over the Niagara Falls. These are all instances of motion. For Aristotle, however, the most important sense of the ἐνέργεια is connected to activities that are not movements; examples of this are seeing, knowing, and happiness. These activities he understands as a state that is not passive but is full of life complete at every instant.[41] Furthermore, the purpose or end of the activity is just itself. Someone sees a mountain: if he is an artist, he may want to paint it; if he is an engineer, he may have to think about tunnels and bridges; if he is a hiker, he may think about climbing the foothills; but in all three cases the activity of seeing is just that—seeing. Movement is not intrinsic to the act, but then neither is inertness. The ultimate aim of liturgy is to move us toward union with God; and liturgical celebrations must have this contemplative dimension.

The liturgy works through a combination of words and symbols, and all through this book I have argued that there must be a return to an awareness of the importance of symbols if the worship of the Church is to regain its grip on the Catholic consciousness. There is a further point to be made. When we talk about symbols, we nearly always seem

[40] It is also sometimes translated by *energy*; that seems to me to leave the way open to understanding *energeia* as *movement* in an obvious sense.

[41] There is an excellent and very accessible discussion of this term in the glossary of Joe Sachs' trans. of *Aristotle's On the Soul; and On Memory and Recollection* (Santa Fe, N.M.: Green Lion Press, 2001).

to mean static entities such as lights, statues, or the vestments and other objects required for the celebration of Mass and the other sacraments. But it is not only objects that both symbolize hidden realities as well as provide the *locus* or site where we encounter these realities; it is also in the planned motion of the liturgy itself that the depths of God's merciful dealings with us are both portrayed and are to be found.

There is a good deal of instinctive opposition to this claim. Movement is closely allied with the idea of ritual, and the idea of ritual is associated almost automatically today with what is meaningless and even with what is frivolous and self-indulgent; ritual is thought to be pantomime in a fairly negative sense. It is not just "smells and bells" that set off alarms; it is what people sometimes refer to as "prancing around". If we are not going to dismiss the rich tradition of liturgical movement with this guilt by association, we have to try to see why this question of motion is so important.[42]

Liturgy, as we have seen, is a human activity, but it is not merely a human activity because God takes the most important role in the celebration of the sacraments. We adore, bless, praise, give thanks, confess our sins, intercede, and present our petitions, yet it is God, Father, Son, and Holy

---

[42] Chap. 6, "The Sense of the Sacred", in John Borella's book *The Sense of the Supernatural*, trans. G. John Champoux (Edinburgh: T & T Clark, 1998), is of the greatest value on the question of liturgy and ritual. He writes: "The spectacular thinning-out of practising members and the rapid, almost total disappearance, in a short time, of the clergy (at least in France) are not due simply to the liturgical reform. But one cannot deny that this is a powerful contributor, especially to the extent that, ... at the beginning, the sacred forms of the liturgy are the first and most effective educators of the sense of the supernatural, without which the grace of faith cannot penetrate the human heart. Now the 1970 reform has had at least one incontestable effect, whether sought for or unexpected: the suppression of *liturgical rituality* as such" (p. 61).

Spirit, who is principally active in the Church's liturgy. It is God who constitutes the people of God in a community with a supernatural dimension, which is therefore more than a naturalistic or social entity; and it is God who displays and makes present the saving death, Resurrection, and Ascension of his Son through the work of the Holy Spirit.

We have seen how Dionysius and the Greek Fathers understood the liturgy within the framework of the going out of God to his creation and of the drawing back by God of this creation to himself. We have also seen how St. Thomas used this *exitus-reditus* to structure both his understanding of reality and his own *Summa Theologiae*. In and through all liturgical action is this mysterious process of God's going out to what is his own in order to draw it back into a likeness of himself; and the liturgy itself should express or reflect this fundamental ontological structure. It is reasonable to ask at this point how we are to understand this movement on God's part and, then, to go on to wonder how liturgical movement can express this activity of *God* and not in fact misrepresent it.

When people talk about the existence of God, they may imagine him as an inert kind of *something*. In their desire to avoid applying anything inappropriate to God, such as imagining him as an old man with a beard, they often end up thinking of him as what they imagine the word *substance* to mean; they talk of substance as though it were rather thin soup or almost liquid jello. It has been one of the many virtues of a revived Thomism to show that *esse* (whose dynamism is akin to the ἐνέργεια spoken of by Dionysius) is the best way to talk about God as he is in himself.[43]

---

[43] *Esse*, says St. Thomas, "signifies the highest perfection of all"; it "is the actuality of all acts and therefore the perfection of all perfections" (St. Thomas

Suppose we admit that being-at-work is the best way to think about God, then how are we to fit in the notion of movement? God may not be an inert something, but, on the other hand, if we are to think about him best as ἐνέργεια, then he is not in motion. Just as ἐνέργεια is complete in itself, so God cannot be developing or changing into something other than he is now, has always been, and always will be.

To answer this briefly, and only from the perspective of our question about liturgy, we have first of all to realize we are dealing here with a question that involves not only God but his creation as well. Now movement is an inescapable aspect of creation, and we are beings who are by nature and in one way or another always changing. Gregory of Nyssa, Dionysius, and Maximus the Confessor thought deeply about this question, and for them *rest* is not the ideal state: "The ideal, rather, is a kind of paradoxical unity between rest and movement, which allows both poles to find their validity and their positive meaning. With Dionysius, both centers of this tension receive their final approval, preserved ... in the highest unity." [44]

The true nature of the ἐνέργεια of God and of his relation to creation is not going to be captured by thinking solely in terms either of rest or of movement; we have to try to use both in a dialectical relationship of mutual correction and refinement. If, then, the liturgy is to exemplify and teach the truths of faith in a profound way, it must do more than reflect the unity and stability of God; it must

Aquinas, *Disputed Questions on the Powers of God*, q. 7, art. 2, reply to obj. 9, adapted from the trans. by the English Dominican Fathers (Westminster, Md.: Newman Press, 1952).

[44] Von Balthasar, *Cosmic Liturgy*, p. 107.

also leave room for that movement toward God that we know as desire. This desire for God is itself God's work, but to us it is movement toward our eventual union with Christ. Movement for Maximus "consists in allowing oneself to be carried by another in the depths of one's being and to be borne toward the ocean of God's rest".[45]

This understanding of the *exitus-reditus* governs Dionysius' understanding of the Eucharist: "[Dionysius] is primarily concerned with the movement of the liturgical action, and sees that movement almost exclusively in terms of God's love outward to us in creation and redemption, drawing us back to him in our own answering movement of love." [46]

If the liturgy is to be shaken out of its routine complacency, then the reintroduction of planned movement into the sanctuary would help to draw people into the outgoing love of God waiting to draw us to himself. The Mass is supposed to be an *action*, but a modern celebration is largely a talk show with nothing much for the people to see or for the priest to *do*. Ritual movement in a liturgy that is understood in at least one sense as an end in itself would help to restore some of that sense that the Church is the House of God and the Gate of Heaven.

With this discussion of the Mass I have come to the end. I have said what I have thought has gone wrong with the Church's dialogue with the modern world and something about how this has affected the liturgy of the Church. The present state of the liturgy reflects the alienation of modern

[45] Ibid., p. 130.
[46] Louth, *Denys the Areopagite*, p. 60. "Both Denys and Theodore are at one in their concern to interpret the *movement* of the liturgical action. There is relatively little arbitrary symbolism of the gestures and robes of the clergy, and so on, that was later to form such a large part of the interpretation of the liturgy, especially in the West" (p. 61).

Catholic thought and practice from the tradition of the Church; but now it also contributes to it. Modern liturgical practices are defective, and they are in place, and they reinforce people's understanding both of their faith and of how the faith should relate to the modern world. This means that the "reform of the reform" will be a long, hard business. How it will happen is at best opaque.

In the *Apology* Plato reports that the Oracle at Delphi said that no man living was wiser than Socrates.[47] No one seems to have been more disturbed by this judgment than Socrates himself, and he did his best to prove the oracle wrong by trying to find someone wiser than himself. He never managed to find such a person and finally came to the conclusion that his wisdom consisted in two things: first of all, he knew that the most important question we all face is how we should live well, and no one else seemed to know this; and, secondly, he also realized[48] that he did not himself possess this knowledge.

If the reader has seen that living well for a Catholic is intimately bound up with liturgy and has also learned that there seems no clear way, humanly speaking, for the present situation to be remedied, then I have not failed in my purpose in writing this book. Newman said that we walk to heaven backward.[49] He applied his words to the individual

[47] "He [Chaerophon] asked if there was anyone wiser than I [Socrates]. Now the Pithia replied that there was no one wiser" (*Apology* 21A, *Plato with an English Translation*, vol. 1 [London: William Heinemann; Cambridge, Mass.: Harvard University Press, 1953], p. 81).

[48] "Socrates is the one exception; if he, too, does not possess this supremely important knowledge, he knows its importance, and he knows his own ignorance of it" (A. E. Taylor, *Socrates: The Man and His Thought* [New York: Anchor Books, 1953], p. 81).

[49] John Henry Newman, "The State of Innocence", *Parochial and Plain Sermons* (San Francisco: Ignatius Press, 1997), p. 1027.

who learns the truth about faith and right conduct through the experience of error. He was not preaching the modern idiocy that we have to sin in order to be virtuous, but he was reminding us that in fact we all make mistakes about the meaning of life and how it should be lived. But things do not stop there, because we then go on to act out these mistaken ideas, and this is true even if or when we are not very clear as to what exactly the ideas are. Bad practice is based on confused and false principles, and it is by an often bitter experience that we finally see the truth a bit more clearly and so find ourselves a little nearer to the Promised Land.

When it comes to liturgy we really do walk to heaven backward without signposts and without any certainties except for the promises of Christ and of his presence with us in the sacraments of his love. If we can learn this truth in a real way, then we will be given the courage to persevere, not only against wickedness, but against nonsense as well.

L'ENVOI

The Mass is the summit of all the Church's activity
    the Mass is the source from which flows all the Church's
    power
    the Mass is the heart of Catholicism.

The heart is wounded
    and the days of the Church, the Body of Christ
    are affliction and bitterness.

This matters not only for the Church
    but for the world
    because the Church brings to mankind
    the truth about existence and the human condition.

But she brings not only truth, for in her hands are the
sacraments
    the only cure for
    the one deep wound in human nature
    that wound from whence flows all sin
    division, despair, and disintegration.

Yet this is not politics
    for the Church must ever be homeless
    in the land where she has never been at home.

See *Sancrosanctum Concilium* 10; Hans Urs von Balthasar, "The Wound has Blossomed", *Heart of the World*; *The Lamentations of Jeremiah*; John Henry Newman, "Revealed Religion", *Grammar of Assent*; Karl Löwith, "History of the Bourgeois-Christian World", *From Hegel to Nietzsche*.

BIBLIOGRAPHY

Abbot, Walter M., S.J., ed. *The Documents of Vatican II*. New York: Herder and Herder, 1966.

Allison, Henry E. *Lessing and the Enlightenment*. Ann Arbor: University of Michigan Press, 1966.

Antonaccio, Maria, and William Schweiker, eds. *Iris Murdoch and the Search for Human Goodness*. Chicago and London: University of Chicago Press, 1996.

Aristotle. *Aristotle's On the Soul and On Memory and Recollection*. Translated by Joe Sachs. Santa Fe, N.M.: Green Lion Press, 2001.

_____. *Politics*. Translated with notes and appendices by Ernest Barker. Oxford: Clarendon Press, 1946.

Armstrong, Karen. *A History of God*. New York: Alfred A. Knopf, 1993.

Arnaud, Pierre. *Le "Nouveau Dieu": Préliminaires à la politique positive*. Paris: J. Vrin, 1973.

Arndt, William F., and F. Wilbur Gingrich. *A Greek-English Lexicon of the New Testament and Other Early Christian Literature*. 5th ed. Chicago and London: University of Chicago Press, 1958.

Avineri, Shlomo. *Hegel's Theory of the Modern State*. Cambridge: Cambridge University Press, 1972.

_____. *The Social Thought of Karl Marx*. Cambridge: Cambridge University Press, 1969.

Barth, Karl. *Ad Limina Apostolorum*. Translated by Keith R. Crim. Richmond: John Knox Press, 1968.

_____. *From Rousseau to Ritschl*. Translated by Brian Cozens. London: S.C.M. Press, 1959.

Berger, Peter L. *The Desecularization of the World*. Grand Rapids, Mich.: William B. Eerdmans, 1999.

Berkeley, George. *Selections from Berkeley Annotated*. Edited by A. C. Fraser. Oxford: Clarendon Press, 1899.

Berlin, Isaiah. *Karl Marx: His Life and Environment*. New York: Oxford University Press, 1963.

Bernard, R., O.P. *La Foi*. Vol. 1. Paris: Desclée, 1963.

Bibby, Reginald W. *Fragmented Gods: The Poverty and Potential of Religion in Canada*. Toronto: Irwin, 1987.

_____. *Restless Gods: The Renaissance of Religion in Canada*. Toronto: Stoddart, 2002.

_____. *Unknown Gods: The Ongoing Story of Religion in Canada*. Toronto: Stoddart, 1993.

Blanning, T. C. W. *The Culture of Power and the Power of Culture: Old Regime Europe, 1660–1789*. Oxford: Oxford University Press, 2002.

_____. *The Eighteenth Century*. Oxford: Oxford University Press, 2000.

Blumenberg, Hans. *The Legitimacy of the Modern Age*. Translated by Robert M. Wallace. Cambridge, Mass.: M.I.T. Press, 1999.

Book of Common Prayer. Cambridge: Cambridge University Press, 1969.

Borella, John. *The Sense of the Supernatural*. Translated by G. John Champoux. Edinburgh, T & T Clark, 1998.

Boswell, James. *The Journals, 1761–1795*. Selected and introduced by John Wain. London: Heinemann, 1990.

Bouyer, Louis. *Dictionary of Theology*. Translated by Rev. Charles Underhill Quinn. New York: Desclée, 1965.

_____. *The Paschal Mystery*. Translated by Sister Mary Benoit, R.S.M. Chicago: Henry Regnery, 1950.

Britt, Rev. Matthew, O.S.B., ed. *The Hymns of the Breviary and Missal*. New York: Benziger Brothers, 1922.

Brown, David. "Sexuality and Constitutional Choice: The Case for Same-Sex Marriage". In R. E. Hauser, ed., *Temperance: Aquinas and the Post-Modern World*. Grand Bend, Ind.: University of Notre Dame Press, forthcoming.

Brown, Peter. *The Body and Society: Men, Women, and Sexual Renunciation in Early Christianity*. London and Boston: Faber and Faber, 1990.

Bruce, Steve. *God Is Dead: Secularization in the West*. Oxford: Blackwell Publishers, 2002.

Bugnini, Annibale. *The Reform of the Liturgy, 1948–1975*. Collegeville, Minn.: Liturgical Press, 1990.

Byatt, A. S. *Degrees of Freedom: The Early Novels of Iris Murdoch*. London: Vintage Press, 1994.

Casanova, José. *Public Religions in the Modern World*. Chicago and London: University of Chicago Press, 1994.

Cassian, John. *Institutes of the Coenobia*. Translated by Philip Schaff. *Nicene and Post-Nicene Fathers*, 2nd series, vol. 11. Grand Rapids, Mich.: Eerdmans, 1979–1983.

Cassirer, Ernst. *Kant's Life and Thought*. Translated by James Haden. New Haven and London: Yale University Press, 1981.

———. *The Philosophy of the Enlightenment*. Princeton, N.J.: Princeton University Press, 1968.

Catechism of the Catholic Church. 2nd ed. Vatican City: Libreria Editrice Vaticana, 1997.

Cessario, Romanus, O.P. *The Godly Image: Christ and Salvation in Catholic Thought from Anselm to Aquinas*. Petersham: St. Bede's Publications, 1990.

Chadwick, Owen. *The Secularization of the European Mind in the Nineteenth Century*. Cambridge: Cambridge University Press, 1975.

Chapman, Ronald. *Father Faber*. Westminster, Md.: Newman Press, 1961.

Chappell, V. C., ed. *Hume: A Collection of Critical Essays*. New York: Doubleday, Anchor Books, 1966.

Chenu, M.-D., O.P. *Toward Understanding Saint Thomas*. Translated by A. M. Landry and D. Hughes. Chicago: Henry Regnery, 1964.

Clark, Francis, S.J. *Eucharistic Sacrifice and the Reformation*. London: Darton, Longman and Todd, 1960.

Collingwood, R. G. *An Essay on Metaphysics*. Oxford: Clarendon Press, 1940.

———. *The Idea of History*. Oxford: Clarendon Press, 1946.

Comte, Auguste. *Catéchisme positiviste*. Edited by Pierre Arnaud. Paris: Garnier-Flammarion, 1966.

Conradi, Peter J. *Iris Murdoch: A Life*. New York and London: W. W. Norton, 2001.

Copleston, Frederick. *History of Philosophy*. Vol. 8. New York: Image Books, 1977.

Corbon, Jean. *The Wellspring of Worship*. Translated by Matthew J. O'Connell. San Francisco: Ignatius Press, 2005.

Cowling, Maurice. *Religion and Public Doctrine in Modern England*. Vol. 2, *Assaults*. Cambridge: Cambridge University Press, 1985.

Daniélou, Jean, S.J. *Prayer as a Political Problem*. Edited and translated by J. R. Kirwin. New York: Sheed and Ward, 1967.

Darnot, Robert. *George Washington's False Teeth*. Cited in a review by Munro Price, *Times Literary Supplement*, August 8, 2003.

Derrida, Jacques. *Dissemination*. Translated by Barbara Johnson. Chicago: University of Chicago Press, 1981.

Dix, Dom Gregory. *The Shape of the Liturgy*. New York: Seabury Press, 1983.

Duffy, Eamon. "Rewriting the Liturgy". In *Beyond the Prosaic—Renewing the Liturgical Movement*. Edited by Stratford Caldecott. Edinburgh: T & T Clark, 1998.

Durrwell, F. X. *The Resurrection*. Translated by Rosemary Sheed. London: Sheed and Ward, 1964.

Eliot, T. S. *Four Quartets*. London: Faber and Faber, 1979.

Fabro, Cornelio. *God in Exile*. Edited and translated by Arthur Gibson. Westminster, Md.: Newman Press, 1968.

Fackenheim, Emil L. *The Religious Dimension in Hegel's Thought*. Bloomington, Ind.: Indiana University Press, 1967.

Farrow, Douglas, ed. *Recognizing Religion in a Secular Society*. Montreal and Kingston: McGill-Queen's University Press, 2004.

Ferrari, G. R. F. *Listening to the Cicadas: A Study of Plato's Phaedrus*. Cambridge: Cambridge University Press, 1987.

Ferry, Luc. *Man Made God: The Meaning of Life*. Translated by David Pellauer. Chicago: University of Chicago Press, 2002.

Fisichella, Rino, ed. *Il Concilio Vaticano II: Recezione e attualità alla luce del Giubileo*. Cinisello Balsamo [Milan]: San Paolo, 2000.

Flew, Antony. *The Presumption of Atheism*. London: Elek Books, 1976.

Fogelin, Robert J. *A Defense of Hume on Miracles*. Princeton, N.J.: Princeton University Press, 2003.

Forster, Michael N. *Hegel's Idea of a Phenomenology of Spirit*. Chicago and London: University of Chicago Press, 1989.

Francis, Christopher, and Martin Lynch, eds. *A Voice for All Time*. Bristol: Association for Latin Liturgy, 1994.

Francis de Sales, St. *Treatise on the Love of God*. Translated by Henry Benedict Mackey, O.S.B. Westminster, Md.: Newman Press, 1951.

Gauchet, Marcel. *The Disenchantment of the World: A Political History of Religion*. Translated by Oscar Burge. Princeton, N.J.: Princeton University Press, 1999.

Gay, Peter. *The Enlightenment: An Interpretation*. 2 vols. London: Weidenfeld and Nicolson, 1967.

Gilley, Sheridan. *Newman and His Age*. London: Darton, Longman and Todd, 1990.

Gilson, Étienne. *The Unity of Philosophical Experience*. New York: Charles Scribner's Sons, 1947.

The Gospel according to Luke. Introduction, translation, and notes by Joseph A. Fitzmyer. Anchor Bible. Vols. 28–28A. Garden City, N.Y.: Doubleday, 1981–1985.

Habermas, Jürgen. *Knowledge and Human Interests*. Translated by Jeremy J. Shapiro. Boston: Beacon Press, 1971.

Hadot, Pierre. *Philosophy as a Way of Life*. Translated by Michael Chase. Oxford: Blackwell, 1995.

_____. *What Is Ancient Philosophy?* Translated by Michael Chase. Cambridge, Mass: Belknap Press, 2002.

Hague, René. *A Commentary on the Anathemata of David Jones*. Wellingborough, Eng.: Christopher Skelton, 1977.

Hammond, Philip E., ed. *The Sacred in a Secular Age*. Berkeley: University of California Press, 1985.

Hampshire, Stuart. "The Pleasure of Iris Murdoch". *New York Review of Books*, November 15, 2001, p. 24.

Harris, H. H. *Hegel's Development*. Vol. 1, *Toward the Sunlight, 1770–1801*. Oxford: Clarendon Press, 1972.

Hart, David Bentley. *The Beauty of the Infinite: The Aesthetics of Christian Truth*. Grand Rapids, Mich.: Wm. B. Eerdmans, 2003.

Hawkins, Peter S. *The Language of Grace: Flannery O'Connor, Walker Percy and Iris Murdoch*. Cambridge, Mass.: Cowley, 1983.

Hegel, G. W. F. *Early Theological Writings*. Translated by T. M. Knox. Chicago: University of Chicago Press, 1948.

_____. *Hegel's Philosophy of Right*. Translated with notes by T. M. Knox. Oxford: Clarendon Press, 1949.

_____. *Lectures on the Philosophy of Religion*. Translated by E. B. Speirs and J. Burdon Sanderson. New York: Humanities Press, 1974.

_____. *Lectures on the Philosophy of World History: Introduction*. Translated by N. B. Nisbet. Introduction by Duncan Forbes. Cambridge: Cambridge University Press, 1975.

_____. *The Phenomenology of Mind*. Translated with notes by J. B. Baillie. 2nd ed. New York: Humanities Press, 1964.

Heidegger, Martin. *Kant and the Problem of Metaphysics*. Translated by James C. Churchill. Bloomington and London: Indiana University Press, 1962.

Honderich, Ted, ed. *The Oxford Companion to Philosophy*. Oxford and New York: Oxford University Press, 1995.

Hook, Sidney. *From Hegel to Marx*. Ann Arbor: University of Michigan Press, 1962.

Hull, Geoffrey. *The Banished Heart: Origins of Heteropraxis in the Catholic Church*. Sefton, Australia: Robert Burton, 1996.

Hume, David. *Enquiries concerning Human Understanding*. Edited by L. A. Selby-Bigge. 1777; 2nd ed. Oxford: Clarendon Press, 1953.

_____. *Hume's Dialogues concerning Natural Religion*. Edited by Norman Kemp Smith. Oxford: Clarendon Press, 1935.

Israel, Jonathan I. *Radical Enlightenment: Philosophy and the Making of Modernity, 1650–1750*. Oxford: Oxford University Press, 2001.

Jacobs, Alan. "A Bible for Everyone". *First Things*. December 2003.

Jones, David. *The Anathemata*. London: Faber and Faber, 1955.

Kant, Immanuel. *The Critique of Judgement.* Translated by James Creed Meredith. Oxford: Clarendon Press, 1973.

_____. *Foundation of the Metaphysics of Morals.* Translated by Lewis White Beck. Edited by Robert Paul Wolff. Indianapolis and New York: Bobbs-Merrill, 1969.

_____. *Immanuel Kant's Critique of Pure Reason.* Translated by Norman Kemp Smith. London: Macmillan, 1950.

_____. *Kant's Critique of Practical Reason.* Translated by T. H. Abbot. 6th ed. London, New York, and Toronto: Longmans, Green, 1948.

_____. *The Moral Law: Kant's Groundwork of the Metaphysic of Morals.* Translated by H. J. Paton. London: Hutchinson's University Library, 1961.

_____. *The Philosophy of Immanuel Kant.* Edited by Carl J. Friedrich. New York: Modern Library, 1949.

_____. *Religion within the Limits of Reason Alone.* Translated by Theodore M. Greene and Hoyt H. Hudson. New York: Harper & Row, 1934.

Kelly, George Armstrong. *Idealism, Politics and History: Sources of Hegelian Thought.* Cambridge: Cambridge University Press, 1969.

Kenny, Anthony. *The Legacy of Wittgenstein.* Oxford: Blackwell, 1987.

_____. *Wittgenstein.* London: Penguin Books, 1975.

Kerr, Fergus, O.P. *Immortal Longings.* London: SPCK, 1997.

Kierkegaard, Søren. *Concluding Unscientific Postscript.* Translated by David F. Swenson and Walter Lowrie. Princeton, N.J.: Princeton University Press, 1943.

Knowles, David. *The Religious Orders in England.* Vol. 3, *The Tudor Age.* Cambridge: Cambridge University Press, 1959.

Kocik, Thomas M. *The Reform of the Reform? A Liturgical Debate: Reform or Return?* San Francisco: Ignatius Press, 2003.

Kołakowski, Leszek. *Main Currents of Marxism*. Translated by P. S. Falla. 3 vols. Oxford: Clarendon Press, 1981.

Lacey, Nicola. *A Life of H. L. A. Hart: The Nightmare and the Noble Dream*. Oxford: Oxford University Press, 2004.

Lafont, Ghislain, O.S.B. *Structures et méthode dans la "Somme théologique" de Saint Thomas d'Aquin*. Paris: Desclée de Brouwer, 1961.

Lang, U. M. *Turning towards the Lord: Orientation in Liturgical Prayer*. San Francisco: Ignatius Press, 2004.

La Taille, Maurice de. *The Mystery of Faith*. New York and London: Sheed and Ward, 1940.

Lenzer, Gertrud. *Auguste Comte and Positivism*. New York: Harper & Row, 1975.

Liturgy, Participation and Music. Ninth International Colloquium on the Liturgy. CIEL (International Centre for Liturgical) Studies. Paris, November 2003.

Louth, Andrew. *Denys the Areopagite*. London and New York: Continuum, 1989.

Löwith, Karl. *From Hegel to Nietzsche*. Translated by David E. Green. New York: Anchor Books, 1967.

Lubac, Henri de. *The Splendor of the Church*. Translated by Michael Mason. San Francisco: Ignatius Press, 1999.

Lukács, György. *Marxism and Human Liberation*. Edited and with an introduction by E. San Juan, Jr. New York: Dell, 1973.

———. *The Young Hegel*. Translated by Rodney Livingstone. London: Merlin Press, 1975.

Lyotard, Jean-François. *The Postmodern Condition: A Report on Knowledge*. Translated by Geoff Bennington and Brian Massumi. Minneapolis: University of Minnesota Press, 2002.

Malcolm, Norman. *Wittgenstein: A Religious Point of View?* Ithaca, N.Y.: Cornell University Press, 1994.

Marion, Jean-Luc. *God without Being*. Translated by Thomas A. Carlson. Chicago: University of Chicago Press, 1995.

Martin, C.B., and D.M. Armstrong. *Locke and Berkeley: A Collection of Critical Essays*. New York: Doubleday, Anchor Books, 1968.

Martin, David. *Christian Language and Its Mutations*. Aldershot: Ashgate, 2002.

——. *Christian Language in the Secular City*. Aldershot: Ashgate, 2002.

Martin, Gottfried. *Kant's Metaphysics and Theory of Science*. Translated by P.G. Lucas. Manchester: Manchester University Press, 1955.

Martinez, German. *Signs of Freedom: Theology of the Christian Sacraments*. Mahwah, N.J.: Paulist Press, 2003.

Marx, Karl. *Early Writings*. Translated and edited by T.B. Bottomore. Toronto: McGraw-Hill, 1964.

Marx, Karl, and Friedrich Engels. *Basic Writings on Politics and Philosophy*. Edited by Lewis S. Feuer. New York: Doubleday, Anchor Books, 1959.

McCabe, Herbert, O.P. *God Matters*. London and New York: Mowbray, 1987.

——. *God Still Matters*. London and New York: Continuum, 2002.

McLelland, David. *The Young Hegelians and Karl Marx*. London: Macmillan, 1969.

McManners, John. *Church and Society in Eighteenth-Century France*. 2 vols. Oxford: Clarendon Press, 1998).

McTaggart, John McTaggart Ellis. *Studies in Hegelian Cosmology*. New York: Garland, 1984.

Milbank, John. *Theology and Social Theory beyond Secular Reason*. Oxford, U.K., and Cambridge, Mass.: Blackwell, 1990.

Milbank, John, Catherine Pickstock, and Graham Ward, eds. *Radical Orthodoxy*. London and New York: Routledge, 1999.

Mill, John Stuart. *Selected Writings of John Stuart Mill*. Edited with an introduction by Maurice Cowling. New York and Toronto: New American Library, 1968.

Miłosz, Czesław. *To Begin Where I Am*. New York: Farrar, Straus and Giroux, 2001.

Monk, Ray. *Ludwig Wittgenstein: The Duty of Genius*. London: Vintage, 1991.

Morris, Charles R. *American Catholic*. Toronto: Random House, 1997.

Müller, Gerhard Ludwig. "Can Mankind Understand the Spirit of the Liturgy Anymore?" Zenit.org. October 10, 2002. http://www.tcrnews2.com/liturgymuller.

Murdoch, Iris. *Existentialists and Mystics*. London: Chatto & Windus, 1997.

_____. *The Fire and the Sun*. Oxford: Oxford University Press, 1978.

_____. *Metaphysics as a Guide to Morals*. London: Penguin Books, 1993.

Murphy, Francesca Aran. *Art and Intellect in the Philosophy of Etienne Gilson*. Columbia and London: University of Missouri Press, 2004.

Neiman, Susan. *Evil in Modern Thought*. Princeton, N.J.: Princeton University Press, 2002.

Newman, John Henry. *An Essay on the Development of Christian Doctrine*. New York: Image Books, 1960.

_____. *Fifteen Sermons Preached before the University of Oxford between A.D. 1826 and 1843*. London: Longmans, Green, 1900.

_____. *Grammar of Assent*. Introduction by Étienne Gilson. New York: Doubleday, Image Books, 1958.

_____. *The Idea of a University.* New York: Image Books, 1959.

_____. *Newman the Oratorian: His Unpublished Oratory Papers.* Edited with an introduction by Placid Murray, O.S.B. Dublin: Gill and Macmillan, 1969.

_____. *Parochial and Plain Sermons.* San Francisco: Ignatius Press, 1997.

Nichols, Aidan, O.P. *The Holy Eucharist.* Dublin: Veritas Publications, 1991.

_____. *Looking at the Liturgy.* San Francisco: Ignatius Press, 1996.

_____. *A Pope and a Council on the Sacred Liturgy.* Farnborough: Saint Michael's Abbey Press, 2002.

Nussbaum, Martha C. *The Fragility of Goodness.* Revised ed. Cambridge: Cambridge University Press, 2001.

_____. *Love's Knowledge.* New York and Oxford: Oxford University Press, 1990.

O'Connor, Flannery. *The Habit of Being.* Edited by Sally Fitzgerald. Toronto: McGraw-Hill Ryerson, 1979.

Oldmeadow, Harry, ed. *The Betrayal of Tradition: Essays on the Spiritual Crisis of Modernity.* Bloomington, Ind.: World Wisdom, 2005.

Pears, David. *Wittgenstein.* London: Collins, 1971.

Pelczynski, Z. A., ed. *Hegel's Political Philosophy: Problems and Perspectives.* Cambridge: Cambridge University Press, 1971.

_____, ed. *The State and Civil Society.* Cambridge: Cambridge University Press, 1984.

Peter Chrysologus. *Saint Peter Chrysologus: Selected Sermons, and Saint Valerian: Homilies.* Translated by George E. Ganss, S.J. Fathers of the Church, vol. 17. New York: Fathers of the Church, 1953.

Pickstock, Catherine. *After Writing: On the Liturgical Consummation of Philosophy.* Oxford: Blackwell, 1998.

Plamenatz, John. *Karl Marx's Philosophy of Man*. Oxford: Clarendon Press, 1975.

Plato. *The Dialogues of Plato*. Translated by B. Jowett. Introduction by Raphael Demos. 2 vols. New York: Random House, 1937.

_____. *The Republic of Plato*. Translated with notes by F. M Cornford. Oxford: Clarendon Press, 1955.

Pseudo-Dionysius. *The Complete Works*. Translated by Colm Luibhéid. New York: Paulist Press, 1987.

Rahner, Hugo, S.J. *Greek Myths and Christian Mystery*. Translated by Brian Battershaw. New York: Biblo and Tannen, 1971.

Rahner, Karl. *The Church and the Sacraments*. Freiburg: Herder, 1967.

Rahner, Karl, and Angelus Häussling. *The Celebration of the Eucharist*. Freiburg: Herder; Montreal: Palm Publishers, 1967.

Rahner, Karl, et al., eds. *Sacramentum Mundi*, 6 vols. Montreal: Palm Publishers, 1968–1970.

Rahner, Karl, and Herbert Vorgrimler. *Theological Dictionary*. New York: Herder and Herder, 1965.

Ratzinger, Joseph. *God Is Near Us: The Eucharist, the Heart of Life*. Edited by Stephan Otto Horn and Vinzenz Pfnür. Translated by Henry Taylor. San Francisco: Ignatius Press, 2003.

_____. *Milestones: Memoirs 1927–1977*. Translated by Erasmo Leiva-Merikakis. San Francisco: Ignatius Press, 1998.

_____. *The Spirit of the Liturgy*. Translated by John Saward. San Francisco: Ignatius Press, 2000.

Reid, Alcuin, O.S.B., ed. *Looking Again at the Question of the Liturgy with Cardinal Ratzinger*. Farnborough: Saint Michael's Abbey Press, 2003.

_____. *The Organic Development of the Liturgy*. Farnborough: Saint Michael's Abbey Press, 2004.

Rist, John M. *Augustine*. Cambridge: Cambridge University Press, 1996.

_____. *Real Ethics*. Cambridge and New York: Cambridge University Press, 2002.

Rorem, Paul. *Pseudo-Dionysius*. New York and Oxford: Oxford University Press, 1993.

Rose, Gillian. *The Broken Middle*. Oxford: Blackwell, 1992.

Rose, Margaret A. *The Post-Modern and the Post-Industrial*. Cambridge: Cambridge University Press, 1991.

Ross, James F. "Together with the Body I Love". *Proceedings of the American Catholic Philosophical Association* 75 (2002).

Scruton, Roger. *Modern Philosophy*. New York: Allen Lane, Penguin Press, 1995.

_____. *A Short History of Modern Philosophy*. 2nd ed. London: Routledge, 1995.

Shanks, Andrew. *God and Modernity: A New and Better Way to Do Theology*. London and New York: Routledge, 2000.

_____. *What Is Truth? Towards a Theological Poetics*. London and New York: Routledge, 2001.

Sheehan, Thomas. *Karl Rahner: The Philosophical Foundations*. Athens, Ohio: Ohio University Press, 1987.

Smith, Norman Kemp. *A Commentary on Kant's "Critique of Pure Reason"*. London: Macmillan, 1930.

Stein, Edith (St. Teresa Benedicta of the Cross). *The Science of the Cross*. Translated by Hilda Graef. Chicago: Regnery, 1960.

Stern, Karl. *The Third Revolution*. New York: Image Books, 1961.

Taylor, A. E. *Socrates: The Man and His Thought*. New York: Anchor Books, 1953.

Taylor, Charles. *A Catholic Modernity?* New York and Oxford: Oxford University Press, 1999.

———. *The Ethics of Authenticity*. Cambridge, Mass.: Harvard University Press, 2002. Originally published in Canada in 1991 under the title *The Malaise of Modernity*.

———. *Hegel*. Cambridge: Cambridge University Press, 1975.

———. *Human Agency and Language*. Cambridge: Cambridge University Press, 1985.

———. *Philosophical Papers*. 2 vols. Cambridge: Cambridge University Press, 1985.

———. *Sources of the Self*. Cambridge, Mass.: Harvard University Press, 1989.

Thomas Aquinas. *Disputed Questions on the Power of God*. Translated by the English Dominican Fathers. Westminster, Md.: Newman Press, 1952.

———. *Summa Theologiae*. Cambridge, Eng.: Blackfriars; New York: McGraw-Hill, 1964–1969.

———. *Summa Theologica*. Translated by the Fathers of the English Dominican Province. New York: Benziger Brothers, 1946–1948.

Tucker, Robert C. *The Marxian Revolutionary Idea*. New York: W. W. Norton, 1969.

Voegelin, Eric. *From Enlightenment to Revolution*. Durham, N.C.: Duke University Press, 1975.

Von Balthasar, Hans Urs. *Cosmic Liturgy: The Universe according to Maximus the Confessor*. Translated by Brian E Daley, S.J. San Francisco: Ignatius Press, 2003.

———. *The Glory of the Lord: A Theological Aesthetics*. Vol. 2, *Studies in Theological Style: Clerical Styles*. San Francisco: Ignatius Press, 1984.

———. *Heart of the World*. Translated by Erasmo S. Leiva. San Francisco: Ignatius Press, 1979.

Waddell, Helen. *Mediaeval Latin Lyrics*. London: Penguin, 1952.

Warnock, G.J. *Berkeley*. Handsworth: Penguin Books, 1953.

Waugh, Evelyn. *Brideshead Revisited*. Boston: Little, Brown, 1999.

Weinandy, Thomas G., Daniel A. Keating, and John P. Yocum, eds. *Aquinas on Doctrine: A Critical Introduction*. London and New York: T & T Clark International, 2004.

Wiley, Basil. *The Seventeenth-Century Background*. Garden City, N.Y.: Doubleday, Anchor Books, 1953.

Wilson, A.N. *Iris Murdoch as I Knew Her*. London: Hutchinson, 2003.

Wilson, Bryan. *Religion in Sociological Perspective*. Oxford and New York: Oxford University Press, 1982.

Wittgenstein, Ludwig. *Philosophical Investigations*. Translated by G.E.M. Anscombe. Oxford: Blackwell, 1958.

Wollheim, Richard. *The Mind and Its Depth*. Cambridge, Mass., and London: Harvard University Press, 1993.

Wood, Allen W. *Hegel's Ethical Thought*. Cambridge: Cambridge University Press, 1990.

——. *Kant's Moral Religion*. Ithaca: Cornell University Press, 1970.

Wright, N.T. *The Resurrection of the Son of God*. Minneapolis: Fortress Press, 2003.

Wuthnow, Robert. *After Heaven: Spirituality in America since the 1950s*. Berkeley: University of California Press, 1998.

INDEX